PUBLIC LIBRARY
W9-BYK-352

WITHDRAWN

You've Got Ketchup *on Your* Muumuu

EUGENE EHRLICH

You've Got Ketchup *on Your* Muumuu

An A-to-Z Guide to English Words from Around the World

Henry Holt and Company | New York

Henry Holt and Company, LLC
Publishers since 1866
115 West 18th Street
New York, New York 10011

Henry Holt® is a registered trademark of Henry Holt and Company, LLC.

Published in Canada by Fitzhenry & Whiteside Ltd.,
195 Allstate Parkway, Markham, Ontario L3R 4T8.

Library of Congress Cataloging-in-Publication Data
Ehrlich, Eugene H.
You've got ketchup on your muumuu: an A-to-Z guide to English words from around the world / Eugene Ehrlich.—1st ed.
p. cm.
ISBN 0-8050-6163-0
1. English language—Foreign words and phrases Dictionaries.
2. Language and languages—Influence on English Dictionaries.
I. Title.
PE1670.E37 2000 99-39458
422'.4'03—dc21 CIP

Henry Holt books are available for special promotions and premiums. For details contact: Director, Special Markets.

First Edition 2000

Designed by Paula Russell Szafranski

Printed in the United States of America

1 3 5 7 9 10 8 6 4 2

To grandmothers everywhere who enrich the lives of their grandchildren by reading to them and showing their deep love. Especially to Ellys, Juliet, Anne, Joyce, and Cynthia—all masters of their art. But most of all to Norma, the greatest of all.

PREFACE

"Neither a borrower nor a lender be."

—POLONIUS, IN SHAKESPEARE'S *HAMLET*

Old Polonius was talking about prudence in managing one's finances, not about borrowing and lending words.

But just as English words are increasingly taken into other languages, English throughout its history has continually picked up words from other languages and treated such words as its own, calling them English. This two-way exchange between borrowers and lenders is what economists and others might call a win-win transaction. Neither side loses, both sides win.

English, the language spoken in England and many parts of the world that once were part of the British Empire, has long been an active borrower and lender, largely because of successive invasions of England by the Romans, Angles, Saxons, Jutes, and French. These invaders all brought with them their own languages and left behind a legacy of useful vocabulary that was assimilated, or absorbed, into English.

Later, especially as international trade flourished, English vocabulary continued to expand and incorporate words of disparate world languages.

Thus it was that early English settlers of the countries now called Canada and the United States brought with them a language whose vocabulary had already been substantially enriched by borrowings from other languages. In addition, because the settlers had to find names for plants, animals, and practices that were new to them, and because of the influence of native American languages, British English and American English began to diverge.

Before long, settlers were speaking of *moccasins* and **wampum** and *wigwams* and *tepees* and **sachems**. Lexicographers appropriately identify such words as American in origin, but there also were among the early settlers people of Dutch and Spanish and French extraction, who were contributing words from their own languages. And over the centuries, as immigrants arrived in ever greater numbers from countries all over the world, American English came to embrace a growing selection of foreign terms ripe for borrowing.

One example of a recent English adoption of a foreign word is seen in the Russian word **samizdat**.

About three decades ago—no more than a few seconds in linguistic time—reports began to appear in English-language magazines and newspapers of the clandestine publishing of banned writings in the Soviet Union. The Russian term for this activity is **samizdat,** which means "self-published." Quickly, **samizdat** was adopted as the term of choice by British and American reporters and essayists writing about this Russian phenomenon. Considering the subsequent demise—perhaps dormancy—of the Soviet Union, it is likely that from now on this term will appear only in the writings of political analysts and historians. But **samizdat** will not disappear entirely from the English vocabulary for a long time.

Now consider **dénouement**, an English word of older provenance, borrowed from French near the end of the eighteenth century. Its literal meaning, "unraveling or unknotting," has become most often associated with the unraveling or resolution of the complications of the plot of a play or novel. An indication of the complete acceptance of this French term in English can be seen in the increasing use of the spelling **denouement**. The dropping of the acute accent implicitly suggests that now this useful term is *ours*, not *theirs*. Incidentally, the word **provenance**, used above, meaning "place or source of origin," is itself a nineteenth-century adoption from the French.

And so it is that, along with countless other words, English has adopted the delightful Italian *ciao*, which is used as a word of greeting or leave-taking; the German noun *Lederhosen* adopted as *lederhosen*, literally "leather trousers," with the English meaning of leather shorts with shoulder straps worn by men, especially in Bavaria; the Yiddish noun **kvetch**, meaning a "chronic complainer," also used as a verb, with the same meanings in English; the familiar Latin noun phrase *rigor mortis*, literally, "stiffness of death," well understood by generations of British and American detective story devotees; and the Turkish noun *yashmaq*, taken into English as **yashmak**, meaning the double veil worn in public by Muslim women to cover the face. And let us not forget the many dozens of words dealing with food—primarily borrowings from French cuisine, as one might expect.

The goal of this book is to explore interesting words with origins in other languages that have made or are making their way into English, enriching our vocabulary and helping English increase its usefulness and prominence among speakers, readers, and writers all over the world. It must be pointed out that words are not considered here that came into British English and American English by way of the predecessors of the English language—Anglo-Saxon, Old English, and Middle English.

And, as it might be asked: When does a word from a foreign

language become an English word? The only answer must be when lexicographers recognize its use in English writing, and that writing might well begin in the menus of restaurants, the published statements of public officials, and the like. When the frequency of such uses reaches the point at which dictionaries begin to define these introduced English words, a new linguistic star is being born.

As the reader will see, many of the words discussed in this book have long been used in English, while others are recent arrivals. Some have lost their foreign pronunciations over time, but others have not. And some have pronunciations in British English that differ from their American pronunciations. For the convenience of American readers, entry words in this book are given American pronunciations.

A word must be said about the criteria for selecting some words and excluding others as entries for this dictionary. The principal attribute considered in making this selection is the intrinsic interest of candidate words, and the author has appointed himself first and final arbiter of how well this characteristic is met. The second attribute considered is that of offering words originating from a large variety of foreign languages. How well this goal has been achieved is left to the reader to judge.

Pronunciation Key

In the system used here to pronounce entry words and certain additional words within entries, the effort has been made to keep to a minimum the number of special symbols needed. In addition it must be pointed out that only one pronunciation has been provided for each of these words.

The sounds used are represented as much as possible by the sounds made by letters of the English alphabet. The most important exception is the use of the schwa (ə) to represent the neutral vowel sound:

ə *as in a*go, tak*e*n, stenc*i*l, salm*o*n, s*u*ppose, circ*u*s

a *as in* apt, sap

ah *as in* calm, father

ahr *as in* ark, harm

air *as in* care, pair

aw *as in* all, saw

ay *as in* ail, tame

b *as in* bob, nab

ch *as in* chest, church

d *as in* dud, dug

e *as in* bet, egg

ee *as in* ease, me

eer *as in* beer, ear, tier

f *as in* far, fluff

g *as in* gave, hag

h *as in* half, he

i *as in* is, quick

ī, Ī *as in* my, tie, bite

j *as in* jump, judge, magic

k *as in* cuff, cluck

kh *as in* German *ach* and Scottish *loch*

l *as in* left, lull

m *as in* come, merry, room

n *as in* now, nun, span

n French final, almost unpronounced n *as in vin, garçon*

ng *as in* hang, sing, singer

o *as in* hot, on, socks

oh *as in* bone, coat, soak

oi *as in* boy, toil

oo *as in* boon, too

oor *as in* poor, tour

or *as in* for, tore, warn

ow *as in* cow, out

p *as in* put, pop, trap

r *as in* hear, rap, rare

s, ss *as in* sop, spice, twice

sh *as in* hush, sheep, shush

t *as in* pat, tip, toot

th *as in* bath, fourth, thin

th *as in* bathe, mother, this

u *as in* utter, supper, up

ü *as in* French *rue* and *vue*

ur *as in* first, her, spur

uu *as in* book, full, look

v *as in* live, valve, very

w *as in* quiet, quite, west

y *as in* yard, you

z *as in* zest, hazy, please

zh *as in* leisure, pleasure

Finally, it should be noted that fully stressed syllables are represented by capital letters, syllables of lesser stress by small capital letters, and unstressed syllables by lower case letters. For example, **abalone** is pronounced AB ə LOH nee.

You've Got Ketchup *on Your* Muumuu

A

abacus AB ə kəss

From Greek abax, *meaning a "drawing board."*

In English since the fourteenth century, meaning "a frame for making arithmetic calculations, with balls or beads sliding on wires"; in Japanese called a *soroban* (SOH roh bahn), from Chinese *suanpan*, literally, a "count board": "The **abacus** has the advantage of presenting a running subtotal each time an addend is inserted, so as soon as the final addend is inserted, the total is presented."

abalone AB ə LOH nee

From American Spanish.

In English since 1840, in both languages meaning an "edible mollusk with a shell lined with mother-of-pearl": "Years ago, visitors to the San Francisco waterfront slurped oysters and **abalones**, all the while discussing the relative merits of each."

abat-jour AH bah *ZH*UUR

From French, literally, it "throws down the daylight"; meaning a lamp shade.

In English since 1830 meaning a "lamp shade" or "reflector"; also, "a skylight or sloping aperture to admit light from above": "The architect failed to design the framing needed to accommodate the promised number of **abat-jours** (AH bah *ZH*UURZ)."

abattoir AB ə TWAHR

From French, meaning a "slaughterhouse."

In English since early in the nineteenth century with the same meaning, but only infrequently used in ordinary speech: "When would he get over his revulsion at the sounds and smells of the **abattoir** where he finally had found work?"

That people today find any use for the English word "abattoir" may suggest a preference for the pleasant sound of this word and the cover it provides for the explicit ugliness conveyed by the word "slaughterhouse."

absinthe AB sinth

Also given as ***absinth****, in French spelled* absinthe, *meaning "wormwood," a bitter herb with tonic qualities, as well as a green liqueur made from vermouth, wormwood, and other herbs.*

In French, and in English since the beginning of the seventeenth century, "absinthe" has been used to mean a delicious green liqueur: "Rose knew she would never have the chance to sit with other artists, sipping **absinthe** and dreaming of sudden success as a painter."

Most Western countries now ban this drink, which has an alcoholic content of 68 percent.

Small wonder.

accouchement ə KOOSH mənt

From French, meaning "childbirth."

In English since the beginning of the nineteenth century, with the same meaning.

The French word *accouchement* derives from elements that may literally be translated as "brought to bed," a phrase not unknown in English in the sense of awaiting childbirth: "Each day that went by brought the young woman closer to her **accouchement**, which would change her life forever."

In earlier times "accouchement" was hit upon as an acceptable term for an event that English had a tough time dealing with —witness other euphemisms for childbirth: "confinement"; "delivery"; and "lying-in"; not to mention "blessed event." After all, until recently people never spoke of, nor did newspapers ever write of, a woman's pregnancy. Instead, many people resorted to whispering that a woman was "anticipating"; "expecting"; "in a family way"; "in an interesting condition"; "in a delicate condition"; or, falling back on French for inspiration, **enceinte** (which see). Those with a propensity for more colorful language would say a woman "has one in the oven"; she's "knocked up"; even she's "wearing her apron high."

afflatus ə FLAY təss

From Latin, literally, a "breathing on."

In English since the mid-seventeenth century, meaning "divine inspiration" or just plain old "inspiration." The meaning "divine inspiration" is understood when we use "afflatus" to characterize the mysterious force that gives rise to a poetic impulse, but anyone who uses "afflatus" in this sense had better be sure of his grounds for making this claim: "The writers' workshops he attended that winter promised him everything but **afflatus**, and that was what he needed most."

There ain't hardly no poets around these days who are divinely inspired.

aficionado ə FISH yə NAH doh

From Spanish aficionado, *literally, "amateur"; the past participle of* aficionar, *meaning "to engender affection."*

In English since the mid-nineteenth century, meaning "a devotee or fan of any sport or pastime," originally said especially of a person devoted to bullfighting. The feminine form of the Spanish and the English word is **aficionada** (ə FISH yə NAH də). "They opened a bar across the street from where the cockfights were held, and almost at once, the **aficionados** made it their drinking headquarters."

It is worth pointing out that **amateur** (AM ə CHUUR), a French word from Latin *amator*, meaning "lover," was taken into English about one hundred years before "aficionado" and was welcomed by our omnivorous language. "Amateur" now has as its principal meaning in both French and English "someone who participates in a sport or other activity for the love of it, not for pay." A secondary meaning of "amateur" is "someone who lacks skill in a particular activity."

agent provocateur AY jənt prə VOK ə TUR

From French, literally, "inciting agent."

The plural in English as well as in French is ***agents provocateurs*** (AY jəntss prə VOK ə TUR). It carries the same meaning in French as it has in English since late in the nineteenth century: "a secret agent employed to incite suspects to overt action that will make them liable to punishment": "Because it was becoming too difficult to recruit the necessary number of **agents provocateurs**, the department chiefs decided to set up a school and award certificates in troublemaking, which they called 'government service.'"

aide-de-camp AYD də KAMP

From French, literally, "camp helper." In English since the late seventeenth century, also given in American English as ***aid-de-camp****, with the same meaning as in French: "a subordinate military officer acting as confidential assistant to a senior officer."*

In a highly regarded French-English dictionary, **aide-de-camp** is defined as "aide-de-camp."

This term has largely been replaced by **aide**, which clearly carries the suggestion that a person so described is not to be confused with a military orderly. The latter person is an officer of low rank who performs menial duties for an officer of high rank: "Much to his chagrin, the new **aide** found he was expected to play cards with the colonel for half the night."

Lurking within the "aide"/"orderly" distinction seen in military life is a comparable spirit abroad in the corporate world, where much is made of the difference between "administrative assistant" and "secretary." Just refer to someone as "secretary" these days and see how quickly a friendly atmosphere turns dark.

And then see what may happen when you ask this same person whether he or she can get you a cup of coffee.

aide-mémoire AYD mem WAHR

From French, literally, "aids memory"; meaning a "memorandum."

In English since the mid-nineteenth century, plural **aides-mémoire** (AYDZ mem WAHR), with the same meaning, more completely a "memorandum summarizing a discussion, agreement, or action." The term is used particularly in diplomacy: "Immediately after the meeting concluded, I was expected to prepare an **aide-mémoire** for my government's use."

Lest we forget.

alfresco al FRESS koh

From Italian al fresco, *literally, "in the fresh (air)."*

In English since the mid-eighteenth century, as an adverb meaning 1. "in the open air"; "out-of-doors": "We hope for good weather this weekend, so we'll be able to lunch **alfresco**."

2. As an adjective meaning "outdoor": "**Alfresco** dining will be impossible if the weather is as poor as predicted."

And as it almost always is.

alter ego AWL tər EE goh

From Latin, literally, "another I."

In Latin, and in English since the sixteenth century, meaning a "second self"; an "inseparable friend"; and a "perfect substitute or deputy": "Soon enough he found himself no longer satisfied with the role of **alter ego** he was expected to play."

amateur See **aficionado.**

ancien régime ahn SYAN ray *ZH*EEM

From French, literally, "old rule," referring particularly to the French system of government before the Revolution of 1789.

In English since the end of the eighteenth century, meaning a "superseded regime." Thus, we may write, "How I long for the days of the **ancien régime**, before mergers and acquisitions became common and our little company was still family-owned."

angina pectoris an JĪ nə PEK tə riss

From Latin, literally, "spasm of the chest."

In English given initially as **angina**—meaning "throat inflammation"—since the end of the sixteenth century. Later, toward the end of the eighteenth century, it became known as **angina pectoris**. The addition of **pectoris** gave English a dignified name for the severe chest pain that results when a diseased heart is subjected to overexertion.

Today, once again called "angina" by those who know it well, and applied broadly to any attack of painful spasms: "My doctor gave me a prescription for pills to take immediately when an attack of **angina** begins."

angst **ahngkst**

From German Angst *meaning "fear" or "anxiety."*

In English since the mid-nineteenth century, meaning "anxiety" or a "feeling of dread, remorse, or guilt, especially neurotic fear": "He appears doomed to irrepressible **angst** even though the battle experiences he blames for his condition occurred decades ago."

The word "angst" may have become fashionable in English speech because of the glut of twentieth-century psychoanalysts whose first language was German and had to adapt—resisting all the way—to learning English. "Angst," thus, came into English as a vestige of German psychoanalytical terminology.

Which also gave us the fifty-minute hour, eventually to be replaced by the forty-five-minute hour.

annus mirabilis **AHN əss mə RAB ə liss**

From Latin, meaning "year of wonders."

In English since late in the seventeenth century, plural **anni mirabiles** (ANĪ mə RAB ə leez), meaning "remarkable or auspicious year."

The classic "annus mirabilis" in English history is generally taken as the year 1666, memorable for the Great Fire of

London and England's victory over the Dutch, and impelling John Dryden, in 1667, to publish his poem "Annus Mirabilis." "Breathes there a young writer who does not dream that acceptance of his first novel for publication will surely lead to his **annus mirabilis**?"

It is interesting to note that England's Queen Elizabeth II, unhappy over highly publicized family problems that had befallen the House of Windsor and alluding to Dryden's phrase, used **annus horribilis** (haw RIB i liss), "awful year," to characterize a year recently past.

She could not, with Charles Dickens in mind, say, "It was the best of times, it was the worst of times."

No way. It wasn't the best of times in any sense.

anomie AN ə MEE

From French anomie, *from Greek* anomia, *meaning "disregard of law."*

In English since the end of the sixteenth century, also given as **anomy**, meaning "a condition of individuals or society characterized by an absence of social values."

This term comes into use particularly as a vogue word from the pens and mouths of social scientists searching for a way to characterize the causes of social unrest and unruly behavior of adolescents. Thus, one may read such mouthfuls as "Incipient **anomie** is an alarming sign of a society on the edge of disintegration."

In other words, when law and order break down, things don't look too good.

apéritif ah PAIR i TEEF

From French, literally, an "opener."

In French, and in English since the end of the nineteenth century, meaning "an alcoholic drink taken to stimulate the appetite before a meal."

The word is also given in English as **aperitif** (ə PER i tif), an indication that the word is getting ready to write "paid" on its debt to French: "By the time Alfred had drunk three **aperitifs**, we knew he wouldn't make it to the dinner table."

Or to an upstairs bedroom.

apparatchik AH pə RAH chik

From Russian apparatchik, *plural* apparatchiki, *meaning "party bureaucrat."*

In English since the end of World War II, plural **apparatchiks**, meaning "Russian Communist Party bureaucrat," also "Russian Communist agent or spy." The term has also come to be applied loosely to any bureaucrat: "Few journalists were unaware that former **apparatchiks** were in full control of the so-called new Russian economy."

The Russian word combines *apparat*, meaning the "Russian Communist Party machine," with the suffix *-chik*, meaning "agent." In English, **apparat** (AP ə RAT) means "an organization or power structure, especially in politics or government": "It was becoming increasingly apparent that the **apparat** was still flourishing and was still intent on having its way."

You can bet on it.

arriviste AR ee VEEST

From French, meaning a "go-getter."

In English since the beginning of the twentieth century, meaning "a person who has recently acquired wealth or position, especially one who has done so by dubious means and without gaining concomitant esteem": "Some readers perceive

Fitzgerald's Gatsby as an **arriviste**, nothing more and nothing less."

See also **parvenu**.

ashram AHSH rəm

From Sanskrit asrama, *meaning "hermitage."*

In English since the beginning of the twentieth century, meaning "a place of religious retreat or instruction in Hinduism"; also the persons instructed there: "You won't believe it, in the middle of Nebraska there's an honest-to-goodness **ashram**!"

auto-da-fé AW **toh dah** FAY

From Portuguese auto-da-fé, *plural* autos-da-fé; *and from Spanish* auto-de-fe, *plural* autos-de-fe. *Both, literally, "act of the faith."*

In English since the beginning of the eighteenth century, meaning 1. "a judicial sentence of the Inquisition": "The entire community knew what was in store when people gathered apprehensively in the public square to listen to the reading of the **auto-da-fé**."

2. "The execution of the sentence of a court characterized as the Inquisition, especially the burning of condemned heretics at the stake": "Once he became chairman of the Senate Committee of the Judiciary, any nominee brought before him knew he faced an **auto-da-fé**."

The Spanish Inquisition, an effort of the Catholic Church to root out heresy, was established in 1478 and finally abolished in 1834. Its inquisitor-general, from 1487, was a Dominican monk named Tomás de Torquemada (1420–98), who turned the Inquisition into an instrument of the state.

It was Torquemada who persuaded the Spanish monarchs Ferdinand and Isabella to expel the Jews from Spain in 1492 and, during his term of office, found time to have approximately two thousand heretics burned at the stake.

Small wonder that the name Torquemada has ever since been associated with **autos-da-fé** and become synonymous with a cruel persecutor.

avatar AV ə TAHR

From Sanskrit avatara, *literally, a "passing down."*

In Sanskrit, and in English since late in the eighteenth century. In Hindu mythology meaning the "descent of a deity to earth in visible form"; also meaning "manifestation; phase; incarnation": "Several Sikhs I know have named their first-born sons **Avatar**, presumably in hope that they will prove to be incarnations of a deity."

You never know.

B

babel BAY bəl

From Hebrew babhel, *meaning "Babylon."*

In English since early in the seventeenth century, meaning "a scene of noise and confusion"; also, "thorough confusion of sounds or voices": "The young teacher was taken aback at the **babel** that confronted her when she first entered her new classroom."

As a proper noun, **Babel** is an ancient city and tower, mentioned in Genesis 11:4–9, which recounts the origin of separate human languages. The ancient city may have been located in the land of Shinar, today's Sumer, and the builders of the tower—the Tower of Babel—intended it to reach all the way to heaven.

Until this project was undertaken, all people spoke a single language, but God saw the building of the tower as the beginning of human ambition. Whereupon, God "did there confound the language of all the earth," creating linguistic havoc and scattering people all over the earth. It was this so-called confusion of tongues that prevented the tower builders from communicating easily with one another.

And ever since, all over the world, people speaking a great variety of languages have struggled to communicate with one another.

A problem that shows no sign of abatement.

babushka bə BUUSH kə

From Russian bábushka, *meaning "grandmother"; from* bába, *"old woman"* + -ushka, *a diminutive suffix.*

In English since early in the twentieth century, meaning 1. "a woman's scarf folded diagonally and worn as a head covering tied under the chin": "She always wore a **babushka** when she stood at her outdoor market stall."

2. "An elderly Russian woman, especially a grandmother": "I am always struck by the stolidity written on the faces of Moscow's **babushkas** working doggedly at their street-sweeping jobs."

Even during the cold Russian winters.

bagel BAY gəl

From Yiddish beygel, *from dialectical German* Beugel, *meaning "a ring."*

In English as **bagel** since early in the twentieth century, meaning "a leavened, doughnut-shaped, firm bread roll, usually with a glazed surface": "Whether served with a generous dollop of cream cheese, a slice of onion, and some lox or smoked salmon, or merely buttered to accompany a morning cup of coffee, the **bagel** is constantly growing in popularity."

But unlike the almost universal pizza, "bagel" is not yet reported in languages other than English.

Their loss.

baksheesh BAK sheesh

From Persian bakhshish, *meaning "gift."*

In English since the early seventeenth century, in the Near or Middle East meaning a "tip," "present," or "alms." Also used as a verb meaning "give a tip": "Beggars in American cities are said to seek handouts, in Cairo **baksheesh**, but in both cultures, persistence and location—especially location—are the key to success."

banal bə NAL

From French banal, *an adjective meaning "trite, well-worn, commonplace."*

In English since early in the nineteenth century with the same meanings: "The actor had a gift for uttering the most **banal** thoughts, but in his deep, sonorous voice, managed to deceive listeners into thinking he was saying something original."

The related English noun **banality** means "anything trite or trivial; a commonplace": "The **banality** of his eulogy was soon apparent to all but the poor widow, who was so overcome by grief that she had not listened at all but said afterward the minister's words were golden."

The most interesting linguistic aspect of "banal" is the struggle of English-speakers over the years to find what may be considered a single, natural pronunciation of the word. Are we comfortable treating the word as English, or are we really attempting to pronounce a French word? Read on.

In French *banal* is pronounced bah NAHL. In British English it is pronounced ba NAL or bə NAHL or BAY nəl. In American English it is pronounced bə NAL or bə NAHL or BAYN əl. Even though most lexicographers eschew foisting a single, so-called "correct," pronunciation of any word on dictionary users, might it not be time—at least among those of us who speak American English—to settle on one way of pronouncing this useful, but pesky, word?

Perhaps bə NAL would fit the bill, since Americans pronounce "banality" bə NAL i tee. Makes sense.

bar mitzvah, bat mitzvah. See **mitzvah.**

barrio BAHR ee OH

From Spanish, meaning a "municipal district or quarter."

In English since the end of the nineteenth century, meaning in the United States "an inner-city area populated largely by Spanish-speaking residents": "Once he had thoughts of leaving his beloved **barrio**, but its people, its sounds and smells held him throughout his life, and he knew he could never leave."

The United States has traditionally been a haven for immigrants, who tend to live close together for comfort and support until they find the strength and prosperity that enable them to disperse into the general population. It is not uncommon for a large city, therefore, to have its Chinatown or its Little Italy, and even its Japantown.

Many cities also have their "barrios," where Spanish is the language of choice, and English is not often heard. But unlike a "ghetto," originally a Jewish district in some European cities and now, in the United States and England, populated by members of any national or ethnic group, a "barrio" is and may always be thought of by its inhabitants as an urban district for persons of Hispanic extraction.

beau monde boh MAWND

From French, literally, "fine world."

In English since the beginning of the eighteenth century, meaning "the people who make up the coterie of fashion"; "high society": "There they were, in all their outrageously expensive finery, trying hard to be taken as members of the **beau monde**, an aspiration never to be realized."

Late in the nineteenth century, New York City's **beau monde** was dubbed "The Four Hundred." The members of this most exclusive social set were said to number four hundred because Mrs. William Astor, preeminent society leader of her day, had a ballroom that could comfortably accommodate no more than four hundred guests. She therefore carefully pruned her invitation list to precisely this number, in the process creating a roster of the highest of high society.

And newspaper society reporters from then on, with no one keeping a precise count, referred to New York City's "beau monde" as "The Four Hundred."

Mrs. Astor's position as arbiter of the "beau monde" slipped markedly during the Great Depression of the 1930s, and the term "The Four Hundred" gave way to "café society." The new designation had nothing to do with one's position in high society—a social stratum that had so diminished in importance that it had virtually vanished from public view. Rather, "café society" suggested the preoccupation by the tabloid press with the men and women who seemed to spend all their nights drinking and being seen at the Stork Club, El Morocco, and other exclusive watering places.

Sure enough, in just a few years, the term "café society" itself became passé, and occasionally from then on was replaced in the press by "glitterati"—a fanciful coinage, by linguists called a "portmanteau" word or "blend," combining the words "glitter" and "literati." But "beau monde" retains its currency, perhaps because its French origin appeals to many who see anything French as glamorous.

bel canto BEL KAN toh

From Italian, literally, "fine song," meaning "singing characterized by full, rich, and flowing style."

In English since the end of the nineteenth century with the same meaning: "When the couple went to the opera, it was Verdi and his **bel canto** they wanted to hear, not the bellowing of Wagner."

Take note that **bel canto** is applied exclusively to a style of operatic singing concentrating on beauty of sound and vocal technique.

"Bel canto" is not applied to anything one might hear in a nightclub or at a so-called rock concert.

belles-lettres bel LET rə

From French, literally, "fine letters," meaning "literature" or "great literature."

In English since the beginning of the eighteenth century, meaning "studies or writings of the purely literary kind, especially literature that may be termed polite or excessively refined": "Few modern essayists who publish in serious journals would characterize their writings as **belles-lettres**."

English, since early in the nineteenth century, has also had the noun **belletrist** (bel LE trist), meaning "someone who writes belles-lettres": "It was when Harry began to refer to himself as a **belletrist** that I knew he had moved emotionally as well as physically out of our old neighborhood."

The adjective **belletristic** (BEL li TRISS tik) has also been used in English at least as long, and the noun **belletrism** appeared in English in the 1930s. Both "belletristic" and "belletrism" may be thought of as examples of the evolution of the English "belles-lettres," not the French.

In short, when English finds a good thing in a foreign language, it does not hesitate to go off on its own in enriching the English vocabulary.

And, of course, this independence of spirit is not restricted to the English language.

bidet bee DAY

From French, originally meaning a "pony," now a "low basin for washing the genitals."

In English since the early seventeenth century, with both the original French meaning and, especially, the modern French meaning: "Whatever did their young sons think when they saw that the family bathroom in their new home came equipped with a **bidet**?"

The connection between "pony" and "basin for washing" can be seen in the posture assumed by the bidet user, who straddles the basin while washing.

Facing the water tap, of course.

Bildungsroman BIL duungz roh MAHN

From German Bildungsroman, *literally, "formation novel"; plural* Bildungsromane; *meaning "a type of novel dealing with one person's early life and development."*

In English since the beginning of the twentieth century, plural **Bildungsromans**, with the same meaning as in German: "Thomas Mann's *The Magic Mountain* (1924) and Charles Dickens's *David Copperfield* (1850) are excellent examples of the **Bildungsroman**."

The reader may wonder why the English term **Bildungsroman** retains the initial capital letter of the original German. One can only respond by suggesting that the term is still more German than English, since it has not been in popular use but finds use primarily among scholars and literary critics. And, as we observe, scholars, literary critics, and highfalutin journalists are fond of flaunting their fluency—real or pretended—in other languages.

But if we are patient, we may one day see the capital letter—even the entire word—gradually disappear from English.

Use it or lose it!

blasé blah ZAY

From French blasé, *meaning "exhausted by enjoyment"; in modern French-English dictionaries translated into English as* "blasé."

This suggests that English has no other word to express the meaning of this adjective and that the French transplant has really taken root: "'You are much too young to convince anyone you are **blasé**,' she said."

But what has **blasé** meant since it entered English at the beginning of the nineteenth century? "Indifferent to or bored with life," also given as "unimpressed, as or as if from an excess of worldly pleasures."

And that says it well. But not in a single word.

Game, set, and match for "blasé."

bodega boh DAY gə

From American Spanish, meaning "grocery store"; formerly, in Spanish, meaning "wine shop."

In English since the mid-nineteenth century, with the meaning of "wine shop," and since the mid-twentieth century, in American English especially, meaning "grocery store," particularly one in an urban Hispanic neighborhood: "Mr. Ruiz ran his **bodega** as a friendly neighborhood hangout for his steady customers."

The term **bodega** must not be misinterpreted by the reader. For the uninitiated, "grocery store" may invoke an erroneous image of the classic American supermarket, now found throughout Europe and elsewhere. The typical "bodega" is more accurately characterized as a mom-and-pop establishment, often open far into the night—a modest store staffed by members of the owner's family and offering fruits, vegetables, cigarettes, beer, and especially merchandise they believe to be primarily of interest to neighborhood customers.

In this usage, "bodega" is well within the classical American protocapitalistic tradition of starting small, working hard, and sacrificing any possible social life or comforts for the sake of one's children's futures.

Which augurs well for the survival of true entrepreneurship, a phenomenon that bears no relation to Wall Street or initial public stock offerings.

bon mot See **mot juste.**

boondocks BOON DOKSS

From Tagalog bundok, *meaning "mountain."*

In English since World War II, when United States troops in the Philippines misheard the word *bundok* as **boondocks** and made it their own, with the meaning of "backwoods, a remote rural area; a rough or isolated region": "For months we have been stuck in the **boondocks**, with nothing to do but clean our rifles."

And wait for letters from home.

borscht bawrsht

From Yiddish borsht, *from Russian* borshch, *meaning "soup with red beets as its principal ingredient."*

In English since late in the nineteenth century, also given as **borsch** and **borschch**, meaning "any of various eastern European soups made primarily with beets and cabbage":

"Tamara's recipe for **borscht** is considered unsurpassable by her Russian immigrant friends."

Borscht, properly prepared, is delicious and may be served hot or cold, and with or without a dollop of sour cream and a boiled potato.

Summer or winter, yum!

boudoir BOO dwahr

From French, literally, a "sulking place," meaning "a woman's small private room."

In English since the late eighteenth century, meaning especially "a woman's bedroom or an elegant room to which a lady may retire to find solitude or to receive intimate friends": "I spent the entire morning in my **boudoir**, lacking the energy to go out and face the day."

Sometimes it seems there's nothing better than full-fledged sulking.

bravura brə VYUUR ə

From Italian, meaning "spirit" or "dash."

In English since the late eighteenth century, with two noun meanings: 1. "a brilliant performance or an attempt at brilliance": "The music the great soprano chose for her recital made it clear we would be present at nothing short of **bravura**."

2. "A piece of music requiring great skill and spirit of the performer": "For the orchestra's first concert of the season, the conductor made it clear she would not be satisfied with anything but **bravura**."

3. As an adjective, meaning "spirited, florid, brilliant" and said especially of vocal performances: "Her **bravura** Covent Garden debut in the role of Mimi brought offers from opera houses on the Continent."

brut broot

From French brut, *literally, "raw," meaning "very dry, unsweetened," said especially of Champagne.*

In English since the end of the nineteenth century, with the same meaning: "The caterers said they would supply a **brut** Champagne of a vintage year."

And why "Brut" was chosen as the name of a men's aftershave lotion and cologne is beyond me.

Which is why I write books such as the one you are reading now instead of creating names for commercial products.

C

cabana kə BAN ə

From Spanish cabaña, *meaning "cabin."*

In English since the turn of the twentieth century especially in American English, meaning a "cabin" or "cottage," especially "a small cabin or tentlike structure on a beach or adjacent to a swimming pool": "Ray's job was to sweep out all the **cabanas** every Monday and keep the grounds clean."

While the ostensible function of a beach or pool **cabana** is to provide shelter from the sun, as well as privacy while changing one's clothing before and after swimming, its primary use for most people is to afford privacy while reading, playing cards, ogling bikini beauties, dallying, drinking, gossiping, or closing big business deals.

Anything but dressing to swim or changing clothes after swimming.

cachet ka SHAY

From French, literally, "something compressed to a small

size," but carrying the meaning of "a seal" in addition to the English meanings about to be given.

In English since the middle of the seventeenth century, having a variety of meanings, most especially 1. "prestige, superior status": "Membership in that club carried with it a certain **cachet**."

2. "A stamp of individuality, a distinguishing mark": "Unfailing goodwill is the **cachet** of the competent social worker."

In centuries past, under the French monarchy, *lettres de cachet*, "sealed letters," could be issued by the king under the royal seal—the *cachet*. We remember these letters as orders to punish or imprison a king's subject without trial. This practice was abolished as one important step toward the democracy made possible by the successful French Revolution launched in 1789.

café au lait kaf AY oh LAY

From French, meaning "coffee with milk."

In English since the late eighteenth century, with the same meaning: "Breakfast for him was a brioche, **café au lait**, and a cigarette." Also meaning "the color of coffee with milk," said especially of a person of light brown complexion: "Her extraordinarily attractive **café au lait** skin made her the most sought-after model of the season."

A word must be said now about the American predilection for anything thought to be elegantly Continental in style (see **couturier**). Consider the proliferation in cities all over the country of coffeehouses run supposedly in the Continental style. In addition to serving exotic types of coffee at high prices, these establishments encourage patrons to linger over their coffee cups for as long as they wish while trying to meet interesting people, reading newspapers, or gossiping with friends.

In an earlier time, one of the coffees served might have been **café au lait,** with milk heated or scalded before being combined with hot coffee. Alas, it was not to be. The phrase was beaten out by an Italian term—most Americans had earlier learned to eat Italian food and drink **espresso** (e SPRES oh), which they typically mispronounced as though it were spelled "e x p r e s s o." So, not surprisingly, American coffeehouses stayed with the winner: Instead of serving café au lait, they served the Italian *caffè latte* (in English pronounced KAF ay LAT ay), usually abbreviated as *latte*. And what is *caffè latte*? You guessed it: coffee with milk, heated or scalded.

canapé KAN ə pee

From French, literally, a "covering" or "netting"; meaning an open sandwich.

In English since the end of the nineteenth century, meaning "a thin piece of bread or toast or a cracker topped with cheese or other savory food—a cocktail accompaniment": "**Canapés** should be avoided when you know you will soon be sitting down to a well-cooked dinner of challenging proportions."

While it is easy enough to see how a French term literally translated as a "covering" or "netting" might in time come to mean "a cracker covered with a cheese spread," it must be pointed out that the French word *canapé* has "sofa" as a third meaning. In fact, in British English today, **canapé** also has this meaning. So the plot thickens.

There is an easy solution. What did the literal covering or netting of the French *canapé* cover? A bed. And it is a short step from covering a bed to covering a cracker.

As long as you don't eat the crackers in bed.

cappuccino KAP uu CHEE noh

From Italian, literally, a "Capuchin"; meaning a Capuchin friar as well as an espresso coffee with steamed milk.

In English since the mid-twentieth century with the coffee meaning: "Coffee devotees drink **cappuccino** only at a reliable Italian coffeehouse, in the Italian language called a *caffè* (pronounced kah FAY)."

But how did **cappuccino** go from "Capuchin" to "coffee"? "The color of the coffee—delight of the Starbucks crowd—was thought by some long ago to be close to the color of the habit worn by a **cappuccino**, a Capuchin friar."

Something to think about next time you make your way through the whipped cream or steamed milk topping to sip the coffee with its **soupçon** (which see) of powdered cinnamon.

cause célèbre KAWZ sə LEB rə

From French, literally, "famous case," meaning "a celebrated or notorious lawsuit."

In English since the mid-eighteenth century, plural **causes célèbres** (KAWZ sə LEB rəz), with the same meanings; also any controversy that attracts great public attention. "**Causes célèbres** are the lifeblood of tabloid newspapers and commercial television."

caveat KAV ee AHT

From Latin, literally, "let him beware."

In English since the sixteenth century, a noun meaning "a warning, admonition, or caution": "Before opening the art auction, the auctioneer announced a **caveat** disclaiming responsibility for the provenance of any works to be sold."

Two well-known Latin caveat phrases have come into legal English: **caveat emptor** (EMP tər), "let the buyer beware";

and **caveat venditor** (VEN di tər), "let the seller beware." These phrases warn the buyer, or the seller, that he or she alone is responsible if disappointed in the outcome of the transaction.

chacun à son goût sha KUN a saw*n* GOO

From French, literally, "each to his own taste."

In English since the late eighteenth century, with the same meaning: "When I saw Fred add mayonnaise to his onion soup, I almost gagged before managing to mutter malevolently, '**Chacun à son goût**.' "

It must be pointed out that while some sources give the phrase as **chacun a son goût**, meaning "everyone has his own taste," there is ample substantiation for the use of **à**, meaning "to," rather than **a**, meaning "has." And if you consult a modern French dictionary, you will also find **chacun son goût** translated as "every man to his own taste."

So here you have three chances to express each to his own taste, meaning, "Don't bother arguing with me when we are discussing matters of taste." Or, as the Romans said, *de gustibus non est disputandum*, "there's no disputing about tastes."

Come to think of it, you can always try "One man's meat is another man's poison."

chaise longue SHAYZ LAWNG

From French, literally, "long chair," meaning a deck chair.

In French, and in English since the end of the eighteenth century, and often given in English as **chaise**, meaning "a low chair for reclining, with seat extended to support the legs": "I was surprised to find she had sold her comfortable **chaise longue** to the people who bought her apartment."

The French plural is *chaises longues*, the English plural **chaise longues** (LAWNGZ).

Perhaps reflecting the idle comfort implicit in the image of someone lolling—lounging?—in a chaise longue, many Americans have mispronounced this term as though it were spelled "chaise lounge" (CHAYZ LOWNJ). And permissive dictionaries roll over and play dead in the face of such abomination, giving this **solecism** (which see) the honor of its own entry.

A profanation of a furniture design and linguistic standards that surely moved Western civilization ahead.

chef-d'oeuvre she DURV **rə**

From French, literally, "chief (piece of) work"; meaning "masterpiece."

In English since the beginning of the seventeenth century, plural **chefs-d'oeuvre** with pronunciation unchanged, meaning "a masterpiece, especially in art, music, or literature": "Emily was convinced that the painting then standing on her easel would become known as her **chef-d'oeuvre**."

See also **oeuvre**.

cheongsam CHAWNG **sahm**

From Chinese chángshan, *literally, "long dress," meaning "a traditional form of Chinese women's garment with high neck and slit skirt."*

In English since the mid-twentieth century with the same meaning: "For parties his Chinese wife wore colorful **cheongsams** that never failed to attract attention."

And observant men at those parties, practiced at gawking unobtrusively, were always grateful.

chichi SHEE SHEE

From French, meaning "a fuss."

In English since the beginning of the twentieth century as an adjective meaning 1. "pretentious; trendy; frilly or showy": "What used to be high fashion has been transformed into unbelievably **chichi** gowns unfit to wear except at a minor-league charity ball."

2. As a noun meaning "fussiness; pretentiousness," said of a person, thing, or behavior: "Most of us find his **chichi** insufferable."

chutzpah *KH*UUT spə

From Yiddish khutspa, *meaning "unmitigated impudence or gall."*

In English since the end of the nineteenth century, also given as **chutzpa, hutzpa**, and **hutzpah**, a slang term with the same meaning: "The cabbie had the **chutzpah** to demand a large tip after taking us from Kennedy Airport to Manhattan by way of the Bronx, virtually doubling the fare and the time it took to make the trip."

Proving that a little bit of chutzpah can take you a long way.

cinéma vérité SIN ə mə VER i TAY

From French cinéma-vérité, *literally, "cinema-truth," translated from Russian* kinoprávda, *with the same literal meaning.*

In French, as in English since 1960, meaning "a documentary film technique recording actual persons and events without directorial control": "When **cinéma vérité** is most effectively produced, the people whose actions and conversations are filmed are unaware of the presence of the camera."

So happy is English with **cinéma vérité** that it has no other one- or two-word way of expressing its meaning. But how does our favorite French-English dictionary define the French *cinéma-vérité*? As "cinéma-vérité," of course.

cloisonné KLOI zə NAY

From French cloisonné, *past participle of* cloisonner, *meaning "to partition"; from the noun* cloison, *meaning "division"; hence,* cloisonné *as a noun means "enamel in which colors of a pattern are kept apart by thin metal strips or the like."*

In English, also called **cloisonné enamel**, since the mid-nineteenth century, with the same noun meaning: 1. "The couple have long collected **cloisonné** and by now have quite a valuable collection."

2. As an adjective, **cloisonné** means "pertaining to cloisonné": "For their first anniversary, Julian bought Dorothy a beautiful **cloisonné** bowl."

coffee klatsch KAW fee KLOCH

From German Kaffeeklatsch, *from* Kaffee *"coffee"* + Klatsch *"noise," meaning "gossip over cups of coffee."*

In English since the end of the nineteenth century, meaning "a gathering of friends for informal conversation or gossip, whether or not coffee is served": "Would our neighborhood social life ever be the same if the **coffee klatsch** were abandoned?"

It is worth noting that the German word *Klatsch* is taken to mean "gossip" in addition to "noise," so there is no mistaking the nature of the conversation heard at an authentic coffee klatsch.

cojones kə HOH nayss

From Spanish cojones, *literally, "testicles," but also—not surprisingly—meaning "courage."*

In English since the 1930s, with the same pair of meanings, but with the second meaning better rendered vulgarly as "balls" or colloquially as "guts": "Do you have the **cojones** to stand up to your boss?"

Clearly a locution equating courage with manliness. Sorry about that!

cologne See **eau de Cologne.**

corpus delicti KOR pəss di LIK tī

From Latin, literally, "body of the offense."

In English since the early nineteenth century, meaning in law "the basic elements or facts of a crime": "No progress will be made in the investigation until the **corpus delicti** has been revealed."

In a murder case, for example, the **corpus delicti** is the death of the murdered person. Also given as tangible evidence of a crime—for example, the corpse of a murdered person.

Now you're ready for your next television encounter with Helen Mirren et al.

coup de grâce koo də GRAHSS

From French, literally, "blow of mercy."

In French, and in English since the end of the seventeenth century, plural **coups de grâce** (koo də GRAHSS), meaning 1. a "death blow," especially one delivered mercifully to end suffering: "The hunter always carried a pistol so he could administer the **coup de grâce** to a wounded animal."

2. "Any finishing or decisive stroke": "When the company president announced there would be substantial reductions in the number of employees at headquarters, all Jake could do was wait for the **coup de grâce** he knew was imminent."

Thus, while a bullet in the brain of a dying enemy soldier may be construed as a "coup de grâce," so may a pink slip and a three-pointer by the home team in the final moment of a hard-fought basketball game.

A cautionary word on the pronunciation of "coup de grâce." This phrase and the plural "coups de grâce" are properly pronounced koo də GRAHSS, as shown above, not koo də GRAH.

Again, notice that "coup" and "coups" are both pronounced koo, not koop or koops.

So, in English as well as in French, "grâce" is grahss, and "coup" and "coups" are koo. Except in such English uses as "The country saw three **coups** (kooz) in a single year."

coup d'état KOO day TAH

From French, literally, "a blow concerning the state."

In French, and in English since the mid-seventeenth century, meaning "a sudden and decisive action in politics, especially one resulting in a change of government illegally or by force." (The plural **coups d'état** in English is pronounced KOO day TAHZ; in French, koo day TAH.) "Anyone plotting a **coup d'état** had better prepare for the possibility that the plot may go awry."

Many a plot has boomeranged with dire consequences for the plotters.

couturier koo TUUR ee AY

From French, literally, "one who sews," meaning a "fashion designer"; the French feminine form, **couturière**, *once meant "seamstress" and now also means "fashion designer." So attitudes and social practices are changing.*

The English word **couturier**, in the language since the end of the nineteenth century, means "a person who designs, makes, and sells fashionable clothes for women": "Some of the gowns available from celebrated **couturiers** can only be worn by superthin models."

Couturière (koo TUUR ee ER), in English since early in the twentieth century, means "a woman who is a couturier," formerly known as a "modiste": "Sally was rapidly becoming known in Los Angeles as a first-class **couturière**."

Both "couturier" and "couturière" are related, as one would expect, to the French noun **couture**, literally, "sewing" or "seam." "Couture" (koo TUUR) has also come into English since the beginning of the twentieth century, meaning "dressmaking" both in English and French, especially the design and making of fashionable garments: "The Fashion Institute of Technology aims to train its students not in ordinary dressmaking, but in **couture**."

But if you wish to set up shop as a couturier or couturière in New York City, you had better be prepared to pay the kind of rent charged on Fifth Avenue or on Madison Avenue.

That's where the action is for **haute couture** (in English pronounced OHT koo TUUR)—high fashion, that is—whether you speak English or French. But a designer's knowledge of French and the talent to speak English with a French accent can be translated into higher prices charged.

crème de la crème KREM də lah KREM

From French, literally, "cream of the cream," meaning "the élite, the very best"; "the choicest parts or members."

In English since the mid-nineteenth century with the same meanings, applied especially to the very pick of society: "Most metropolitan newspapers ignore the social lives of less than fashionable people, preferring instead to publish photographs of society balls, where the **crème de la crème** disport themselves in the best gowns that haute couture offers—or offers for rent!"

See also **beau monde**.

croissant krwah SSAH*N*

From French, literally, "crescent," meaning in French, and in English since the end of the nineteenth century, "a rich, buttery, crescent-shaped roll of puff pastry": "Nothing is better in the morning than a heavenly ***croissant*** *and a proper café au lait."*

The **croissant** is a fine creation of French bakers—and a disaster in the hands of most American bakers. Having no time or inclination for the ardors of preparing puff pastry, they settle for ordinary leavened dough and end up with just another bread roll in the shape of a crescent.

No wonder the American so-called croissant is often used in place of sliced bread in making sandwiches.

Ugh!

This baking failure is matched by the word's failure of pronunciation. The French and proper American pronunciation, as shown above, is krwah SSAH*N*, which is corrupted by many Americans as krə SANT or as krə SAHNT. Double ugh! As for the British, they go along with Americans except for their almost predictable shift in stress, making it KRWAH ssah*n*.

They almost get it right.

cul-de-sac KUL də SAK

From French, literally, "bottom of a sack," meaning "dead end" or "blind alley." One of the best French-to-English metaphors.

In English since the beginning of the nineteenth century, plural **culs-de-sac** (KULZ də SAK), with the same meanings: "We had a small house on a suburban **cul-de-sac**." "Finally, it became clear to us that our investigation had reached a **cul-de-sac**."

D

dacha DAH chə

From Russian dácha, *literally, a "grant of land," meaning "a small summer house or villa in the country."*

In English since the end of the nineteenth century with the same meaning, but used only to apply to such a house or villa in Russia: "Most **dachas** are far from sumptuous, actually resembling shacks rather than summer houses in the American style."

Readings of Russian literature and news reports give the impression that every self-respecting public official in the former Russia and Soviet Union had a **dacha**, which was supplied by the government. Perhaps the protocapitalism now seen in modern Russia may find the burgeoning capitalist class paying hard cash for things like summer homes. Unless an uncertain economy causes the rosy future to collapse.

dachshund **DOKS huunt**

From German Dachshund, *from* Dachs *"badger"* + Hund

"dog," literally, "badger hound," so called from its original breeding purpose. Its comparatively long snout and body enable it to pursue a badger—in American suburbs more likely a squirrel or chipmunk—that has taken refuge in a burrow.

In English since the nineteenth century, the **dachshund**, a short-legged, frankfurter-shaped dog is not thought of as anything but a pet: "Jon was inordinately fond of his annoying little **dachshund**, much to the discomfiture of his siblings."

In English the first letter of its name, unlike its name in German, is not capitalized. The initial letter of any German noun is capitalized.

danse du ventre DAHNSS dü VAHN trə

From French, literally, "dance of the belly," meaning "a belly dance." In this Oriental dance a woman dances with midriff—or more—exposed, emphasizing movements of the pelvis and abdominal muscles.

In English since the end of the nineteenth century, plural **danses du ventre**, with the same meaning and pronunciation: "Clubs that offer a program of shapely young women dancing authentic **danses du ventre** attract enthusiastic crowds night after night."

As well they might.

debauchee DEB aw CHEE

From French débauché, *past participle of* débaucher, *a verb meaning "debauch." Thus, the French* débauché *and its feminine form* débauchée, *mean "debauched."*

A **debauchee**, in English since the mid-seventeenth century, means "a person addicted to excessive indulgence in sensual pleasures"; "one given to debauchery." Notice that the word "person" is used in this definition, indicating that "debauchee"—the English suffix "-ee" knows no gender—may be either male or female: "As might have been expected, the congregation reacted strongly when stories representing their pastor as a **debauchee** began to appear on TV news programs."

In modern times, a debauchee may even be a young person, even though it usually takes some years of riotous living to qualify for full membership in the society of dissolute persons.

déclassé DAY kla SAY

From French déclassé, *past participle of* déclasser, *used as an adjective, meaning "lowered in status" or "downgraded."*

In English since late in the nineteenth century, meaning "having come down in the world"; also, "reduced or degraded from one's social class": "Once the family had lost its money, both parents and their three children were considered **déclassé**."

In English, **déclassé** is also used as a noun, meaning "one who has come down in the world or the like": "By openly avoiding the company of **déclassés**, he revealed himself to be an insufferable snob."

décolleté DAY kol TAY

From French décolleté, *past participle of* décolleter, *used as an adjective, meaning "low-necked"; "with neck bared."*

In English since the early nineteenth century, given also as **decollete**, as an adjective meaning "low-necked" or "with plunging neckline," said of a woman's dress. Also, said of a woman, meaning "wearing a low-necked dress," which exposes the neck and shoulders—and often more: "I wonder whether the Oscar awards are designed to honor motion picture excellence or to titillate TV audiences with visions of how extreme **décolleté** gowns can become."

An English and French noun associated with "décolleté" is **décolletage** (DAY kol TAH*ZH*), also given in English as **decolletage** since late in the nineteenth century, meaning "cleavage exposed by the low-cut neck of a dress": "I wonder why the designer ever suggested so much **décolletage** for a wedding gown." Also a low-cut neck of a dress: "Everybody is still talking about Mrs. Gordon's **décolletage** at the inaugural dance—seldom had so much been covered by so little."

Gosh, in these days of unrestrained public display, this doesn't seem worth having a special word for.

dégagé DAY gah *ZHAY*

From French dégagé, *past participle of* dégager, *used as an adjective.* Dégagé, *feminine form* dégagée, *literally, "released," "set free"; "extricated."*

In English since the end of the seventeenth century, meaning 1. "unconstrained, easy; casual, jaunty, especially in manner or style": "Hugh's **dégagé** air puts everyone at ease and never fails to impress his dinner guests."

2. "Detached; without emotional involvement": "Spectators at the murder trial wondered at the defendant's **dégagé** manner, which he maintained even when the judge sentenced him to life imprisonment."

A cool cucumber.

déjà vu DAY *zh*ah VOO

From French, literally, "already seen," meaning "old hat"; something seen too often before.

In English since the beginning of the twentieth century, meaning 1. "disagreeable familiarity or sameness": "As Henrietta approached the end of her distinguished publishing career, most of the novels she was asked to edit gave her the sense of **déjà vu**—same predictable plots, same old characters, same deadly dull writing."

2. In psychology, "the feeling of having already experienced something that is actually encountered for the first time": "The patient complained that, increasingly, he experienced **déjà vu** when he traveled to places he had never seen before."

Déjà vu helped establish Yogi Berra, one of the great Yankee baseball sluggers of his time, as a much-quoted phrasemaker even when many of his phrases had actually been invented by others.

It was Yogi who said—or did not say—"It's **déjà vu** all over again." And immediately launched this borrowing from French as an integral part of our language, to be offered again and again in public statements by people who may or may not know why the line is a rib-tickler.

Try to beat that!

démarche day MAHRSH

From French, literally, "gait," meaning "a step or move."

In English since the end of the seventeenth century, a word with three meanings: 1. "An action or gesture by a diplomat, especially a formal appeal, protest, or the like": "Even though the ambassador demanded time to make his **démarche**, the Security Council refused to reopen the matter."

2. "A statement, protest, or the like presented to public officials by private citizens, interest groups, etc.": "After the mayor's tiebreaking vote was made public, our group decided to make a **démarche** to force reconsideration of the zoning case."

3. "A procedure, maneuver": "As the press reported our case, an appeal to the governor would be nothing more than a **démarche**, with no chance of success whatever."

demimonde DEM ee MAWND

From French demi-monde, *literally, "half-world," meaning "a group whose activities are ethically or legally questionable."*

In English since the mid-nineteenth century, also given as **demi-monde**, with this same meaning 1. "She could not escape the effects of her early association with the **demimonde** of Hollywood performers and gossip columnists."

2. "A class of women of doubtful reputation because of indiscreet behavior or sexual promiscuity": "Some publishers thrive on issuing lurid novels detailing the adventures of the **demimonde**."
3. "Prostitutes or courtesans in general": "By then Nana had earned full status in the **demimonde** and knew she could never realize her dream of a brilliant marriage."
4. "A group characterized by lack of success or status": "If he is recalled at all, it will be as a member of the **demimonde** of failed novelists."

A term associated with demimonde is **demimondaine** (DEM ee mawn DAYN), in English since the end of the nineteenth century, in French as *demi-mondaine*, meaning "a woman of the demimonde."

demi-vierge DEM ee vee AIRZH

From French, literally, "half-virgin," plural demi-vierges; *meaning "a virgin in name only."*

In English since the beginning of the twentieth century, sometimes also given as **demi-virgin**, meaning "a woman who behaves in a sexually provocative and permissive way but retains her virginity": "A fraternity house on our campus posts names of known **demi-vierges** on its bulletin board, striking out names when frat members report a change in the status of the women."

Nasty boys.

denouement DAY noo MAHN

From dénouement, *literally, "an untying," meaning "outcome" or "conclusion."*

In English since the mid-eighteenth century, also given as **dénouement**, meaning "the final resolution of the intricacies of a drama or novel"; also, "the final solution of a mystery or other complication": "The **denouement** of the governmental intrigue known as Watergate awaits the death of the informant known as Deep Throat."

Probably the best-kept inside-the-Beltway secret of all time.

derrière DAIR ee AIR

From French, a preposition meaning "behind," but also a noun meaning "buttocks" or, for the fastidious, a "behind."

In English as a noun since the late eighteenth century with the same noun meaning, and also given as **derriere**: "To the consternation of all, the dowager arrived drunk and promptly slipped and fell on her **derrière**."

It is characteristic of many languages, including English, that socially acceptable terms are often sought to replace expressions that may—or do—give offense. Thus, "buttocks" in French and later in English was expressed as **derrière**, and was also in French called *postérieur* and in English called "posterior."

Any reader can readily supply a number of objectionable, if not vulgar, expressions for this valuable feature of the human body. And, to everyone's surprise, words once considered less than genteel have a way of creeping into civilized discourse.

A good example of this phenomenon is the word "butt," meaning "buttock," in American slang since the mid-nineteenth century. It suddenly reached the nobody-bats-an-eye point of general acceptance toward the end of the twentieth century when an ordinarily conservative U.S. president vowed he would "kick some butt."

A good way to sound masculine and show leadership qualities.

détente day TAHNT

From French, literally, "loosening, relaxation"; meaning "a relaxing of tension, especially between nations."

In English since the beginning of the twentieth century, also given as **detente**, with the same meaning: "Some small nations proclaim their desire for **détente**, but are said to prefer continuing low-level warfare, which increases their chances of being given international attention and infusions of financial aid from abroad."

Seems hard to believe.

deus ex machina DAY əss ekss MAH kə nə

From Latin deus ex machina, *from Greek, literally, "god from a machine."*

In English since late in the seventeenth century, meaning an intervention of some providential event just in time to rescue someone from difficulties: "A sudden, unexpected surge in stock prices turned out to be our **deus ex machina**, preventing what otherwise would have been a precipitate plunge into bankruptcy."

Deus ex machina was in ancient Greek theater a machine that could lower the statue of a god onto the stage just in time to enable the god to do his thing. Usually this meant rescuing the protagonist from what appeared to be certain death or destruction.

Don't laugh at the ancients. Today's TV and movie fans readily accept the modern and equally improbable equivalents of deus ex machina.

dharma DAHR mə

From Sanskrit, literally, a "decree, custom, duty"; in Buddhism and Hinduism meaning "moral law and truth."

In English since the end of the eighteenth century, according to Indian and Buddhist teaching meaning "religious law; social custom"; "correct behavior, virtue, and justice": "Ever since he took that course in Eastern philosophy, he has seemed obsessively preoccupied with **dharma**."

Not to be confused with **karma** (which see).

discotheque DISS kə TEK

From French discothèque, *meaning a record collection or cabinet; also meaning a dance hall.*

In English since the mid-twentieth century, also given as **discothèque** and as **disco**, meaning "a club for dancing to live or recorded music": "My favorite **discotheque** is going to install a sophisticated sound system and elaborate lighting."

And ear protection for the dancers?

distingué DISS tang GAY

From French distingué, *feminine* distinguée, *meaning "distinguished," "elegant," "refined, eminent."*

In English since the beginning of the nineteenth century, meaning "distinguished," especially in regard to appearance or manner. English also observes the difference between the masculine and feminine forms of this adjective: "The Governor's wife, ever **distinguée** (DISS tang GAY) in a stunning gown, welcomed each guest warmly and individually."

distrait di STRAY

From French distrait, *feminine* distraite, *meaning "absentminded, inattentive."*

In English since the mid-eighteenth century, meaning "inattentive" because of distracting worries, preoccupations, etc.; also, "distraught": "All through the reception, the consul seemed uncharacteristically silent, even **distrait**, except when his aides appeared at his side to whisper in his ear."

Secrets of state?

doch-an-dorrach DO*KH* ən DAHR ə*kh*

From Gaelic deoch an dorais, *literally, "drink of the door."*

In English since the late eighteenth century, meaning "stirrup cup" or "drink taken at parting"; also given as **doch-an-dorris**, **deoch an doris**, and other transliterations: "Now that the designated driver has become institutionalized in our culture, the **doch-an-dorrach** has become more widespread."

You can be sure, of course, that the drink taken is not a cup of coffee, but something a good deal stronger. Whiskey—preferably Scotch (in which case the spelling "w h i s k y" is preferred) or Irish—comes to mind, although Kentucky bourbon and Canadian whisky (with the same preference for "w h i s k y") will also be welcome.

For persons returning home by automobile, it goes without saying that the designated driver, by definition, will not take part in this splendid ritual.

The driver's loss and the benefit of the rest of us.

dolce far niente DAWL che fahr NYEN te

From Italian, literally, "sweet to do nothing."

In Italian, and in English since the early nineteenth century, meaning "pleasing inactivity, pleasant idleness": "After a difficult semester of teaching and exhausting work on her book, she looked forward to an entire summer of **dolce far niente**."

You can't beat it.

dolce vita DAWL che VEE tə

From Italian la dolce vita, *literally, "the sweet life," meaning a life of physical pleasure, luxury, and self-indulgence both in Italian and in English since 1960, when* La dolce vita, *the great film of Federico Fellini, was first shown.*

"With stocks at an all-time high, the couple pursued their version of **dolce vita** without any thought of what tomorrow might bring."

It should be noted that Fellini in his film represented modern Roman high life as anything but sweet, instead offering a cynical portrayal of the self-indulgence of his characters.

doppelgänger DOP əl GANG ər

From German Doppelgänger, *literally, "double-goer."*

In German, and in English since the mid-nineteenth century, meaning "a ghostly double or counterpart of a living person"; also, "a ghost": "Joan's novels depict a world of wraiths and **doppelgängers** besieging the occasional intruder from the world of normal people and institutions."

Also given in English as **doppelganger** and as **doubleganger** (DUB əl GANG ər). Whichever way one spells this word, you can be sure it is the stuff of which paperback bestsellers are made.

doyen doi EN

From French, literally, "dean"; feminine doyenne.

In French, and in English since the mid-seventeenth century, meaning "senior member of a group": "Philip saw himself as the undisputed **doyen** of watercolorists summering on Cape Cod."

The French feminine form of this noun did not come into English as **doyenne** (doi EN) until much later, at the beginning of the twentieth century. Which says something about how a male-dominated society has regarded women.

dressage drə SAH*ZH*

From French, literally, "training," especially of horses.

In French, and in English since the early twentieth century, meaning 1. "a series of intricate steps, gaits, etc., taught to an exhibition horse": "From the first time André saw a trained horse perform **dressage**, he knew what career he wanted to follow."

2. "The art of training a horse in obedience and in precision of movement": "He spent summers all through college conducting classes for skilled equestrians who wanted to learn **dressage**."

3. **Dressage** is sometimes applied figuratively to the training of people, rather than horses, in the sense of knocking someone or some group into shape: "The Speaker of the House soon found some party **dressage** had to be applied to his recalcitrant followers."

The pronunciation of "dressage" is of interest. In French it is dre SAH*ZH*, with the letter "r" pronounced in the customary throat-clearing way. In American English dressage is pronounced drə SAH*ZH*, as shown above, but in British English, whose speakers so often prefer to accent the first syllable of a two-syllable word, it is DRE sah*zh*.

Both the British and the Americans make the "r" sound without bringing up phlegm.

du jour də *ZHUUR*

From French, literally, "of the day."

In English since the late twentieth century, used to form often-ironic, pseudo-French phrases, as "scandal du jour," "headline du jour," "soup (correctly *soupe*) du jour," "spin du jour," and "coffee du jour."

The existence of **du jour** enables sardonic phrasemakers to practice their art.

Such phrases have their source in **plat du jour** (which see).

dungaree DUNG gə REE

From Hindi dungri, *a kind of coarse cloth.*

In English since the beginning of the seventeenth century, meaning "blue denim." The plural, **dungarees** (DUNG gə REEZ), means blue jeans and blue denim work clothes: "Some large law firms treat Fridays as informal dress days, and **dungarees**—expensive designer dungarees, to be sure—are seen in most departments."

E

eau de Cologne OH də kə LOHN

From French, literally, "water of Cologne," meaning "a mildly scented perfume."

In English since the beginning of the nineteenth century, now given usually as **cologne**, meaning "a mildly scented toilet water": "As long as **eau de Cologne** is applied sparingly, most people consider its scent attractive."

The distinction drawn between "perfume"—generally considered to impart a strong, rich aroma—and "toilet water"—generally lightly scented—may reflect a perceived difference between the sexes: Women may use perfume—often calling it a "fragrance"—but real men use toilet water, generally calling it "aftershave lotion."

Eau de Cologne was first produced in the eighteenth century by an Italian chemist living in the German city of Cologne, near the Belgian border and called *Köln* in German. Incidentally, in German "eau de Cologne" is called *Kölnischwasser*, literally, "water of Köln," but is defined in German dictionaries as "eau de Cologne."

Could it have been the French **cachet** (which see) that influenced the naming of this product? Or was it the preeminence of the French language in Europe, especially among people of good breeding or good education, at the time when eau de Cologne first was produced?

eau de vie OH də VEE

From French, literally, "water of life," meaning "brandy."

With the same meaning in English since the mid-eighteenth century: "Mike nightly assured himself that a treat of an ounce or two of **eau de vie** was his rightful perquisite for the stressful life he led."

A word about the quality of **eau de vie**: It is generally taken to be a coarse, incompletely purified variety of brandy, nothing like the ambrosia that is very special old pale brandy, abbreviated V.S.O.P.

Remember, however, that "eau de vie" translates literally as "water of life," and whatever it may lack in quality it makes up in efficacy. And who could take exception with the downing of a drink with such a comforting name?

éclat ay KLAH

From French, literally, "splinter, fragment, burst, flash, brilliance."

In French, and in English since the mid-seventeenth century, with several meanings: 1. "brilliance of success, reputation, etc.": "Her early career was marked by the **éclat** of stardom in film after film."

2. "Brilliant or elaborate display": "The coronation, conducted with great **éclat** only one month after the end of a long war, gave a welcome lift to our country's spirits."

3. "Acclamation, acclaim": "The final curtain came down to thunderous **éclat**."

O happy day!

élan ay LAHN

From French, meaning "vigor" or "spirit."

In English since the late nineteenth century, meaning "dash"; "impetuous ardor": "Whatever else you say about the team, you must admire the players' **élan**, which often carries them to victory even against superior opponents."

But not without at least a handful of excellent athletes.

El Dorado EL də RAH doh

From Spanish El Dorado*, literally, "The Gilded."*

Originally a name given to a fictitious king and, especially, to his equally fictitious capital and country believed by Spanish explorers to exist on the Amazon. The city, named El Dorado, alternatively called Manoa or Dorado, was supposed to have houses roofed with gold.

El Dorado, in English since the end of the sixteenth century, means "any place that offers opportunities of getting rich quickly": "The promoters looked upon the Indian reservation as an **El Dorado**, where roulette, blackjack, slot machines, and the rest would line their pockets with gold and even make some work for Native Americans."

So, long before impoverished Central Europeans dreamed of going to the United States to find streets paved with gold, adventurous Spaniards felt impelled to travel to South America in search of golden roofs.

Streets of gold, roofs of gold—why be fussy?

El Niño **See niño.**

embarras de richesses ahn ba rah də ree SHESS

From French, literally, "embarrassment of riches."

In English since the mid-eighteenth century, meaning "a confusing overabundance of wealth." Lest this definition confuse you, consider a second definition: "the state of having more money than one knows how to handle": "Once Sally's husband had died, she would come to know an **embarras de richesses** as well as a plethora of suitors."

Are you willing to risk an **embarras de richesses**? Win a multimillion-dollar lottery and find out.

embonpoint ahn bawn PWAN

From French, literally, "in good condition"; meaning "stoutness"; "portliness."

In English since the mid-seventeenth century, meaning "excessive portliness"; "stoutness": "Once Ralph reached the age of forty, he began to be inclined to **embonpoint**, and no program of exercise he tried could erase this undesired poundage."

Today, we are so accustomed to viewing stoutness as synonymous with poor health that the French word's literal meaning, "in good condition," may confuse us. It should be recalled that plumpness was long considered a sign of good health and community standing, and anyone who characterized a person as "plump" was paying that person a compliment.

In the good old days, people ate heartily without worrying about the risk of heart attacks or any other of Shakespeare's thousand natural shocks that flesh is heir to.

So, along with fashions and habits, our perceptions change. And give rise to billion-dollar diet industries.

emeritus i MER ə təss

From Latin, an adjective, literally meaning "earned."

In English since the late eighteenth century, meaning "retired from active professional duty, but retaining the title of one's position," especially said of a university professor or high academic official: "After forty years of service to the university, he retired as **Emeritus** Professor of English Literature." The feminine form **emerita** (i MER ə tə) is also used: "Rose now is **Emerita** Professor of Physics."

Emeritus, along with emerita, is also a noun, meaning "a person having emeritus status": "Is he certain he will be named an **emeritus**?"

émigré EM i GRAY

From French émigré, *past participle of* émigrer, *"to emigrate." As a noun meaning "an emigrant," especially a political or literary exile.*

In English since the late eighteenth century, with the same noun meaning: "Even today, American tourists gather at certain Parisian cafés to drink where James Baldwin and other **émigrés** once sat."

English also uses **émigré** as an adjective: "Various **émigré** committees soon formed to lend political and financial support to the exiled foreign leaders struggling to support themselves far from home."

éminence grise ay mee nah*n*ss GREEZ

From French, literally, "gray eminence"; meaning "confidential adviser."

In French, and in English since the mid-nineteenth century, plural **éminences grises** (ay mee nah*n*ss GREEZ), meaning "a person wielding unofficial power," especially through another person and often surreptitiously: "What the inexperienced new mayor sorely needs is an **éminence grise** to guide him through the murky waters of Los Angeles politics."

The English translation "gray eminence" is sometimes used instead of **éminence grise**, and this will have to be dealt with in deciphering "éminence grise."

The story begins with the French word *éminence*—in English, "Your Eminence"—a title of respect, usually capitalized, that is accorded cardinals and so can be translated as "cardinal." Père Joseph (1585–1642) was confidential agent and private secretary to Cardinal Richelieu and, in recognition of the power he wielded, was given the sobriquet *éminence grise*. But why *grise*? An éminence grise does not have to have gray hair.

When *grise* is applied to a person it means "anonymous"; "unidentifiable." And that's the key to what is meant by "éminence grise," making its meaning that of an anonymous person, or a power behind the throne.

In English we might even call such a person a "shadow cardinal"; a "shadow mayor"; a "shadow president"; etc.

Clear enough?

enceinte ahn SANT

From French, literally, "ungirdled"; meaning "pregnant."

In English since the beginning of the seventeenth century, with the same meaning: "For the first five years of our marriage, Norma was happily **enceinte** practically all the time."

But why use the word **enceinte** instead of "pregnant"? One explanation is that "enceinte" is clearly thought preferable by persons who like to show their sophistication and so are quick to call a spade anything but a "spade." Some persons of refined sensibilities may even find the mere idea of pregnancy messy and objectionable.

Not surprisingly, therefore, cognate words are found in other Romance languages—consider *encinta* in Portuguese and Spanish, and *incinta* in Italian. So the word "pregnant"—itself of French origin, but not obviously French—must be avoided on the grounds of being insufficiently obscure.

Quick, Henry, an English euphemism!

Here are a few: Pregnant women, besides being said to be "enceinte," are in a "delicate condition" or in an "interesting condition," or "in a family way," or "expecting." Lest we forget, women are also said "to have one in the oven" and to be "knocked up," not to mention many other inelegant phrases.

See also **accouchement**.

en famille ah*n* fa MEE yə

From French, literally, "in family."

In French, and in English since the early eighteenth century, meaning "in or with one's family"; "at home": "It had long been their practice, except in extraordinary circumstances, to dine **en famille**."

enfant terrible ah*n* fah*n* tə REE blə

From French, literally, "terrible child"; meaning "unruly child."

In English since the mid-nineteenth century, plural **enfants terribles** (ah*n* fah*n* tə REE blə), with two meanings: 1. "an incorrigible child, whose behavior is embarrassing": "To the family's dismay, their youngest son proved to be their **enfant terrible**, never missing a chance to display his brattishness before company."

2. "An outrageously bold or outspoken person, who does and says indiscreet or irresponsible things": "Martin was our organization's **enfant terrible**, given to openly discussing

sensitive company intentions during delicate negotiations with our suppliers."

So, you need not outgrow the characterization of "**enfant terrible**" if you wish. But, all things considered, it would be better for you to shed this inclination each morning before you board your commuter train.

Or become a recognized genius whose lapses are always forgiven.

ennui ahn WEE

From French, meaning "boredom"; "world-weariness"; "tedium."

In English since the late seventeenth century, with similar meanings: "a feeling of weariness and discontent resulting from satiety or lack of interest"; "boredom": "After leaving her long, exciting career as war correspondent, she found herself unhappy with the insufferable **ennui** of life as a desk-bound editor."

entente ahn TAHNT

From French, literally, an "understanding."

In French, and in English since the mid-nineteenth century, meaning 1. "a friendly understanding between nations": "The **entente** the foreign ministers reached proved workable for the rest of the century."

2. "The parties to such an understanding": "When the economies of the **entente** began to crumble, the days of the nations' amicable relations were numbered."

Two historic **ententes** were the so-called *ententes cordiales*—*cordiale* meaning "cordial" or "warm"—one signed by Great Britain and France in 1904; the other by Great Britain, France, and Russia in 1907.

espresso e SPRESS oh

From Italian espresso, *literally, "pressed out," plural* espressi; *a shortened form of* caffé espresso.

Espresso first appeared in English during World War II, with the plural **espressos** (e SPRESS ohz), as in Italian meaning 1. "coffee prepared by forcing live steam or boiling water through ground dark-roast coffee beans": "The growing popularity of **espresso** in the United States has fostered development of coffee bars in the European style."

2. "A cup of this coffee": "I was surprised to find that Tom drank at least two **espressos** after every meal of the day."

The pitfall for American coffee drinkers is not overindulgence in this strong coffee, but their strong tendency to pronounce "espresso" as though it were spelled "e x p r e s s o." And some of these well-intentioned persons actually misspell the word as "e x p r e s s o."

esprit de corps e SPREE də KOR

From French, literally, "spirit of the body," the body being an organization or collective group. **Esprit de corps**, *then, means "communal spirit."*

In English since the late eighteenth century with comparable meaning, formally defined as "a sense of unity" and "of common responsibilities," as developed within a group; "fellowship": "Upon being appointed chief executive officer of the failing conglomerate, she resolved that her first goal would be to restore the **esprit de corps** essential for effective teamwork throughout her organization."

So well understood is the English "esprit de corps" that a first-class French-English dictionary uses it to define the French *esprit de corps*.

F

fado FAH doh

From Portuguese fado, *from Latin* fatum, *both, literally, "fate."*

In Portuguese, and in English since the beginning of the twentieth century, a Portuguese folk song typically of melancholy character: "Liam, his sad expression never changing, sat alone for hours in a dark corner of the room, sipping wine and listening intently to the **fados** of the singer and her guitarist."

faience fay AHNSS

From French faïence, *originally meaning "pottery made in the Italian city of Faenza."*

In French, and in English since the beginning of the eighteenth century, also given as **faïence**, meaning "glazed earthenware or pottery, especially a fine variety with highly colored designs": "They happened to chance upon several pieces of **faience** they could afford to buy."

Incidentally, the Italian word for **faience** is *faenza*. Seems fair enough.

fainéant FAY nee ənt

From French fainéant, *from* faire *"do"* + néant *"nothing"; an adjective meaning "idle"; "lazy"; as well as a noun meaning "idler"; "loafer."*

In English since early in the seventeenth century, **fainéant**, also given as **faineant**, has the same meanings and, as an adjective, is often defined as 1. "indolent, inactive; do-nothing": "He had acquired a reputation, well deserved, as a **fainéant** dabbler."

2. As a noun, defined as "an idler, a do-nothing": "After Sylvia's marriage collapsed, she seemed to lose her purpose in life and became a **fainéant**."

3. A related noun is **faineance** (FAY nee ənss), meaning "the state of being a fainéant": "The circumstances of his birth—he was an only child born into wealth to parents who agreeably died young—made it easy for him to embrace **faineance**."

While Americans are accustomed to condemning a do-nothing Congress, they have the opportunity to convey the same meaning by condemning a "fainéant" Congress. Since "fainéant" is not in common use in English, of course, anyone who uses this word runs the risk of being misunderstood by most people.

But it may be worth the risk if your usage adds to your reputation as a linguist.

fait accompli fe tah kaw*n* PLEE

From French, literally, "accomplished fact."

In English since the mid-nineteenth century, plural **faits**

accomplis (fe za kaw*n* PLEE), meaning "an accomplished fact"; "something already done." This phrase is generally used in English as well as French in the sense of an action carried out before the persons affected learn of it: "Before we could take steps to evict our troublesome tenant, he skipped town, and the matter became a **fait accompli**."

A fait accompli thus enables someone to steal a march on an opponent, preventing the opponent from taking action in time to forestall an expected outcome.

fakir fə KEER

From Arabic faqir, *literally, "poor man."*

In Arabic, and in English since the beginning of the seventeenth century, also given as **fakeer**, meaning 1. "a Muslim or Hindu religious ascetic or mendicant monk commonly considered a wonder-worker": "As I watched, three **fakirs** passed in less than a minute, all looking for a good place to stand in the busy thoroughfare."

2. "A member of any Islamic religious order; a dervish": "The crowd gathered to watch as soon as the **fakir** began to whirl."

The pitfall for the unwary is the confusion of **fakir** with the English word "faker," which has a well-known but entirely different meaning.

farrago fə RAH goh

From Latin, originally meaning "a mash for feeding cattle"; later, figuratively, a "medley" or "hodgepodge."

In English since the early seventeenth century, plural **farragos** or **farragoes**, with the Latin later meanings: "As soon as I finished my presentation, I faced a **farrago** of catcalls, objections, and angry questions, leavened by a welcome smattering of applause."

fasnacht FAWSS NAHKT

From Pennsylvania German fasnacht, *from German* Fastnacht, *literally, "night of fasting," meaning—get this—"a deep-fried raised doughnut."*

In American English, date of introduction unknown, also given as **fastnacht** (FAWST NAHKT): "Visitors to the Amish country soon learn the efficacy of a **fasnacht** taken with a freshly brewed cup of coffee."

People fortunate enough to eat a proper **fasnacht** or two should learn that these sinkers were originally served on Shrove Tuesday as the last sweet treat before Lent.

And if you take an interest in doughnuts, you may be amused to learn that President John F. Kennedy's famous public declaration "*Ich bin ein Berliner*," given during a 1963 speech in West Berlin, Germany, could be and was translated in two ways: 1. "I am a citizen of Berlin" and 2. "I am a doughnut."

Food for thought. At any rate, try a fasnacht. You'll like it.

faux-naïf FOH nah EEF

From French, literally, "false-innocent," meaning "ingenuous."

In English since the mid-twentieth century, 1. a noun meaning "a person who shrewdly affects a pose of simplicity or innocence": "What Lincoln often did while trying a case in court was play the role of **faux-naïf**, misleading an opponent into seeing him as nothing more than a simple country lawyer."

2. As an adjective, meaning "marked by a pretense of simplicity or innocence"; "disingenuous": "We finally understood that what we had thought was innocent behavior was really **faux-naïf** cleverness carefully planned to deceive."

So, by now you have deduced that the French adjective *faux* and its English cousin "faux" mean "false, artificial, or imitation," giving us in addition to **faux-naïf** the next entry, **faux**

pas, and other faux-terms, for example faux pearls, faux tears, and faux anything else you wish to devise.

faux pas foh PAH

From French, literally, "false step"; meaning "foolish mistake."

In English since the late seventeenth century, plural **faux pas** (foh PAHZ), meaning "an embarrassing social blunder or indiscretion": "Terry told her friends she had established a new rule governing her husband's behavior at a dinner party, 'Three **faux pas** and you're out.' "

Faux pas are the least of your worries, you say? Try this: The incomparable *Oxford English Dictionary*, in its entry for "faux pas," gives as one of its early definitions "an act that compromises one's reputation, especially a woman's lapse from virtue." Sounds a bit too strict for me.

Other times, other customs!

favela fə VEL ə

From Brazilian Portuguese, meaning a "shack" or "shanty."

In English since the mid-twentieth century, meaning "a Brazilian slum or shantytown in or near a city": "Tourist guides shun our pathetic **favela** unless specifically asked to take visitors there."

It is worth noting that the **favela** is literally "a shrub," whose name derives from *fava*, a type of bean. Today, anyone fortunate enough to live in an ethnically diverse area knows the fava as a type of broad bean, which is an Italian as well as a Portuguese term.

But how did the fava give us a word meaning "slum"? It is said that Favela was the name given to a hill near Rio de Janeiro where shantytowns were built about the end of the last century.

Could its inhabitants have had little besides fava beans to eat?

fedayeen fe dah YEEN

From Arabic fedayeen, *also given as* fedayin, *a plural noun literally meaning "people who undertake perilous adventures."*

In Arabic and in English, the singular form of fedayeen is **fedayee** (fe dah YEE).

In English since the mid-twentieth century, meaning "members of an Arab commando group operating especially against Israel": "Once the news came that **fedayeen** were planning an attack on the settlement, the local people went about only in pairs or small groups and fully armed."

femme fatale FEM fə TAL

From French, literally, "fatal woman."

In French, and in English since the early twentieth century, plural **femmes fatales** (FEM fə TALZ), meaning "an irresistibly attractive woman, especially one who leads men into dangerous situations"; "a siren": "Age had taken its toll on the actress, making it difficult for her to play a credible **femme fatale**, and for the rest of her career she could only act roles suitable for a woman of advanced age."

Alas for those who are too young to grasp the worth of an older, wiser woman.

fete fayt

From French fête, *literally, "a feast."*

In French, and in English since the mid-eighteenth century, also given as **fête**, meaning 1. "a holiday"; "a day of celebration": "The weather was cooperative on the day of the **fete**, and we were able to complete the entire planned schedule of contests and entertainments."

2. "A festive celebration or entertainment": "What started out as a **fete** to honor our new councilman ended as a protracted bout of drinking and brawling."
3. "A religious festival or feast": "The town turned out in force for the **fete** of Saint Denis, patron saint of Paris."
4. As a verb, meaning "entertain at or honor with a fete": "Our benefactor was **feted** on the occasion of her endowment of the splendid new hospital wing."

The rich have the knack of gaining celebrity.

See also **fiesta**.

fiancé FEE ahn SAY

From French, literally, "betrothed."

In French, and in English since the mid-nineteenth century, meaning "a man engaged to be married"; also, "a man to whom a woman is engaged." Thus one may say, "I thought it was time to change my status from **fiancé** to husband"; and "John Stiles is Ellen Demarest's **fiancé**."

The feminine form of **fiancé** is **fiancée**, with the same pronunciation. Substitute "woman" for "man," and "man" for "woman," to make the definition of fiancé fit that of fiancée.

It appears that in today's world the institution of formal engagement to marry is on the way out, having largely been replaced by various other arrangements between and within the sexes.

fiesta fee ESS tə

From Spanish, literally, a "feast."

In Spanish, and in English since the beginning of the nineteenth century, plural **fiestas**, meaning any "festival" or "festive celebration": "The day was approaching for the spring **fiesta**, and schoolchildren spent most of the school day practicing traditional songs and dances."

Also meaning, in Spain and Latin America, "a festive celebration of a religious holiday": "Our initial task of preparation for the **fiesta** will be to take down and clean the statue of Santa Teresa."

fin de siècle **fa*n* də SYE klə**

From French, literally, "end of a century."

In Great Britain the **fin de siècle**, the end of the nineteenth century, was the time when the complacency and conservatism of the Victorian era gave way to the more relaxed Edwardian era. A similar relaxation was observed on the Continent and in the United States as well.

Three meanings of "fin de siècle" have developed in English and in French since late in the nineteenth century: 1. a noun meaning "the end of the nineteenth century": "With the **fin de siècle** at hand, almost as if by prearrangement the new senior class appeared markedly more serious than its predecessors."

2. An adjective, also given as **fin-de-siècle**, meaning "pertaining to concepts of art, society, etc., associated with the end of the nineteenth century": "She wrote a brilliant analysis of **fin-de-siècle** European literature that was well received by her colleagues."

3. Another adjectival meaning is "decadent," particularly with reference to the end of the nineteenth century, and is given both as **fin de siècle** and **fin-de-siècle**: "Marcel Proust was the preeminent chronicler of **fin-de-siècle** French society."

It was interesting to observe a last-minute rush to fin de siècle in journalistic writing as the second millennium drooped to a close.

flagrante delicto See **in flagrante delicto.**

flambé flahm BAY

From French flambé, *"singed"; past participle of* flamber, *literally, "to singe"; "to pass through flame."*

In French, and in English since the beginning of the twentieth century, 1. an adjective meaning "served in flaming liquor, especially brandy, applied to food that is brought alight to the diner": "I always enjoy watching an expert head waiter exhibiting his prowess at preparing crêpe suzettes **flambé**."

2. As a verb, meaning "pour liquor (over a food) and ignite it": "I was continually chagrined at my failure time after time to **flambé** savory dishes my wife prepared."

And regretful of the waste of precious brandy we could ill afford.

flâneur flah NUR

From French flâneur, *from* flâner, *meaning "to saunter idly."*

In French, and in English since late in the nineteenth century, meaning "an idler, a man about town": "After a few years of living the life of a **flâneur**, he found himself so satisfied with his empty existence that he never again sought employment."

Every lazy man's dream.

foie gras fwah GRAH

From French, literally, "fat liver."

In French, and in English since early in the nineteenth century, meaning "the liver of specially fattened geese or ducks, used particularly as a pâté": "Poultry farmers in Poland are said to be supplying large quantities of **foie gras** to French processors, who create a French product with Polish raw materials."

Almost as good as chopped chicken liver adorned with a slice of sweet onion.

See also **pâté de foie gras**.

foo yung foo yung

From Chinese fùh yùhng, *literally, a "hibiscus."*

In English since the mid-twentieth century, known only from its appearance in the phrase **egg foo yung**, so often encountered in the menus of Cantonese restaurants, meaning "a pancake-shaped omelet mixed and cooked with vegetables": "For years I avoided going to Chinese restaurants, because I was allergic to eggs and thought mistakenly that all Chinese food, like **egg foo yung**, was prepared as omelets."

force majeure forss mah *ZH*UR

From French, literally, "superior force."

In English since the mid-nineteenth century, plural **forces majeures** (forss mah *ZH*UR), meaning "irresistible force" or "overwhelming circumstances." **Force majeure** finds its most frequent use as a term in law, meaning "an unforeseen event that may operate to excuse a party from the responsibility of fulfilling a contract": "Our lawyer told us that the ninth paragraph of the contract, dealing with **force majeure**, may be invoked only when a natural disaster occurs."

Think, for example, of a hurricane, a terrible fire, a flood, or the like.

fourragère FUUR ə *ZH*AIR

From French.

In French and, since the early twentieth century, in English military use, meaning "an ornament of cord worn on the shoulder of a uniform as an honorary decoration"; awarded, for instance, to members of a unit that has received a stipulated number of citations for heroism, etc.: "All the members of our artillery battalion, even company clerks who had never gone near an artillery piece fired in anger, wear their **fourragères** proudly."

Few of us really are heroes.

frankfurter FRANK fər tər

From German Frankfurter, *short for* Frankfurter Wurst, *literally, "Frankfurt sausage."*

Frankfurt is the English name of a German city, Frankfurt am Main, and Main is the name of the river on which Frankfurt stands.

In English since the closing years of the nineteenth century, **frankfurter**, also known as **frank** in "franks and beans" and other phrases, means—as every decently raised American child knows—a "hot dog," that is, "a smoked sausage of various meats": "The genius of the **frankfurter** is its ability to rest resigned to its fate within the jaws of a mustard-slathered bun, with or without sauerkraut, chopped onions, or whatever, there to await the crunches of its human predator."

Ah!

fresco FRESS koh

From Italian, meaning "cool" or "fresh."

In Italian, and in English as a noun since the end of the sixteenth century, plural **frescoes** or **frescos**, meaning 1. "the art or technique of watercolor painting on a moist plaster surface": "Once he had mastered the intricacies of **fresco**, he worked primarily in that medium."

2. "A picture or design so painted": "During our stay in Italy we were particularly interested in viewing early **frescoes**."

3. As a verb, meaning "paint in **fresco**": "The original plan called for engaging an artist who would **fresco** all the exterior walls of the structure."

frisson free SOHN

From French, meaning "a shiver," "a shudder," "a thrill."

In English since the late eighteenth century, plural **frissons** (free SOHNZ), meaning "a sudden, passing sensation of excitement"; "a shudder of emotion"; "a thrill": "Hitchcock was master of the art of inducing collective **frissons** in movie audiences."

Momentarily interrupting the crunching of popcorn.

frottage fraw TAH*ZH*

From French, meaning "rubbing"; "friction"; from frotter *meaning "to rub."*

In English since the mid-twentieth century, with three meanings: 1. "a technique in art of rubbing chalk, charcoal, etc., over paper laid on a relieflike surface": "In spring and summer I found myself spending most weekends going about old cemeteries, using **frottage** to record tombstone inscriptions and decorations."

2. "A work of art produced by this technique": "My **frottages** were stored in my father's attic and eventually were thrown out when his house was sold."

3. In psychiatry, "the practice of gaining sexual stimulation by rubbing one's body against something, especially by rubbing against another person": "In a crowded subway car, it is not unusual for a woman to find herself the victim of **frottage**."

English had adopted **frotteur** (fraw TUR) in the late nineteenth century to identify a person given to rubbing against the body of another person, as in the third sense above, before taking in frottage in the twentieth century: "As soon as I saw the man pushing through the crowd toward me, I was gripped by anxiety—certain I was to be the target of a **frotteur**."

G

gabble GAB əl

From Middle Dutch gabbelen, *perhaps onomatopoeic in origin—geese do gabble, don't they?—with the meaning of "jabber."*

In English since late in the sixteenth century as a noun meaning 1. "noisy, unintelligible talk, chatter": "I am rapidly tiring of the children's never-ending **gabble**."

2. As a verb meaning "jabber, prattle, chatter"; "talk volubly and incoherently": "The frightened old man continued to **gabble** after his rescue, despite the fact that no one paid him any attention."

gaffe gaf

From French, meaning "a blunder."

In English since the beginning of the twentieth century, meaning "a social blunder"; "a **faux pas** (which see)": "I immediately knew I had made no ordinary mistake, but a **gaffe** that would spread rapidly through the town and be remembered for years."

And used to embarrass me.

gaga GAH GAH

From French gaga, *also given in French as* ga-ga, *a slang noun meaning "a senile person"; and a colloquial adjective meaning "senile, crazy, and foolish."*

In English since the beginning of the twentieth century, and also given as **ga-ga**, a colloquial adjective meaning 1. "excessively and foolishly enthusiastic": "Tennis fans went **gaga** over the new star, who served ace after ace and seemed to be able to chase down every ball hit at her and make returns flawlessly."

2. "Ardently fond"; "infatuated": "Are you still **gaga** over that beautiful girl?"

3. "Demented"; "crazy"; "dotty": "I think the old guy going around the neighborhood half-naked in winter is really **gaga**."

"Senile" to "enthusiastic" to "infatuated" to "demented." A multipurpose adoption from the French.

gambit GAM bit

From French gambit, *from Spanish* gambito *or Italian* gambetto, *literally, a "tripping up."*

In all these languages, and in English since the mid-seventeenth century, meaning 1. "an opening in the game of chess in which a player seeks to gain advantage by sacrificing a piece": "In a short while, the clever opening became known at the club as Dan's **gambit**, a term that made the boy's chest swell with pride."

2. "Any maneuver by which one seeks to gain an advantage": "Your new friend has more imaginative **gambits** than the leader of a Balkan country."

3. "A remark made to open or redirect a conversation": " 'To tell the truth,' the editor said, using his favorite and totally deceitful **gambit**, 'I put your check in the mail this morning.' "

gâteau ga TOH

From French gâteau, *plural* gâteaux, *meaning "a cake."*

In English since the mid-nineteenth century, also given as **gateau**, plural **gateaux** (ga TOHZ), meaning "a cake," especially a light sponge cake with a rich icing or filling: "When Stan was told a **gâteau** would be served with the coffee, he murmured, 'When did this family stop eating pound cake?' "

At any rate, no matter whether the first letter "a" carries or does not carry a circumflex accent, the English plural form ends in "x."

gauche gohsh

From French, meaning "left, left-handed"; "awkward."

In English since the mid-eighteenth century, an adjective meaning 1. "lacking social grace, sensitivity, or acuteness"; "awkward"; "crude"; "tactless": "My wife could always be counted on to call my attention to any **gauche** remark I made at the dinner table—and always in a voice heard by everyone at our table."

2. The noun **gaucherie** (GOH shə REE), in English since the end of the eighteenth century, means "lack of social grace, sensitivity, or acuteness": "Larry's **gaucherie** is attributable to his lack of early training at home."

3. "An act, movement, etc., that is socially graceless": "The **gaucheries** were piling up so rapidly that I began to wonder whether they were intended as a form of party game."

But how did the French word *gauche*, originally meaning "left," get to mean "awkward"? The simple answer is that in this right-handed world, any left-handed person appears awkward to the rest of us.

The old Romans had a similar proclivity: In Latin, *sinister* means "left" and has a secondary meaning of "perverse" and "unfavorable." And the English adjective "sinister," which came directly from Latin, has the word "left" as one of its secondary meanings, but its most important meaning is "threatening or portending evil."

gegenschein GAY gən SHĪN

From German Gegenschein, *from* gegen *"opposite"* + Schein *"shine" or "glow"; literally, "opposite shine"; in astronomy meaning "counterglow; opposition or reflection."*

In English since the late nineteenth century, also given as **Gegenschein**, an astronomical term meaning "a faint patch of light in the night sky that is a reflection of sunlight by meteoric material": "American astronauts finally succeeded in their attempt to photograph the **gegenschein**."

Imagine.

geisha GAY shə

From Japanese gei *"arts"* + sha *"person."*

In English since the end of the nineteenth century, plural **geisha** and **geishas**, meaning "a Japanese woman trained as a professional singer, dancer, and companion for men": "At supper, **geishas**—one assigned to sit with each guest—ministered to the visiting American businessmen, making certain they had all the food and drink they wanted."

The prevailing wisdom is that geishas, who must go through a long course of instruction, are not to be considered prostitutes, even though many foreigners use the term loosely in that sense. It is also asserted that a geisha eventually will retire from her occupation to become the companion of a rich man, who will support her for life.

A truly precise definition is difficult to come by, since an excellent current Japanese-English dictionary defines the Japanese word *geisha* as the English word "geisha."

And there it must be left.

gemütlich gə MOOT lik

From German, meaning "jovial"; "cheerful."

In English since the mid-nineteenth century, also given as **gemuetlich**, meaning 1. "comfortable and pleasant"; "cozy": "Once we refurnished the apartment, everyone agreed that visitors would find it thoroughly **gemütlich**."

2. "Genial; easygoing": "Much to our surprise, the couple next door, initially seen by us as standoffish, proved marvelously **gemütlich** and a pleasure to be with."

And the English noun **gemütlichkeit** follows logically from the German *Gemütlichkeit*, both meaning "cheerfulness, coziness, geniality."

geneva jə NEE və

From Dutch genever*—through French* genevre *and back to Latin* juniperus, *juniper—meaning "gin." And everyone knows that juniper berries play a big part in giving gin its characteristic flavor.*

In English since the beginning of the eighteenth century, also meaning "gin," but more properly called "Holland gin," or "Hollands": "On the long ferry ride to England, the unruly young Hollanders never stopped singing loudly in praise of drink and gulping bottle after bottle of **geneva**."

Only a dry martini expert—a certification that requires extensive preparation—might care that there is a slight difference in the way gin and **geneva** are distilled. The details of the process are better left to an encyclopedia.

genre ZHAHN rə

From French, meaning "sort, kind."

In English since the early nineteenth century, plural **genres** (*ZH*AHN rəz), meaning 1. "a class or category of artistic endeavor having a particular form, content, technique, or the like": "In her studies she concentrated on the novel, a **genre** that had always interested her."

2. "Paintings, usually of a realistic style, in which scenes of everyday life form the subject matter": "**Genre** was not recognized as a worthy and independent subject matter until the sixteenth century in Flanders, where it was popularized by Pieter Bruegel, the elder."

Whose paintings still fascinate museumgoers.

gestalt gə SHTAHLT

From German Gestalt, *plural* Gestalten, *meaning "form, shape."*

In German, and in English since the early twentieth century, plural **gestalts** and **gestalten** (gə SHTAHLT ən), a term in psychology meaning "an integrated structure perceived as functionally more than the sum of its parts": "If we do not consider all aspects of Barbara's personality as a **gestalt**, we surely will fail to understand the entirety of her motivations."

ghee gee

From Hindi ghi, *from Sanskrit* ghrta; *past participle of* ghr, *meaning "sprinkle."*

In Hindi, and in English since the mid-seventeenth century, meaning "clarified butter," used especially in East Indian cooking: "On his first trip to India, he took an intense dislike to the smell of food being cooked in **ghee**."

And to this day still doesn't frequent Indian restaurants.

giaour jowr

From Turkish gavur, *from Persian* gaur, *from Zoroastrian* gabr, *in all these languages meaning "a non-Muslim."*

In English, as **giaour**, since the mid-sixteenth century, meaning "an unbeliever"; "a non-Muslim, especially a Christian": "Imagine my discomfiture when our guide fell ill, and we knew the three of us would from then on be nothing but hapless **giaours** speaking only English and trying to journey through a remote region of Iran, where we probably would meet no one who spoke English."

Maybe we should head for the nearest international airport.

gigolo *ZHIG* ə LOH

From French, meaning "a paid male escort."

In French, and in English since the early twentieth century, meaning more fully 1. "a man living off the earnings or gifts of a woman"; "a kept man, especially a young man supported by an older woman in return for his companionship and sexual attentions": "According to neighborhood gossip, the wealthy woman had a **gigolo**, and while a few persons quietly envied her, most expressed scorn for the woman and for her young man."

2. "A male professional dancing partner or escort": "While the cruise orchestra played, unescorted women waited to be asked to dance by the ship's officers, but women who were traveling with their **gigolos** never missed a dance."

Gigolo is especially interesting as a word because it is the masculine counterpart of the French *gigole* or *gigolette*, meaning "a woman of the streets or public dance halls." **Gigolette**

is seldom heard in English and has disappeared from the French language.

glitterati See **beau monde and literati.**

gobemouche GAWB moosh

From French gobe-mouches, *from* gober *"to swallow"* + mouche *"a fly"; literally, "swallower of flies," meaning the common bird called a "flycatcher" in English.*

More importantly, in English since the early nineteenth century meaning "a credulous person, especially one who believes any rumor, no matter how improbable": "Conspiracy theorists, **gobemouches** first-class and ever growing in number, can be counted on to swallow every wild claim, no matter how unlikely."

And clutter up the Internet with their foolishness.

golem GOH ləm

From Yiddish goylem, *from Hebrew* golem, *meaning "embryo," "larva," "cocoon."*

In Yiddish, and in English since the end of the nineteenth century, meaning 1. in Jewish folklore, "a figure constructed in the form of a human being and said to have been endowed with life": "The legend of Prague's **golem** still fascinates many modern Jews."

2. "A stupid and clumsy person"; "a blockhead": "Above all, I want a clear-thinking person, not a **golem**, as my executive assistant."

3. "An automaton": "Instead of thinking things through before you act, you behave like an unfeeling **golem**."

gourmet guur MAY

From French, formerly meaning "wine taster" and "wine-

merchant's assistant." Now "an epicure, a connoisseur of fine food and drink."

1. As an English noun since the beginning of the nineteenth century, with the same modern meaning: "Mistaking indulgence of his seemingly insatiable appetite for any food and drink set before him for an imagined ability to tell fine cuisine from bad, Gregory proclaimed himself a **gourmet**."
2. As an adjective, meaning "of or characteristic of a gourmet, especially involving skilled preparation of exotic ingredients or ingredients of high quality": "The proliferation of magazines, books, and television programs devoted to **gourmet** cooking may lead one to conclude that Americans sit down each evening to candlelit dinners of extraordinary quality."
3. As an adjective, said of a kitchen well equipped for the preparation of elaborate meals: "Three months ago, the young couple, both hardworking lawyers, bought a high-priced house complete with a **gourmet** kitchen they have not used yet, not even for making morning coffee."

A word must be said about the mistaken use of **gourmand** (guur MAHND) to mean **gourmet**. A *gourmand* in French is—pure and simple—a "glutton." In English, since the late fifteenth century, "gourmand" originally meant a "glutton"; but by the eighteenth century, unfortunately, it also came to be used to mean a "gourmet."

It is easy to see how two words spelled so nearly alike can be thought of as interchangeable in meaning. But consider that self-respecting gourmets never think of themselves as "gourmands." Consider further that few gourmands are ready to come out of the closet and proclaim themselves persons who are given to eating indiscriminatingly and to excess. Not for them the labels "glutton" and "gourmand."

So gourmands think they really are "gourmets"—a socially acceptable term—and go on eating themselves under the table until the day they are recognized by their internists as victims of heavy-duty overweight and life-threatening levels of cholesterol.

And two valuable English words continue to struggle against what inevitably will be complete loss of separate identities. Alas!

graffiti grə FEE tee

From Italian graffiti, *plural form of* graffito, *literally, "scratches."*

In Italian, and in English since the mid-nineteenth century, meaning 1. "markings painted, sketched, scrawled, etc., on a building wall or the like": "In the City of New York a decade ago, **graffiti** appeared in such profusion on the walls of subway cars that costly chemical techniques had to be developed to eradicate them."

2. As a collective noun, such markings as a whole: "As a result of police vigilance and citizen elbow grease, **graffiti** have ceased to be a problem on our street."

3. **Graffito** is the term of choice for an educated archaeologist who wishes to refer to an ancient drawing or writing scratched on a wall: "Vandals have managed to obscure the prized Mayan **graffito** that survived until this century above the entrance to an ancient tomb."

It must be pointed out that in modern times, so-called **graffiti artists** seem never to stop at a single graffito, so there is little use for the singular form in referring to the current output of these civic despoilers.

grand mal gran mahl

From French, literally, "great sickness."

In French, and in English since the mid-nineteenth century, meaning "a form of epilepsy characterized by convulsions and loss of consciousness": "The child's parents, deeply affected by their son's first **grand mal** seizures, were assured by physicians that they soon would be able to control his epilepsy."

Grand mal contrasts with **petit mal** (which see).

Grand Prix grah*n* PREE

From French, literally, "great prize."

In French, and in English since early in the twentieth century, plural **Grand Prix**, **Grands Prix**, and **Grand Prixes**, all pronounced grah*n* PREE.

Meaning any of various major automobile races over a long, arduous course, especially any of several international races held each year over the same courses: "Whenever I drive alone along a winding road, scarcely wide enough for my little car, I lose myself as Walter Mitty driving in a **Grand Prix**."

gravitas GRA vi TAHSS

From Latin, literally, "heaviness."

In Latin, and in English since the early twentieth century, meaning "seriousness, solemn demeanor": "Seldom have we seen an applicant exhibit such **gravitas**, but we wonder whether he has the requisite mental ability for the demanding job."

It takes more than a solemn demeanor to make it in the big time.

gravlax GRAHV lahkss

From Swedish gravlax, *Norwegian* gravlaks, *from* grava *"bury"* + laks *"salmon."*

In Swedish, and in English since the mid-twentieth century, meaning "boned raw salmon cured by marinating in various spices": "Persons of refined taste mistakenly reject divine lox, smooth-textured cream cheese, and appetite-satisfying bagels as fare fit only for peasants, instead taking pleasure in nibbling on tiny, unsatisfying canapés made with smoked salmon or **gravlax**."

Incidentally, the literal meaning of Swedish *gravlax*, "bury salmon," makes good sense when we consider that in the original Scandinavian method of curing salmon the fish was buried for a time.

A technique no longer needed.

gulag GOO lahg

From Russian Gulág, *an acronym formed from* **G**lávnoe **u**pravlénie ispravítel'no-trudovykh ***lag***erei, *which translates as "Main Directorate of Corrective Labor Camps."*

In English since the mid-twentieth century, meaning 1. "the system of forced-labor camps in the former Soviet Union": "Many Russians and members of other nationalities within the former USSR are alive today who dourly recall the days of the **gulag**."

2. "Any one of these camps": "Aleksandr Solzhenitsyn's *One Day in the Life of Ivan Denisovich* describes in excruciating detail the struggle of one prisoner to survive a typical day in a **gulag**."

3. "Any prison or detention camp, especially for political prisoners": "Many Japanese-Americans recall the camps they were confined in during World War II as nothing less than **gulags**."

It will be interesting to see whether **gulag** will long survive as an English word. So evocative of misery is gulag that my bet is on its survival.

gung-ho gung hoh

From Chinese kungho, *from* kung *"work"* + ho *"harmony," meaning "eager, enthusiastic." According to Hugh Rawson, in his valuable and endlessly entertaining* Devious Derivations *(1994),* ***gung-ho*** *was an abbreviation of the name of the Chinese Industrial Cooperatives in 1939.*

In pidgin English since World War II, an adjective meaning "wholeheartedly enthusiastic and loyal"; "eager, zealous": "When a kamikaze narrowly missed the destroyer ahead of us in the convoy, our **gung-ho** crew was ready for anything that came our way."

Also an adverb meaning "in a successful manner": "Their business was going **gung-ho** until the Fed hiked the prime rate."

guru GUUR oo

From Sanskrit, meaning "an elder, a priest."

In English since the early nineteenth century, with several meanings: 1. "a Hindu spiritual teacher or leader of a religious sect": "I lived in Bombay for six months and there met the most extraordinary **guru** with a following of at least a thousand disciples, most of them Americans."

2. "An intellectual or spiritual guide or leader": "You could hardly think of an unfrocked priest as ideally qualified to act as a young seminarian's **guru**."

3. "Any person who counsels or advises"; "a mentor": "In her first staff job in Congressional politics she found a **guru** in our crafty old senior senator."

4. "A leader in a particular field": "They represented themselves as financial **gurus**, but never provided any verifiable information on their qualifications."

Nor reliable information on their accomplishments.

gusto GUSS toh

From Italian gusto, *from Latin* gustus, *meaning "taste."*

In English since the early seventeenth century, plural **gustoes**, meaning "hearty" or "keen enjoyment, as in eating or drinking, or in action or speech in general": "No matter what the occasion—but especially after funerals—my mother ate with great **gusto**."

Nothing like food to sustain life, especially after the death of a loved one.

H

habeas corpus HAY bee əss KOR pəss

From Latin, literally, "you have the body."

In English since the sixteenth century, meaning "a writ requiring a person to be brought before a judge, specifically for investigation of a restraint on the person's liberty": "Once my lawyer filed for a writ of **habeas corpus**, I knew I would soon be released from confinement."

The phrase is an abbreviation of the opening words of the writ—in Latin *habeas corpus ad subiciendum*, translated freely as "you (the prosecutor) must bring the accused before a court to undergo the action of the law."

Habeas corpus is one of those adopted foreign expressions in English that will never be fully Anglicized. It is firmly established in legal circles and, wherever personal liberties are protected by law, habeas corpus—or the equivalent—will continue to be used to prevent illegal detention of persons suspected of committing a crime.

And readers of detective fiction and the rest of us will continue to understand that this writ is a cornerstone of common law in that it gives lawyers the opportunity to have judges decide whether police officers have detained their clients illegally.

habitué hə BICH oo AY

From French habitué, *the past participle of* habituer, *meaning "to frequent (a place)." Used as a noun,* habitué *means "a habitual visitor or customer of a particular establishment."*

In English since early in the nineteenth century, with the same meaning, but especially that of a regular customer of a restaurant, club, bar, or the like: "It was the kind of place in which almost every customer was surely an **habitué**, and only tourists had to tell the bartender what they wanted to drink."

A word about the accent on the final letter of the English **habitué**. It was there when the word was originally taken from French, and there it remains and probably always will. Without that accent, the English word—like the words "roué" and "passé" and many others borrowed from French—would defy reasonable pronunciation.

Consider what may be happening to the word "café," which was clearly adopted from French and is pronounced ka FAY by most of us in the United States and England. In England today, however, the pronunciation KAF is heard more and more, and the word is sometimes even spelled "cafe."

This pronunciation began as street slang and appears to be gaining popularity. Among the educated, however, KAF is said only jocularly. Yet ROO and PASS for "roué" and "passé" will not travel this accepting route, since these two words are used almost exclusively by educated speakers and writers.

And will never enter street slang, I believe.

hakim hah KEEM

From Arabic, meaning "wise; wise man."

In English since the late sixteenth century, also given as **hakeem**, meaning "wise man," especially in Muslim countries.

Hakim also means "philosopher" and "physician": "I was fortunate to be befriended by a **hakim**, who showed great patience in answering all my questions."

halvah hahl VAH

From Yiddish halava, *in modern Hebrew* halbah; *in modern Greek* khalbas, *in Turkish* helva; *from Arabic* halwah *and Persian* halwa, *all meaning "a sweet confection."*

In English since the mid-nineteenth century, and also given as **halavah** and **halva**, meaning "a sweet candy of Turkish origin, made chiefly of ground sesame seeds and honey": "In my old neighborhood **halvah** was sold in many stores, but the best-tasting variety came from a shop owned by a family of Armenian immigrants."

The mere century-and-a-half life thus far of the English word **halvah** must not be taken as indicating that this delicious confection is a Johnny-come-lately. In the mid-seventeenth century, for instance, English writers in India and Persia remarked on this confection, calling it **hulwa**. Consider further that the Yiddish *halava* can also be traced etymologically to Urdu, which is spoken in Pakistan.

All of this information is supplied here to assure readers that wherever they travel they can expect to find halvah available.

Once tasted, halvah is usually found so enticing that government regulators probably should warn the public that it may become addicting.

hapax legomenon HAP akss li GOM ə NON

From Greek hápax legomenon, *literally, "(a thing) said only once."*

In English since the late nineteenth century, also given as **hapax**; plural **hapax legomena** (HAP akss li GOM ə nə); meaning "a word or phrase of which only one recorded instance is known": "The drudgery of single-minded scholarly pursuit of **hapax legomena** has been vastly reduced through exploitation of the rapid search capabilities of modern computers."

And will sooner or later sound the death knell of this particular variety of obscure pedantry.

hara-kiri HAHR ə KEER ee

From Japanese hara-kiri, *from* hara *"belly"* + kiri *"cutting."*

In Japanese, and in English since the mid-nineteenth century, meaning 1. "ceremonial suicide by ripping open one's abdomen with a sword or dagger, formerly practiced in Japan by members of the warrior class when disgraced or sentenced to death": "The movie's depiction of **hara-kiri** was so realistic that many in the audience were seen to hide their eyes."

2. "Suicide or suicidal action"; "a self-destructive act": "Cabinet members advised the president that the sweeping reforms he contemplated would lead almost immediately to political **hara-kiri**."

Some speakers of American English mispronounce **hara-kiri** charmingly, appearing to say Harry Carey, which was the name of a cowboy star of early Hollywood movies. A tribute to the power of movies as an indoctrination tool, but a mispronunciation to be avoided.

Nevertheless, it must be pointed out that so-called descriptive dictionaries—you surely know by now that the text you are reading is prescriptive—dignify this abomination by including the mispronunciation as part of a dictionary entry spelled "hari-kari."

Ugh!

hashish HASH eesh

From Arabic hashish, *literally, "dry vegetation."*

In Arabic, and in English since the late sixteenth century, also given as **hasheesh** (HAH sheesh), and, colloquially, as **hash** (hash), meaning 1. "the flowering tops and leaves of Indian hemp used as an intoxicant"; "cannabis": "Nothing that our government does seems effective in cutting back on use of the illicit substance **hashish**."

2. "The dried resinous exudate of the flowering tops of this plant": "The typical end user knows little and cares less about how **hashish** is painstakingly gathered and processed."

To satisfy the appetites of smokers.

haute couture See **couturier.**

haut monde OH MAWND

From French, literally, "high world."

In French, and in English since the mid-nineteenth century, meaning "the fashionable world": "Even in times of economic downturn, businesses of the best reputation selling high-priced goods find they never lack for customers among the recession-proof **haut monde**.

See also **beau monde**.

hecatomb HEK ə TOOM

From Latin hecatombe, *from Greek* hekatómbe; *from*

hékaton *"100"* + boûs *"cows," meaning "a great public sacrifice."*

In English since the sixteenth century, meaning "any great slaughter"; especially, in ancient Rome and Greece, a public sacrifice of one hundred oxen to the gods: "Under Pol Pot, a former ruler of Cambodia, not often did a day pass without a bloody **hecatomb** of his countrymen."

And almost assuredly with his approval.

hetaera hi TEER ə

From Greek hetaira, *literally, "a female companion."*

In Greek, and in English since the beginning of the nineteenth century, plural **hetaerae** (hi TEER ee), meaning 1. "a highly cultured courtesan or concubine, especially in ancient Greece": "Because his wife lacked Athenian citizenship, she was classified as a **hetaera**."

2. "A woman who uses her beauty to obtain wealth or social position": "In this era of prenuptial contracts, leading inevitably to handsome divorce settlements, tabloid journalism thrives on lurid accounts—with candid photographs, of course—of the way rich men and their **hetaerae** disport themselves."

An observation conceived in envy.

hiatus hī AY təss

From Latin hiatus, *meaning "an opening, a gap"; from* hiare, *meaning "to open"; "to gape."*

In English since the mid-sixteenth century, plural **hiatuses** or **hiatus**, meaning 1. "a break or interruption in the continuity of a work, action, etc.": "During a power failure, there was an unavoidable **hiatus** in the transmission of the lengthy text of the signed diplomatic agreement."

2. "A missing part"; "gap, lacuna": "The centuries had taken their toll on the crumbling manuscript, thwarting scholars who had done their best to work around the **hiatus** in the valuable document."

hibachi hi BAH chee

From Japanese hibachi, *from* hi *"fire"* + -bachi *"a bowl, a pot."*

In Japanese, and in English since the mid-nineteenth century, meaning a small, Japanese-style charcoal brazier covered with a grill, usually used for cooking: "A backyard **hibachi** is nothing more than a portable barbecue grill."

hibakusha hee BAH kuu SHAH

From Japanese hibakusha, *from* hi- *"suffer"* + baku- *"explode, burst open"* + -sha *"person."*

In Japanese, and in English since the end of World War II, plural **hibakushas** and **hibakusha**, meaning "a survivor of either of the 1945 atomic bomb attacks on Hiroshima and Nagasaki, Japan": "I interviewed a Catholic nun who characterized herself as a **hibakusha**; she had lived in a convent about five miles from the center of Hiroshima when the bomb fell on the city and appeared to have survived the bombing uninjured."

high-muck-a-muck HĪ MUK ə MUK

From Chinook hayo makamak, *literally, "plenty to eat."*

In English since the mid-nineteenth century, meaning "an important, influential, or high-ranking person, especially one who is pompous or conceited": "The **high-muck-a-mucks** in headquarters can't be bothered to come down to our laboratory and find out what we are doing."

It is suggested that the Chinook *hayo makamak* may have been applied derisively to indicate Indians of high status with much disposable wealth. After all, if someone living in the far north has plenty to eat, isn't that person wealthy?

And doesn't this thought suggest that high-muck-a-mucks are nothing new, from one pole to the other?

hogan HOH gawn

From Navajo hooghan, *meaning "home."*

In English since the late nineteenth century, meaning "a Navajo dwelling made of logs and earth and covered with mud or sod": "When a Navajo died, it was the custom for his family to leave his **hogan** forever, without removing the corpse of the deceased."

While such a structure might not attract a modern couple interested in acquiring their dream home, we must recognize that the **hogan** was a truly original North American design.

hoi polloi HOI pə LOI

From Greek, meaning "the many."

In Greek, and in English since the early nineteenth century, meaning "the common people"; "the masses"; "the rabble": "Don't worry, the **hoi polloi** will eventually take over, and life will be good—no worry about getting ahead, no chasing after money, because no one will care about success."

In modern English usage, **hoi polloi** is normally preceded by the article "the," even though the Greek word "*hoi*" means "the."

Some purists insist on using the English "hoi polloi" without the article—demonstrating that they know their Greek—but there is no use arguing with them.

It is enough to tell them that hoi polloi has been taken into

English, and English usage is fully accepting of it. If asked to cite an example of this usage, you might point out that Jimmy Durante, an unsurpassed master of rhetoric, regularly drew laughs in his nightclub act when he referred to less-than-polite hecklers as "duh [the] hoi polloi."

One more point is worth mentioning. Some speakers endow "hoi polloi" with the meaning of "elite snobs." This appalling example of mistaken usage must be firmly resisted.

honcho HON choh

From Japanese hancho, *from* han *"squad"* + -cho *"eldest," meaning "squad or group leader."*

In English slang since World War II, meaning 1. "the boss, the person in charge, especially said of an assertive leader": "Without even asking for a show of hands, Joe installed himself as **honcho**, and everyone was satisfied."

2. As a verb, also slang, meaning "oversee, lead, supervise": "To no one's surprise, and without a dissenting voice, we agreed that Lucy would **honcho** the design team."

hoosegow HOOSS gow

From Mexican Spanish jusgado, *meaning "jail"; from Spanish* jusgado, *meaning "court or tribunal"; from Latin* judicatum, *meaning "judgment" or "precedent."*

In American English slang since the mid-nineteenth century, meaning "jail": "Some youngsters may speak casually of having been thrown into the **hoosegow** for some juvenile prank, but they show poor sense if they invite such treatment a second time."

While American English has many slang words meaning "jail" or "prison," **hoosegow** has a charming air of easy informality, unlike the formidable "slammer" and "can" and "pen," short for "penitentiary." Further, "hoosegow" has the distinction of being derived from a foreign language.

Of much interest at present among those who follow developments in penology is the slang term "country club." It has come into use to describe certain federal prisons affording especially comfortable treatment for so-called Armani—or Gucci—types doing easy time as expiation for major white-collar crimes.

Even when those crimes involve illegal transfers of millions of dollars. No hoosegows for Wall Street types!

hors d'oeuvre or DURV

From French, literally, "outside the work."

In French, and in English since the early eighteenth century, plural **hors d'oeuvre** and **hors d'oeuvres** (or DURVZ), meaning 1. "a small bit of appetizing food, often served on small pieces of toast, for eating when drinks are served": "The **hors d'oeuvre** were so good that I ate my fill without any feeling of guilt, promising myself I would skip dinner that evening."

2. "An appetizer, served before or as the first course of a meal": "Dorothy's great **hors d'oeuvres** of tiny shrimp and delicate smoked salmon covering a mound of delicious egg salad were the best I ever tasted."

houri HUUR ee

From French houri, *from Persian* huri; *from Arabic* hur, *plural of* haura', *meaning "gazelle-eyed."*

In English since the early eighteenth century, plural **houris**, meaning 1. "one of the beautiful virgins provided in paradise for all faithful Muslims": "I sometimes wonder how many terrorists are seduced into performing their despicable acts by visions of **houris** awaiting them."

2. "A beautiful and voluptuous woman": "In his dreams, she was always before him, an unsurpassable **houri** waiting to be taken."

Nothing like a dream for creating perfection.

howdah HOW də

From Urdu haudah, *from Arabic* hawdaj, *meaning "a litter carried by a camel."*

In English since the mid-eighteenth century, also given as **houdah**, meaning in the East Indies "a seat or platform for one or more persons, carried on the back of an elephant": "After a ride lasting half a day, we realized that **howdahs** are not the most comfortable of conveniences for the inexperienced passenger."

But they do build character.

huarache wə RAH chee

From Mexican Spanish huarache *or* guarache, *from Tarascan* kwaraci, *meaning "a leather-thonged sandal." Tarascan is the language of an American Indian people of Michoacán, a state in southwestern Mexico.*

In English since the late nineteenth century, meaning "a Mexican sandal with its upper woven of leather strips": "**Huaraches** were once considered essential for vacationers at Cape Cod and other beach areas, but few people wear them now."

hubris HYOO briss

From Greek hybris, *meaning "insolence, presumption."*

In Greek, and in English since the late nineteenth century, also given as **hybris** (HĪ briss), meaning "excessive pride or self-confidence"; "arrogance": "In ancient Greek tragedy, **hubris** was considered to be directed toward the gods and was by the gods punished."

As you would expect, the noun "hubris" has spawned the useful adjective **hubristic** (hyoo BRISS tik), meaning "insolent, contemptuous." Good to remember.

hula HOO lə

From Hawaiian.

In English since the early nineteenth century, also given as **hula-hula**, meaning 1. "a sinuous Hawaiian dance with intricate arm movements that tell a story in pantomime": "The **hula** was said by Mark Twain to exhibit 'the very perfection of educated motion.'"

2. As a verb, meaning "dance the hula": "They could **hula** for hours, seemingly without effort and never tiring."

3. As an adjective: "I bought my wife a **hula** skirt, which she immediately put back in its box, never to be opened again."

What was I thinking?

I

ichneumon **ik NOO mən**

From Latin ichneumon, *from Greek* ichneúmon, *literally, "a tracker," meaning "a spider-hunting wasp."*

In English since the late sixteenth century, **ichneumon** has meant the mongoose, *Herpestes ichneumon*, of Africa and southern Europe: "**Icheneumons** were admired by Egyptians of an earlier time because those animals kept down crocodile populations."

Ancient Egyptians believed that ichneumons devoured crocodile eggs. This belief led to the naming of the **ichneumon fly**, a wasplike insect that has a habit of depositing its eggs on the larvae of other insects, there to feed on and destroy the host insect larvae.

Crocodile eggs, insect larvae—everyone to his own taste.

icon **Ī kon**

From Latin icon, *from Greek* eikón, *both meaning "likeness, image, figure."*

In English since the late sixteenth century, also given as **ikon**, with several meanings: 1. "a picture, image, or other representation, usually in wood": "The Metropolitan Museum of Art, in New York City, has a large collection of early **icons**."
2. In the Eastern Church, "a representation of some sacred personage, as Christ or a saint or angel, painted usually on a wood surface and venerated as sacred": "The small church we visited had two **icons** that were taken out to the street for the annual celebratory parade in veneration of local saints."
3. "A sign or representation that stands for its object by virtue of a resemblance or analogy to it": "Semiologists today use the term **icon** to refer to a verbal sign that somehow shares the properties of the object it denotes."
4. Also, for the computer literate, "the name given to a picture or symbol that appears on a computer monitor screen and is used to represent a command" as, for example, a file drawer to represent the option of gaining access to filing information: "The ingenuity of computer designers to select realistic **icons** appears limitless."
5. In the hype particularly virulent late in the twentieth century, **icon** has become a favorite word of publicity agents, media persons, and other unabashed mock-sociologists; meaning "a model worthy of emulation." Thus, it may be said of any seven-foot-tall basketball players—you supply the names appropriate here—"Suddenly the Nike and Reebok merchandising geniuses had found the sports **icons** they had been looking for."

Never mind saints and angels. Today we have our own modern icons, representations of esteemed public persons, which are painted electronically on monitor screens and venerated by purchasing the products these celebrities endorse. Who needs theologians?

idée fixe ee day FEEKSS

From French, literally, "fixed idea."

In French, and in English since early in the nineteenth century, plural **idées fixes** (ee day FEEKSS), meaning "a recurrent or obsessing idea, often delusional": "The president's notion that scientists could devise a weapon system capable of shooting down enemy ballistic missiles became an **idée fixe**, and there was no point to discussing the validity of the idea with him."

idiot savant ID ee ət sa VAHNT

From French, literally, "learned idiot."

In French, and in English since the early twentieth century, plural **idiot savants** (ID ee ət sa VAHNTSS), meaning "a mentally defective person with an exceptional skill or talent in a special field." For example, an **idiot savant** may be unable to learn high school subjects but have a highly developed ability to play music or to solve complex arithmetic problems mentally at great speed: "A currently insoluble challenge is that of understanding how some **idiot savants** can perform astonishing feats of rapid computation."

See also **savant**.

igloo IG loo

From Inuit iglu, *meaning "house."*

In English, also given as **iglu**, since the mid-nineteenth century, plural **igloos** and **iglus**, meaning 1. "a dome-shaped Eskimo house that is built of blocks of hard snow": "The **igloo** surely is an ingenious response to the challenge of providing human shelter in the harsh Arctic environment."

2. Also meaning "any structure resembling an igloo": "When the architect supplied a model of the house he wanted to

build for us, it looked like nothing more than a concrete **igloo** and would surely become a laughingstock in a neighborhood of conventional homes."

imam i MAHM

From Arabic imam, *literally, "leader, guide"; from* 'amma, *meaning "to lead the way."*

In English since the early seventeenth century, meaning 1. "the officiating priest of a Muslim mosque": "Once our new **imam** appeared, we saw renewed hope emerge in our depressed village."

2. "A title given to various Muslim religious leaders or chiefs": "Our principal purpose for making the journey was to study the architecture of a shrine where three of history's greatest **imams** are buried."

3. "One of a succession of religious leaders of the Shi'ites, believed to be divinely inspired": "We felt that as long as Iran remained under control of **imams**, there was little hope that conventional intellectual freedom would be encouraged."

imbroglio im BROHL yoh

From Italian imbroglio, *meaning "an entanglement or scrape," from the verb* imbrogliare, *meaning "to confuse."*

In English since the mid-eighteenth century, meaning 1. "a disagreement or misunderstanding": "Despite the best efforts of the courts, there was no way to resolve the company's financial **imbroglio** other than to dissolve the partnership."

2. "A confused or difficult situation, especially used to characterize a political or dramatic situation": "Their life together had become a hopeless **imbroglio**, never to be returned to a semblance of order."

3. "A confused heap": "The child's closet was an **imbroglio** of discarded toys and clothing."

The English word is also spelled **embroglio**, but no matter how you spell or define the word—in English or Italian—an **imbroglio** is inherently messy. And American sportswriters always on the lookout for a new synonym for "fight" or "bout" are fond of "imbroglio."

Incidentally, a modern Italian-English dictionary usually gives "imbroglio," in the sense of "predicament," as one of the English meanings of—you guessed it—the Italian word *imbroglio*.

Yet another example of how thoroughly a foreign word can be absorbed into English.

impasse IM pass

From French, meaning "cul-de-sac," dead end.

In French, and in English since the mid-nineteenth century, meaning especially 1. "a position or situation from which there is no escape"; "deadlock, stalemate, gridlock": "By midnight of the first day of discussions, it had become evident that the negotiating parties had reached an **impasse**."

2. A far less common meaning of impasse is identical with the word's first meaning in French, a "cul-de-sac"; "a road or way that has no outlet": "After hours of driving, we found ourselves at an **impasse**, with night falling and no chance of finding our way."

impresario IM prə SAHR ee OH

From Italian, meaning "organizer, manager."

In English since the mid-eighteenth century, plural **impresarios**, with two meanings: 1. "a person who organizes or manages public entertainments, especially operas and ballet":

"Sol Hurok was undoubtedly one of the most prominent **impresarios** of the twentieth century."

2. "Any manager, director, or the like": "Alan's business card identified him as an **impresario**, but no one could remember seeing him do anything that would merit so grand a title."

Anyone can create his own business card.

imprimatur IM **pri MAH tər**

From Latin imprimatur, *literally, "let it be printed"; from* imprimere, *meaning "to imprint."*

In English since the mid-seventeenth century, a noun with two meanings: 1. "an official license to print or publish a book, pamphlet, etc., especially a license issued by a censor of the Roman Catholic Church": "There is no hope that the book will ever receive an **imprimatur** unless substantial sections are deleted."

Upon finding that a work written on theological or moral subjects, which is under consideration for publication, contains nothing contrary to faith or good morals, the censor supplies his **imprimatur** in these Latin words: *nihil obstat quominus imprimatur*, "nothing hinders it from being printed." The words *nihil obstat*, usually translated as "nothing stands in the way," are often used as an abbreviation of the full phrase.

Of course, the censor may instead withhold his imprimatur.

2. "Sanction or approval"; "support": "The study was published with the **imprimatur** of the American Cancer Society." "Now that the district manager has given the restaffing plan her **imprimatur**, we will begin making new work assignments and complete the reorganization as quickly as possible."

In modern, efficient corporations, one always has to wait for a district manager's approval.

Or for a check that's in the mail.

impromptu im PROMP too

From French impromptu, *from Latin* in promptu, *meaning "in readiness."*

In French, and in English since the mid-seventeenth century, as an adjective, adverb, and noun. As an adjective meaning 1. "made or done without previous preparation": "She was at her best when delivering **impromptu** remarks to groups of her subordinates."

2. "Improvised; suddenly or hastily prepared": "It was obvious our host had been surprised to learn his guests expected to stay very late, and the best he could provide was an **impromptu** supper."

3. As an adverb meaning "without preparation": "Few could tell that her polished sermon had actually been delivered **impromptu**."

4. As a noun meaning "an impromptu musical composition, performance, etc.": "I bought a reissued CD of Horowitz playing my favorite Chopin **impromptus**."

inamorata in AM ə RAH tə

From Italian innamorata, *masculine form* innamorato, *literally, "inflamed with love" and meaning "lover, sweetheart." Both are past participles of* innamorare, *meaning "to fall in love with."*

Inamorata has been in English since the mid-seventeenth century, plural **inamoratas**; and **inamorato** has been in English since the late sixteenth century, plural **inamoratos**.

"Inamorata" means "a woman who loves or is loved"; "a female sweetheart or lover": "It was whispered about that Ellen had long been Tom's **inamorata**."

Women don't tell.

To no one's surprise, "inamorato" means "a man who loves or is loved"; "a male sweetheart or lover": "It took a long time for

Ellen to realize that Tom was telling the world he was her **inamorato.**"

Just like a man.

inchoate in KOH ət

From Latin inchoatus, *meaning "unfinished"; past participle of* inchoare *meaning "to begin; start work on."*

In English as an adjective since the early sixteenth century, meaning 1. "rudimentary; not yet completed or fully developed": "I was shocked to discover that with the invasion timed to begin in just a few days, our plans were still **inchoate.**"

2. "Just begun; incipient": "Much remained to be done before formally launching the **inchoate** revolutionary council."

3. "Not organized; lacking order": "All they had to offer in place of the polished report we expected was an **inchoate** collection of unsupported accusations and claims."

incubus See **succubus.**

inferno in FUR noh

From Italian inferno, *meaning "hell"; "horror"; from Late Latin* infernus, *meaning "hell."*

In English since the early nineteenth century, plural **infernos**, meaning 1. "hell"; "the infernal regions": "So absorbed had I become in the museum's collection of seventeenth-century engravings that I felt I could almost hear the screams of the damned and know precisely what the **inferno** holds in store for wrongdoers."

2. "A place or region that resembles hell": "The **inferno** that is the miles-deep tunnels of South African gold mines demands workers of exceptional strength and courage."

Inferno is an overused word popular with journalists who must too often describe burning structures for their readers. In the search for descriptive words, they avoid "conflagration" as too elevated in tone. Instead they turn to "inferno"—which they inevitably describe as "a raging inferno"—finding the cliché handy and, they think, especially descriptive.

But what's wrong with fire?

in flagrante delicto **in flə GRAN tee di LIK toh**

From Latin, literally, "in blazing crime."

In English as an adverb phrase since the end of the eighteenth century, meaning "in the very act of committing an offense," often abbreviated as **flagrante delicto** and as **in flagrante**.

And what, specifically, is the offense thus described? Divorce lawyers, criminal lawyers, and most readers of the tabloid press know well the nature of the offense left unspecified in this marvelous legal euphemism: "Two or more persons have been discovered in the act of adultery or—even worse?—in an unmentionable sexual act."

In the classic example of **flagrante delicto**, it is the irate spouse of one of the participants in the coupling who will eventually testify in divorce court: "I got home early and went to my bedroom, your Honor, and there I caught them **in flagrante delicto**." IN THE ACT, that is.

The idea is to convince the court to grant the spouse the desired divorce.

But the setting may be a criminal trial. In that case, the spouse is not seeking a divorce, since he or she may have already taken the life of one or both of two lovers, one of them perhaps an errant wife or husband. What the spouse wants is a finding of not guilty, the explanation being that the murder was committed in a moment of understandable outrage:

"And there they were, your Honor, **in flagrante delicto**." IN THE VERY ACT!

What more can one say?

No need to practice golf swings at the time of the murder. Oh, dear!

infra dig IN frə DIG

Short for Latin infra dignitatem, *meaning "beneath (one's) dignity."*

In English since the early nineteenth century, colloquially abbreviated as **infra dig**, with the same meaning, "undignified and unbecoming one's position": "It is surely **infra dig** for a university president to be seen buying pornographic videos."

Even when the videos are wrapped in plain brown paper.

ingénue AN *zhə* NOO

From French, feminine form of ingénu, *meaning "ingenuous"; from Latin* ingenuus, *meaning "native, inborn."*

In English since the mid-nineteenth century, a noun meaning "an artless, innocent girl or young woman, especially a theatrical role portraying such a person as well as an actress playing the role": "The great actress was able to play the **ingénue** well into her late fifties, but finally the effects of advancing age became impossible to hide."

"Ingenue" is also given in English, especially in newspapers, where letters combined with diacritical marks are not welcome. This spelling, which obscures the foreign ancestry of the word, suggests that, sans accent, "ingenue" is being pushed into full acceptance as a thoroughly English word.

And the related **ingenuous**, "naive," and **disingenuous**, "insincere," are surely the most overused words of the end of the second millennium. Drat!

in loco parentis in LOH koh pə REN tiss

From Latin, literally, "in place of a parent."

In English since the late eighteenth century, meaning "in the place or role of a parent": "Boarding schools commonly are empowered to act **in loco parentis** while students are in residence."

One would suppose this role assignment gives absent parents a degree of peace of mind.

Or a feeling of relief from responsibility.

in medias res in MAY dee AHSS RAYSS

From Latin, literally, "into the midst of things."

In English since the late eighteenth century, as an adverb phrase with the same meaning, especially without preamble; into the middle of a narrative: "Teachers of writing encourage students to launch the stories they write **in medias res** so that the reader's attention is grabbed immediately."

Lest the reader get away. Or suffer a sudden attack of terminal boredom.

in petto in PET oh

From Italian, literally, "in the breast."

In Italian, and in English since the late seventeenth century, meaning "undisclosed"; "secretly."

In petto is said of cardinals whom a pope appoints but does not disclose in consistory, that is, in solemn assembly of the entire body of cardinals: "One can only guess at the number of cardinals **in petto**, whose names one day will be made public."

And why would a pope not wish to disclose a cardinal's identity? Think of an appointment of a cardinal living in a country in which an announcement might result in danger for the person so appointed.

insouciance in SOO see ənss

From French, meaning "unconcern," from Latin in *"not"* + sollicitare *"to disturb."*

In English since the late eighteenth century, a noun meaning "the quality of being free from concern"; "indifference": "His studied **insouciance** worries me—doesn't anything bother him, or is he merely affecting indifference?"

The related adjective **insouciant** means "carefree"; "heedless"; "undisturbed"; "nonchalant": "As usual, my criticisms bounced right off my **insouciant** partner, but I think I shall never know whether it is because he rejects the validity of my opinions or because he sees himself as above all criticism."

intelligentsia in TEL i JENT see ə

From Russian intelligéntsiya, *from Polish* inteligencja, *from Latin* intelligentia, *all meaning "intelligence."*

In Russian, and in English since early in the twentieth century, a plural noun meaning "intellectuals considered as a group or class, especially as a cultural, social, or political elite": "Once the **intelligentsia** took control of our movement, I had little hope we would survive as an effective political force."

Brilliant theorists are not often capable administrators.

internecine IN tər NEE seen

From Latin internecinus, *meaning "murderous"; from*

Latin internecare, *meaning "to murder"; "exterminate," from* inter- *"mutually"* + necare *"to kill."*

In English since the mid-seventeenth century, with two principal meanings. 1. "Mutually destructive": "Despite the intervention of United Nations forces, the **internecine** struggle continued unabated, threatening eventual decimation of both warring populations."

2. "Deadly"; "characterized by great slaughter": "During the brief cessation of hostilities, our army rebuilt its forces, intent on pursuing **internecine** warfare that eventually would kill or maim everyone in the enemy nation."

English speakers and writers of the eighteenth century began to use **internecine** in a sense not seen or heard before: 3. "Of or pertaining to conflict or struggle within a group": "No one can recall the actual circumstances that led to our long-standing **internecine** feud."

The word "internecine" provides a good example of a phenomenon that may be thought of as a kind of Gresham's Law of English Usage: bad usage drives out good.

Thus, the increasing popularity of "internecine" in the third sense—considered incorrect by most usage commentators—threatens to rob the word of its first two meanings. Consider again the ultimate Latin basis for "internecine," *inter-* "mutually" + *necare* "to kill." This gives us no justification for defining internecine as conflict within a group.

If it's not too much trouble, use "internecine" only in its first two meanings. Try them. You'll like them.

inveigh in VAY

From Latin invehere, *meaning "to attack."*

In English since late in the fifteenth century, meaning "protest strongly or attack vehemently with words": "The aging U.S.

senator always ended his condemnations of the United Nations by **inveighing** against abortion, Communism, income taxes, school desegration, and any other bugaboo that came to mind."

invidious in VID ee əss

From Latin invidiosus, *meaning "envious, envied, hateful."*

In English since the beginning of the seventeenth century, meaning 1. "calculated to create ill will or resentment"; "hateful": "To the discomfort of guests at a dinner table, Alice would direct **invidious** remarks at her patient husband, who would act as though he had not heard her."

2. "Offensively or unfairly discriminating"; "injurious": "In the midst of arguments with my older brothers, I would often draw **invidious** comparisons between them and the neighborhood bully."

3. "Causing or tending to cause animosity, resentment, or envy": "To my dismay, I was voted Least Cooperative Paralegal of the Month, an **invidious** honor, needless to say."

Issei eess say

From Japanese issei, *from* is *"first"* + sei *"generation."*

In Japanese, and in English since the 1930s, also given as **issei**, plural **Issei** or **issei**, meaning 1. "a Japanese who immigrated to the United States or Canada after 1907 and was ineligible for citizenship until after 1952": "My father-in-law was an **Issei** who never learned to speak English and spent all of World War II confined in a camp, while my brothers and I saw combat with the 442nd Regimental Combat Team."

2. "Any Japanese immigrant to the United States": "Professor Hideki, an **Issei**, is a distinguished scholar who speaks Japanese, English, and several Romance languages perfectly."

See also **Nisei** and **Sansei**.

iterate IT ə RAYT

From Latin iteratus, *past participle of* iterare *meaning "to repeat."*

In English since the early sixteenth century, a verb meaning 1. "utter again or repeatedly": "His only response to each of the charges against him was to **iterate**—and reiterate—'Not guilty!' "

2. "Do over again or repeatedly": "With the introduction of modern electronic computers, we became able to **iterate** complex problems rapidly, each time getting closer to the acceptable value we were seeking."

3. The noun **iteration** (IT ə RAY shən), meaning "repetition," is heard more often than the verb **iterate** and, in problem-solving—especially when using a computer—has the special sense of repeating a procedure again and again, each time moving closer to solution: "Finally, after several dozen **iterations**, we decided there was little to gain by going further."

izzat IZ ət

From Urdu 'izzat, *from Persian; from Arabic* 'izzah, *meaning "glory."*

In English since the mid-nineteenth century, meaning "honor, reputation, prestige": "He casts his votes in the Senate solely on the basis of whether he will be enhancing or damaging his **izzat**."

Not an unusual attitude.

J

jackal **JAK əl**

From Turkish chacal, *from Persian* shaghal, *meaning "a wild animal related to the dog," especially* Canis aureus *of Asia and Africa, a hunter and scavenger traveling in packs.*

In English given as **jackal**, with the same meaning, since the beginning of the seventeenth century.

It was formerly believed that this predatory nocturnal animal traveled in advance of a lion to hunt down prey for the larger animal. And it is this perception of the jackal's role that has expanded the meaning of the word.

When we refer to a person as a "jackal," therefore, we are suggesting that he or she is doing the dirty work for someone else. A jackal in this sense means someone who relieves another person of the drudgery necessary for success: "When the editor finally realized that his real function was not to edit books but to act as his manager's **jackal**, he quit his job."

jactation jak TAY shən

From Latin jactatio, *a noun meaning "bragging"; from Latin* jacere, *meaning "to throw."*

In English as a noun since late in the sixteenth century, meaning 1. "boasting, bragging": "I soon tired of his **jactations** about his combat experiences in a war long past, especially since I knew he had spent the entire war in Philadelphia."

2. In medicine, "a restless tossing of the human body": "Neurologists he consulted were mystified by his **jactation**, which caused him such embarrassment."

3. A related word is **jactitation**, literally, "a throwing out"; from Latin *jactare*, meaning "to throw about." In medicine meaning "jactation," second definition above. In law meaning "a false boast or claim that causes injury to another": "My attorney advised me to abandon the idea of a lawsuit against my business competitor for **jactitation**, since the man's boasting had not caused me substantial injury."

Everybody wants to sue everybody these days.

j'adoube *zh*ah DOOB

From French, meaning "I'm adjusting."

In French, and in English since the beginning of the twentieth century, the expression used in chess when a player is about to touch a chessman without intending to make a move: "When a player wishes to adjust a chessman, he must say **j'adoube** or words to that effect."

For example, "I'm adjusting my knight."

Why? "Because it is making me uncomfortable by not facing directly ahead."

Compulsive behavior.

jaguar JAG wahr

From Portuguese jaguar, *from the Tupi word* jaguara, *also given as* yaguara. *Tupi is a language spoken by the Tupi Indians of northern Brazil.*

In Portuguese, and in English since the beginning of the seventeenth century, meaning "a large spotted yellowish-brown, carnivorous feline, *Panthera onca*, of tropical America": "The **jaguar** was once widespread in tropical America, but is now greatly reduced in number and is considered an endangered species in some areas."

Ironically, an automobile that formerly was a darling of smart and moneyed motorists was named for the jaguar—suggesting the silent speed and grace of this great animal—but lately this Jaguar has fallen in popularity and may itself one day be considered an endangered automotive species.

Alas!

jai alai HĪ LĪ

From Spanish jai alai, *from Basque* jai *"festival"* + alai *"merry."*

In Spanish, and in English since the beginning of the twentieth century, meaning "a game resembling handball," played by teams using curved wicker baskets (*cestas*) strapped to the wrist, and a small ball (*pelota*): "**Jai alai** today is played on a court called a fronton, enclosed on three sides, before spectators who sit outside the remaining side, where they are protected by a thick, transparent glass wall."

This fast-moving game, far removed from its Basque linguistic roots as a merry festival, is now most often a professional sport that lends itself to betting by spectators and is popular in many countries.

The term and its ancillary terms have the added advantage of providing entries for crossword puzzles.

jalapeño HAH lə PAYN yoh

From Mexican Spanish chile jalapeño, *meaning "chili of Jalapa," Jalapa being the capital of the state of Veracruz, in Mexico.*

In English since the 1930s, plural **jalapeños**, and given also as **jalapeno** and **jalapeno pepper**, meaning a hot green or orange-red pepper, the fruit of *Capsicum annuum*, which is used especially in Mexican cuisine: "How would Tex-Mex devotees and the scorched palates of millions of masochistic North Americans survive without their daily **jalapeño** fix?"

De gustibus non est disputandum.

jalousie JAL ə SEE

From French jalousie, *from Italian* gelosia, *both, literally, "jealousy."*

In French, and in English since the end of the sixteenth century, meaning 1. "a louvered blind or shutter that can admit light and air but exclude rain and sunlight": "**Jalousies** have all the advantages of Venetian blinds without the inconvenience of troublesome cords needed to raise and lower the blinds."

2. "A window made of glass slats or louvers performing similar functions": "Architects came up with a design for what they called a California room, walled with **jalousies**, which made maximum use of ambient light without overexposure of occupants to harmful effects of sunshine."

Incidentally, modern Italian-English dictionaries define *gelosia* as "jalousie," giving additional strength to the linguistic dictum "What goes around, comes around."

janissary JAN ə SER ee

From French janissaire, *from Italian* gianizzero; *from Turkish* yeniçeri, *from* yeni *"new"* + çeri *"militia."*

In French, and in English since the late sixteenth century, also given as **janizary**, plural **janissaries** and **janizaries**, meaning 1. "a member of a military unit of the Turkish army abolished in 1826 after the unit revolted against the Sultan": "Without the support of most of its officers, the revolt of the **janissaries** collapsed."

2. "Any soldier in the Turkish army": "She was exceedingly proud of her son, resplendent in the uniform of a **janissary**."

3. "A member of any group of loyal guards, soldiers, or supporters." It is this third meaning that is most often intended in modern writing: "The opposition leader, surrounded by ten fierce **janissaries**, entered the committee room precisely at the scheduled time with bayonets fixed, making it clear they would protect their leader with their lives."

It is interesting to note that, in addition to the French, Italian, and Turkish forms of "janissary," there are Portuguese, Spanish, German, and Dutch forms. Especially interesting lexicographically is the fact that the Italian *gianizzero*, in addition to meaning "janissary," is defined as an "underling."

The meanings of words, as you may already know, depend heavily on the point of view of the speakers and writers of a given language. One man's loyal guard, soldier, or supporter (third definition above) may be another man's underling.

And that's what keeps newspaper columnists and historians employed.

jejune ji JOON

From Latin jejunus, *meaning "empty, poor, mean."*

In English since the beginning of the seventeenth century, meaning 1. "without interest or significance"; "dull"; "insipid": "There are readers who will buy and read any **jejune** paperback novel as long as the cover illustration is sufficiently lurid."

2. "Juvenile; immature; childish": "We agree it is a parent's responsibility, not a grandfather's, to criticize **jejune** behavior in a grown grandson."
3. "Lacking knowledge or experience"; "uninformed": "The **jejune** young man's attempt to launch a publishing house was doomed to failure."
4. "Deficient or lacking in nutritive value": "Unfortunately, in his attempt to lose weight he followed a **jejune** quack diet that left him seriously malnourished."

An interesting word related to **jejune** is the physiological term **jejunum** (ji JOO nəm), meaning "the middle portion of the small intestine." But how are these two words related? Recall that the Latin *jejunus*, neuter form *jejunum*, has "empty" as one of its meanings. Well, long ago it was believed mistakenly that the jejunum was empty after death.

If only someone had looked.

je ne sais quoi *zh*uun say KWAH

From French, literally, "I don't know what."

In French, and in English since the mid-seventeenth century, a noun phrase meaning "an indefinable, elusive quality, especially a pleasing one"; "that certain something": "Winsome Audrey Hepburn had the **je ne sais quoi** all movie fans found irresistible."

Even after gracing our language for hundreds of years, this ineffable French contribution to English has never been given anything approaching an English pronunciation. Anyone attempting to pronounce the phrase as though it originated in English would commit an abomination.

If not an act of sacrilege.

jeunesse dorée *zhuu* NES daw RAY

From French, literally, "gilded youth."

In French, and in English since the early nineteenth century, meaning young people of wealth and fashion: "Our country club jumps on Saturday nights, when the **jeunesse dorée** dance to music completely unsuitable for the rest of us, and once the music stops at midnight, the action transfers to the town's all-night diner."

Have you noticed that the **jeunesse dorée** seem to be growing younger as each new generation emerges?

jihad ji HAHD

From Arabic jihad, *literally, "effort, struggle, strife."*

In English since the mid-nineteenth century, also given as **jehad**, meaning 1. "a holy war undertaken as a sacred duty by Muslims": "The imam called for a **jihad** on his country's neighbors, because they had made peace with his country's enemies."

2. "Any vigorous emotional crusade for an idea or principle": "It was not long before the government's **jihad** against illicit drugs proved unsuccessful and had to be abandoned."

Perhaps what the world needs is a jihad to end all jihads.

judo JOO doh

From Japanese judo, *from* ju *"gentle"* + do *"way."*

In Japanese, and in English since the late nineteenth century, meaning 1. "a method of defending oneself without the use of weapons, based on **jujitsu** (which see)": "She became highly skilled in **judo** at Smith College, where courses in the method were offered as part of the physical education program."

2. "The sport of fighting by this method": "The annual county-wide games include many exhibitions of **judo**."

3. As an adjective, meaning "of or pertaining to this sport": "He entered many **judo** tournaments before finally beginning to win his share of victories against experienced opponents."

juggernaut JUG ər NAWT

From Hindi Jagganath, *from Sanskrit* Jagganatha, *literally, "lord of the world, that is, the god Vishnu or Krishna."*

In English since the early seventeenth century, also given as **Juggernaut**, meaning 1. "any large, overpowering destructive force or object, such as war, a giant battleship, or a powerful football team": "In the Rose Bowl this year we will have to face the Nebraska Cornhuskers, a **juggernaut** that has not been scored on all season long."

2. "Anything requiring blind devotion or cruel sacrifice": "Once the extent of their child's handicaps became apparent, the young couple knew they would sooner or later be crushed by the **juggernaut** of around-the-clock nursing care and other extraordinary medical expenses they would face throughout their lives."

3. As **Juggernaut**, also given as **Jagganath** (JUG ə NAHT), in India, an idol of Krishna, drawn annually on an enormous cart under whose wheels the faithful are said to have thrown themselves to be crushed: "I have seen **Juggernauts** three times and, fortunately, have yet to see anyone throw himself under the wheels of the cart."

This third meaning of **Juggernaut** surely makes clear how the term came to have its first two meanings.

jujitsu joo JIT soo

From Japanese jujitsu, *also given as* jujutsu; *from* ju *"gentle"* + jutsu *"technique."*

In Japanese, and in English since the late nineteenth century, also given as **jiujitsu**, **jiujutsu**, and **jujutsu** (joo JUUT soo);

meaning "a method of defending oneself without the use of weapons by using the strength and weight of an adversary to disable him—or her": "Police officers in many towns are taught **jujitsu** and are encouraged to earn black belts."

But also to practice pistol marksmanship.

Just in case.

jungle JUNG gəl

From Hindi jangal, *from Pali and Prakrit* jangala, *literally, "a rough, waterless place."*

In English since the late eighteenth century with many meanings: 1. "a wild land overgrown with dense vegetation and a tract of such land": "Scientists collect plants of South American **jungles**, anticipating they will prove valuable in treating disease." "They are doing all they can to keep out lumber companies who are interested only in clear-cutting **jungles** for timber."

2. "A piece of swampy, thickset forestland": "Why they decided to build a house in that wet **jungle** is beyond me."

3. "Any confused mass or agglomeration of objects; a jumble": "Once the hurricane had passed, nothing remained but a **jungle** of wrecked trailer homes, smashed almost beyond recognition and piled atop one another."

4. "Something that baffles or perplexes; a maze": "How can one be surprised at the jury's failure to find meaning in the **jungle** of DNA gobbledegook to which they had been subjected for days on end?"

5. "A scene of violence and struggle for survival": "Many of our states persist in sentencing criminals to spend their lives confined in prison **jungles**, where mayhem, gang warfare, rape, and murder are everyday matters."

6. "A place or situation of ruthless competition": "I cannot

understand how anyone can choose to pursue a career in the **jungle** that is Washington politics."

Yet many appear to thrive on it.

junta HUUN tə

From Spanish and Portuguese junta, *from Italian* giunta, *all meaning a "meeting." And French has its* junte, *meaning* ***junta****, as defined below.*

In Spanish, and in English since the early seventeenth century, meaning 1. "a small group ruling a country, especially just after a **coup d'état** (which see)": "Few members of the **junta** had had any experience in government."

2. Especially in Spain and Latin America, "a deliberative or administrative council": "His legal education and experience were ideal preparation for appointment to the **junta**."

K

kabob kə BOB

From Arabic kabob, *Hindi* kabab, *Turkish* kebap, *and from Urdu and Persian as well, all meaning "roast meat."*

In English since the mid-seventeenth century, also given as **cabob**, **kebab**, **kebob**, and **kabab**, usually given in the plural **kabobs**, meaning "small pieces of meat or seafood broiled, usually on a skewer, often with tomatoes, green peppers, etc.": "My eldest son is highly skilled in managing lamb **kabobs** over a pan of charcoal, invariably bringing them to juicy succulence."

See also **shish kebab**.

kabuki kah BOO kee

From Japanese kabuki, *from* ka *"song"* + bu *"dance"* + ki *"skill."*

In Japanese, and in English since the end of the nineteenth century, meaning 1. "a popular drama of Japan, dating from the seventeenth century, characterized by elaborate costuming and stylized acting, music, and dancing": "For centuries all roles in **kabuki**, whether male or female, have been played by males."

2. Also called **Grand Kabuki**, public performances of this type of drama: "Westerners, usually those who do not understand spoken Japanese and are seeing **kabuki** for the first time, may find themselves charmed by the visual spectacle but unable to sit through an entire performance, which can last several hours."

Not unlike persons new to opera who make the mistake of choosing to cut their teeth on a Richard Wagner epic.

kachina kə CHEE nə

From Hopi kacína, *meaning "supernatural."*

In English since the end of the nineteenth century, also given as **katcina** and **katchina**, meaning 1. "any of various Hopi Indian ancestral spirits, impersonated in rituals by masked dancers": "The **kachinas** are believed to visit pueblos periodically to bring rain and food to the tribe members."

2. A masked dancer performing as a spirit in a Hopi ritual: "The men **kachinas** are elaborately painted and costumed for the tribe's annual ceremonies."

3. Also known as **kachina doll**, in English since the midtwentieth century, a Hopi Indian doll carved to represent a kachina: "**Kachina dolls** are made by craftsmen to be given to tribal children."

And to be sold to tourists who typically understand little of the dolls' significance.

Kaddish KAH dish

From Hebrew Kaddish, *from Aramaic* qaddish, *literally, "holy."*

In English since the beginning of the seventeenth century,

plural **Kaddishim** (kah DISH im), meaning in Judaism 1. "a liturgical prayer, recited daily at prayer services and on certain other occasions": "I have no understanding of what the words of the **Kaddish** mean, yet I am always moved when I recite the prayer."

2. Also called **Mourner's Kaddish**, the **Kaddish** recited by a person in mourning and on the anniversary of a death: "Only one person in the synagogue—a boy of thirteen—rose when the time arrived for saying the **Kaddish**."

3. As **Kaddishim**, meaning "persons who recite this prayer": "**Kaddishim** will now rise to recite in unison the Mourner's Kaddish."

kamikaze KAH mi KAH zee

From Japanese kamikaze, *from* kami *"god"* + kaze *"wind."*

In Japanese lore the **kamikaze** was the divine wind that suddenly arose one August night in 1281 and destroyed the navy of the invading Mongols. In 1896, Lafcadio Hearn wrote of this long-ago night and how the kamikaze sank the fleets of Kublai Khan.

In Japanese, and in English since the waning months of World War II, meaning 1. "Any Japanese air force pilot given the suicidal mission of flying an aircraft laden with explosives into an enemy target": "I watched transfixed as the **kamikazes**, one after another, piloted their planes straight down at the destroyers protecting our convoy, but fortunately landing wide of our ships."

2. An airplane used for this purpose: "The **kamikaze** carried so great an explosive load that it could barely reach its intended target."

3. "A person or thing that behaves in a wildly reckless or destructive manner": "On my arrival in Naples for the first

time, I rode in a cab driven by a **kamikaze** and made it out alive."

4. As an adjective: "She drove her Mitsubishi automobile with the suicidal confidence of a **kamikaze** pilot."

Never thinking about a round trip.

kanaka kə NAK ə

From Hawaiian, literally, "a person."

In Hawaiian, and in English since the first half of the nineteenth century, meaning "a native Hawaiian or a South Sea Islander": "All the people living nearby on the beachfront are **kanakas**, and some of them invite us now and then to delicious family dinners."

kaput kah PUUT

From German kaputt, *originally meaning "trickless, in the card game piquet"; from French* être capot, *meaning "to be without tricks," a condition comparable to that of a gin rummy player who has been schneidered, or of a baseball team that has been shut out. In German now meaning "broken"; "rendered useless"; "worn out."*

In English slang since the end of the nineteenth century, an adjective meaning 1. "ruined"; "done for"; "demolished": "After many months of trying to operate my small business with little working capital, I realized that it was **kaput** and I had no way of getting back on my feet."

2. "Unable to operate or continue": "With the temperature nearing 100 degrees and our air conditioner suddenly **kaput**, I knew Arizona held no further fascination for me."

3. As **go kaput**, meaning "cease functioning"; "break down": "As Mario had predicted, my old Volvo suddenly **went kaput**, and I had no way of getting to work."

Kaput does not make for happy campers.

And piquet is hardly ever played today, except in old movies.

karaoke KAH rah OH kə

From Japanese karaoke, *from* kara *"empty"* + oke *"shortening of* okesutora, *meaning orchestra."*

In Japanese, and in English since late in the twentieth century, meaning 1. "a form of entertainment originating in Japan, in which people sing the lyrics to popular songs against recorded music": "Wednesday and Saturday nights are given over to **karaoke** at my club, and you can be sure that those are nights when I stay away."

2. Also functions as an adjective, as in **karaoke bar** and **karaoke singing**.

So the great tradition that gave the world **kabuki** now has given us untalented soloists—half drunk, to be sure—crooning "Smoke Gets in Your Eyes" and all the rest.

Banzai!

karma KAHR mə

From Sanskrit karman, *meaning "act, deed"; "fate."*

In English since the early nineteenth century, meaning 1. In Hinduism and Buddhism, "fate, destiny": "It is not given to us to know our **karma**."

2. "Good or bad emanations felt to be generated by someone or something": "Whenever he drew near, I felt only good **karma** coming from him."

A favorite fancy of young people fascinated by Eastern philosophy.

kasha KAH shə

From Russian kásha.

In Russian, and in English since the end of the eighteenth century, meaning 1. "a porridge made from hulled and crushed buckwheat or other grains": "My father always enjoyed his weekly dish of **kasha**, which my mother served with a generous pat of butter slowly liquefying on top."

2. "Buckwheat groats before cooking": "Just as Southerners dote on their grits, New Englanders their pancakes, and Asians their rice, my father's generation of East European immigrants had a passion for **kasha**."

Once a poor person's nourishing fare, today a health food. Go figure.

ketchup KECH əp

From Malay kəchap, *from Chinese* kéjap, *meaning "fish sauce."*

In English since the beginning of the eighteenth century, also given as **catchup** (KACH əp) and **catsup** (KAT səp), meaning 1. "a condiment consisting of puréed tomatoes, onions, vinegar, etc.": "A hamburger without **ketchup** is like chili without peppers or tennis without a net."

2. Any of various other condiments or sauces: "I think of honey **ketchup**, walnut **ketchup**, and all the other nouveaux **ketchups** as culinary abominations."

And the same goes for barbecue sauce and steak sauce.

kibbutz ki BUUTSS

From Modern Hebrew kibus, *from Hebrew* quibbus, *literally, "a gathering."*

In Hebrew, and in English since the 1930s, plural **kibbutzim** (ki BUUTSS sim), meaning "an Israeli collective settlement owned communally by its members": "Many **kibbutzim** still have accommodations for tourists who wish to experience life on a **kibbutz** and are willing to pay modest fees for room and board."

Kibbutz leads naturally to **kibbutznik** (ki BUUTSS nik), a Yiddish word that appends to the Hebrew stem the Slavic noun suffix **-nik** taken into Yiddish, here denoting a person who supports (something). Consider beatnik, nudnik, peacenik, and many other English words.

The Russian word *sputnik*, meaning "traveling companion," gives us another example of the Slavic *-nik* appended to a stem, this time Russian, to form a word. It is the familiar name of any of a series of Earth-orbiting satellites launched by scientists of the Soviet Union between 1957 and 1961.

kibitz KIB itss

From Yiddish kibetsn, *from German* kiebitzen *meaning, at cards, "to look over players' shoulders as a spectator"; from German* Kiebitz, *literally, "a lapwing or plover," meaning a "busybody."*

In informal English since the early twentieth century, as a verb meaning 1. "act as a kibitzer": "We will never again allow him or anyone else to **kibitz** during our card games."

2. "Offer advice or criticism to as a **kibitzer**": "Our retired chief executive officer apparently cannot refrain from publicly **kibitzing** every business decision made by our board of directors."

But **kibitzer** has been used twice above, so it must be defined. This noun, as you might expect, came into informal English at the same time as **kibitz**—after all, someone has to do the **kibitzing**.

Kibitzer, thus, means 3. "a spectator at a card game who looks at the players' cards over their shoulders, especially one who offers unwanted advice": "His reputation as **kibitzer** par excellence had preceded him, and he never failed to live up to it."

4. "A giver of unwanted or uninvited advice"; "a busybody":

"When I am hard at work in my kitchen preparing elaborate dishes, a **kibitzer** is the last thing I want or need."

5. "A person who jokes, chitchats, or makes wisecracks, especially while others are busy": "He never seemed to understand that funny remarks by **kibitzers** are not welcome when serious topics are being discussed."

So kibitz has been a linguistic gold mine.

kielbasa **kil BAH sə**

From Polish kielbasa, *Czech and Serbo-Croatian* kolbása, *Bulgarian* kulbása, *Russian* kolbasá, *all meaning "sausage."*

In Polish, and in English since the mid-twentieth century, meaning "a type of highly seasoned smoked Polish sausage of coarsely chopped beef and pork": "It is not unusual to find **kielbasa** listed prominently on the menus of establishments that proclaim themselves purveyors of authentic Texas barbecue."

So, even as we bite into a garlic-enriched kielbasa, we remember with gratitude the Polish patriot Thaddeus Kosciusko, who helped win the American Revolution.

kimono **kə MOH nə**

From Japanese kimono, *meaning "clothing, garb"; from* ki *"wearing"* + mono *"thing."*

In English since the late nineteenth century, plural **kimonos**, meaning 1. "a loose, wide-sleeved Japanese robe, fastened at the waist with a wide sash": "When I found that all the family's antique **kimonos** were for sale, I realized that the Oyama family had fallen on hard times."

2. "A woman's loose dressing gown": "My mother never called her dressing gowns anything but **kimonos**, a term that was common among her friends."

Many Americans pronounce **kimono** as though it were spelled "kimona," and this pronunciation is now listed first in some highly respected American dictionaries.

Yet another sad bow to popular inclinations.

kiosk KEE osk

From French kiosque, *meaning "a stand in a public park"; from Turkish* kösk, *from Persian* kushk, *both meaning "a villa."*

In English since the early seventeenth century, meaning 1. "a small structure used as a newsstand, refreshment stand, etc.": "When I think of Paris, I see in my mind's eye the colorful **kiosks** along its boulevards."

2. "A thick, columnlike structure for posting notices, advertisements, etc.": "The **kiosks** are usually plastered with notices of musical events, poetry readings, and the like."

3. In English, in Turkey and Iran, "an open pavilion or summerhouse": "They no longer could afford to keep their place in the country, with its charming **kiosk**, where they took afternoon tea in good weather."

4. In Britain, "a telephone booth": "The familiar red **kiosk** was a particularly welcome refuge during a rain shower, especially for young lovers."

It is interesting to note that cognates abound for "kiosk": Italian has *chiosco*, Spanish has *quiosco*, and German has *Kiosk*—which proves that if you build a better word for a structure, the languages of the world will beat a path to your door.

kirsch keersh

From German Kirsch, *literally, "cherry"; a shortened form of* Kirschwasser, *literally, "cherry water," meaning "cherry brandy."*

In English as **kirsch** and as **kirschwasser** (KEERSH VAH sər) since the early nineteenth century, meaning "an unaged brandy distilled from a fermented mash of cherries": "The imminent conclusion of an evening meal at their house is invariably announced by the appearance of a bottle of **kirsch** with small glasses brought to the table on a silver tray by our host."

Sweet, but good.

kitsch kich

From German Kitsch, *meaning "rubbish, trash"; "something thrown together."*

In English since the early twentieth century, meaning 1. "something of tawdry design or content made to appeal to undiscriminating taste": "When a prominent critic labeled Johnson's paintings little more than **kitsch**, the young artist fell into despair."

2. Also used as an adjective, meaning "pertaining to kitsch"; "tasteless": "Every example of **kitsch** doodads can be seen in the new shop in the mall."

klatsch See **coffee klatsch.**

knish knish

From Yiddish knish, *from Polish* knysz *and Russian* knish, *all meaning "a kind of bun or dumpling."*

In English since the early twentieth century, plural **knishes**, meaning in Jewish cookery "a fried roll of dough with a filling of meat, kasha, or potato": "Any New York City politician knows a candidate must run the gauntlet of three-times-a-day **knishes**, pizzas, and egg rolls if he or she is to have any chance of electoral success."

Good reason for a politician to consider anorexia as preparation for political campaigns.

kosher KOH shər

From Yiddish kosher, *from Hebrew* kasher, *literally, "right, proper."*

In Yiddish, and in English since the mid-nineteenth century, also given as **kasher** (kah SHAIR), an adjective meaning 1. in Judaism, "allowed to be eaten or used, according to dietary or ceremonial laws": "My family ate only **kosher** meat until we moved to a backwater town that did not have enough Jewish residents to support their own butcher."

2. In Judaism, adhering to the laws governing such fitness: "Do you know where there is a **kosher** restaurant?"

3. As an informal adjective, meaning "proper, legitimate"; "genuine, authentic": "Are you certain all our political contributions are really **kosher**?"

4. As a verb, meaning "make (something) kosher": "The final step before cooking meat is to **kosher** it by salting to draw out any blood it may retain."

kowtow kow tow

From Chinese ketou *or* k'ot'ou, *literally, "knock (one's) head"; from* ke *"knock"* + tóu *"head."*

In English since the late eighteenth century, also given as **kotow** (koh tow), meaning 1. "act in an obsequious manner"; "show servile deference": "Nothing annoys me more than an employee who always **kowtows** to his employer, especially when the employer hardly ever shows him any respect or warmth."

2. In the former Chinese custom, "to touch the forehead to the ground while kneeling, as an act of servility": "As soon as the old warlord entered the room, all his aging warriors **kowtowed**."

Servile enough for you?

kreplach **See won ton.**

kvetch kvech

From Yiddish kvetshn, *literally, "to squeeze, pinch"; adapted from the German noun* Quetsche, *meaning "crusher, presser."*

In English as a slang verb since the mid-twentieth century, also given as **kvetsch**, meaning 1. "complain, especially chronically": "It seemed that he was happy only when he had something to **kvetch** about."

2. **Kvetch** is also used as a slang noun, sometimes given as **kvetcher**, meaning "a person who kvetches": "I finally lost patience with the **kvetch**, who managed to carry on in his inimitable carping manner even when there was no obvious reason for his complaints."

Who needs a reason?

L

laconic lə KON ik

From Latin Laconicus, *from Greek* Lakonikós, *both translated as "Laconian," meaning "pertaining to ancient Laconia (Sparta) or its people"—more of this soon.*

In English since the late sixteenth century, meaning "using few words"; "expressing much in few words"; "pithy, concise": "There is much to be said for brief remarks, but far better are **laconic** statements, which pack much meaning into few words, unlike brief statements which may convey little."

When we realize that the Spartans were noted for their brusque and aphoristic speech, the derivation of **laconic** is comprehensible. And the noun **laconism** (LAK ə NIZ əm), also given as **laconicism** (lə KON ə SIZ əm), is understandable as meaning 1. "laconic brevity": "His marked **laconism** was incorrectly construed as incivility."

2. "A laconic utterance or sentence": "After half a century together, the woman and her husband communicated largely in **laconisms**."

Perhaps the best-known American laconism is the one attributed to U.S. General Anthony Clement McAuliffe. In December 1944, during World War II, while McAuliffe's troops were defending the Belgian town of Bastogne, he received an enemy message demanding surrender. Despite the fact that McAuliffe's troops were completely surrounded by German forces, the general replied in one word: "Nuts," which may hold the record for American laconisms.

It must be pointed out, however, that witnesses to the episode have said the general's reply actually comprised two words: a blunt and unmentionable phrase that was later sanitized for home consumption.

Incidentally, as far as is known, the world champion laconism is the reply made by the ephors (magistrates) of Sparta in the fourth century B.C. to a message sent by Philip of Macedon: "If I enter Laconia, I will level Lacedaemon (Sparta) to the ground."

The magistrates' full reply? "If."

Those Spartans wasted no words.

lacrosse lə KRAWSS

From Canadian French la crosse, *literally "the crook," the stick used in playing* **lacrosse**. *Incidentally, the French word* crosse *is taken in religion to mean "crosier," a bishop's staff, and the lacrosse player's crook resembles the bishop's crosier.*

In English since the early eighteenth century, meaning "a game played by two teams that attempt to send a ball into the opponent's goal": "**Lacrosse**, originated by Indians of North America and today popular as an intercollegiate sport, was brought from Canada and the United States to England by the mid-nineteenth century."

An early instance of reverse English.

lacuna lə KYOO nə

From Latin lacuna, *meaning "ditch, pit, hole, gap, deficiency"; from Latin* lacus, *meaning "lake."*

In English since the mid-seventeenth century, plural **lacunae** (lə KYOO nee) or **lacunas**, meaning "a gap or missing part, as in a manuscript or a logical argument"; "hiatus": "The scholars deciphering the Dead Sea Scrolls encountered numerous **lacunae**, and the great effort required to fill in the missing words added years to the time needed to accomplish the valuable project."

lager LAH gər

From German Lager-Bier, *literally, "stored beer"; from* Lager *"storehouse"* + Bier *"beer."*

In English since the mid-nineteenth century, also given as **lager beer**, meaning 1. "a kind of light beer aged for weeks or months before use": "In a British pub, devotees may experience the pleasures of quaffing a pint of flavorful **lager** on tap from a barrel kept in a cool cellar."

For the uninitiated, it must be pointed out that refrigeration obscures whatever natural flavor a beer may have.

2. **Lager** is also used as a verb, meaning "to age (beer), usually by storing for weeks or months": "Some breweries lack the huge storage capacity needed to **lager** their beer."

Of interest is a related British term, **lager louts**, meaning "hooligans who create disturbances—and worse—after having drunk too much beer."

The lesson? Know your limit and quit while you're ahead.

lagniappe lan YAP

From Louisiana French lagniappe, *from American Spanish* la ñapa, *meaning "the addition"; from Quechua* yapa, *literally, "that which is added."*

In English since the mid-nineteenth century, chiefly in Louisiana and Texas, also given as **lagnappe**, meaning 1. "a small gift given with a purchase to a customer"; "a bonus": "A successful real estate agent, eager to build client satisfaction, will present a modest house plant as **lagniappe** soon after her client moves into a newly purchased home."

2. "A gratuity or tip": "Give the parking attendant **lagniappe** when you arrive, and there is a good chance your car fenders will go unscathed until the functionary returns your car."

3. "An unexpected or indirect benefit": "There is always the chance that an airline will bump aged customers up to the comfort of business class or first class by way of **lagniappe**."

And most of us can use all the lagniappe we get.

laissez faire LESS ay FAIR

From French, literally, "allow (people) to do"—as they will, that is.

In English since the early nineteenth century, also given as **laisser faire** (LESS ay FAIR), meaning 1. "the theory or belief that government should intervene as little as possible in economic affairs": "Adam Smith, the eighteenth-century Scottish economist who wrote *Wealth of Nations*, advocated a **laissez faire** policy for Britain and free trade among nations."

2. "The doctrine of noninterference in the affairs of others": "Some psychotherapists follow a policy of **laissez faire**, never telling clients what they should do, instead encouraging them to make their own life decisions."

3. By inserting a hyphen within this phrase, we have the adjective **laissez-faire**, also given as **laisser-faire**: "**Laissez-faire** policies may have been helpful a century or more ago, but once wholesale mergers and huge combinations became

common, it also became obvious that close government regulation was essential."

And the fight goes on between the advocates of laissez faire and their opponents.

lama LAH mə

From Tibetan blama—*in Tibetan pronunciation, the* b *is not sounded—literally, "superior one."*

In Tibetan, and in English since the mid-seventeenth century, meaning "a priest or monk in Tibetan and Mongolian Buddhism": "Many **lamas** were subjected to extreme persecution when the People's Republic of China initiated aggressive policies against Tibet."

lasagna lə ZAHN yə

From Italian lasagne, *meaning "a variety of macaroni"; from vulgar Latin* lasania, *meaning "a cooking pot"; from Latin* lasanum, *meaning "a chamber pot"; from Greek* lásana, *meaning "a trivet."*

In Italian, and in English since the mid-nineteenth century, also given in English as **lasagne**, meaning 1. "large, flat, rectangular strips of pasta": "There's not much of an art to arranging **lasagna** in layers; what takes know-how is preparing the sauce needed for the dish."

2. An Italian baked dish consisting of layers of this pasta, cheese, tomato sauce, and, usually, chopped meat: "Thanksgiving dinner in some Italian-American homes may include a generous pan of **lasagna** or a large bowl of spaghetti in addition to a turkey and the traditional vegetables."

In reading the etymology of lasagna given above, you must have been somewhat surprised, particularly by *lasanum*, the Latin ancestor of the Italian *lasagne*.

latrine lə TREEN

From French latrine, *from Latin* latrina, *short for* lavatrina, *meaning "a place for washing; a toilet."*

In French, and in English since the early seventeenth century, meaning "a toilet or something intended to be used as a toilet": "Just as I left the comparative safety of the landing craft in my first invasion, what I needed most was the comfort of a **latrine**."

Because **latrine** is generally associated with military life, and rumors—usually false—form the essence of most soldiers' conversations, **latrine rumor** came into English during World War I and persists today, with the meaning of "a baseless rumor."

As one would expect, other languages eager to avoid vulgarity and coarseness have been attracted to "latrine." German has *Latrine*, Italian has *latrina*, and Spanish has *latrina* and *letrine*.

The entire world needs one from time to time, wouldn't you say?

legume LEG yoom

From French légume, *meaning "vegetable"; from Latin* legumen, *meaning "pulse"—a leguminous plant, for example, peas and beans.*

In English since late in the seventeenth century, meaning 1. "any plant of the family *Leguminosae*, especially a plant used for feed, food, or as a soil-improving crop": "**Legumes** are touted as an essential ingredient in the modern diet."

2. The pod or seed vessel of such a plant: "In my childhood I learned to love black-eyed peas and lima beans with no idea they were **legumes**—I thought they were beans."

3. Any table vegetable of this family: "Vegetarians of the world, unite and thrive on **legumes**' vegetable proteins!"

Or on the next fad food.

leprechaun LEP rə KAWN

From Irish leipreachán; *going back to Old Irish* luchorpan, *from* lu *"small"* + corp *"body"* + -an, *a diminutive suffix.*

In Irish, and in English since the end of the sixteenth century, meaning in Irish folklore 1. "a dwarf or sprite": "**Leprechauns** are traditionally said to carry a purse containing a single shilling."

2. A representation of this figure as a little old man who will guide anyone who catches him to a hidden crock of gold: "The fine score and lyrics of the 1947 musical *Finian's Rainbow*, conveying the spirit of Irish folklore and complete with a delightful **leprechaun**, continue to entrance lovers of musical theater."

lese majesty leez MAJ ə stee

From French lèse-majesté, *from Latin* laesa majestas, *meaning "hurt or violated majesty."*

In French, and in English since the mid-sixteenth century, also given as **lèse majesty**, meaning 1. "in law, a crime, especially high treason, committed against the sovereign power"; also, "an offense that violates the dignity of a ruler": "Jeremy Bentham, an English philosopher, held more than one hundred years ago that in a representative democracy there can be no **lese majesty**."

2. "An attack on any custom, institution, etc., revered by numbers of people": "The aging former president, long out of office, is so highly regarded to this day that any criticism of the man is looked upon as **lese majesty**."

Which proves the effectiveness of advertising and public relations.

lettre de cachet **See cachet.**

levee LEV ee

From French levée, *from Medieval Latin* levata, *meaning "embankment."*

In French, and in English since the early eighteenth century, meaning 1. "an embankment designed to prevent flooding of a river": "In years of extremely heavy rainfall, even the powerful **levees** built along the Mississippi may fail."

2. In agriculture, "one of the small ridges built around irrigated fields": "Anyone who has observed rice planting and cultivation is familiar with the **levees** farmers build around their paddies."

An unrelated word, also spelled **levee**, came into English in the seventeenth century from the French *levé*, meaning "rising," from Latin *levare*, meaning "raise."

3. In English this **levee**, in Britain, means "a public court assembly, formerly held in early afternoon, for men only": "Royal **levees** in times past were held at St. James's Palace." (See the fifth definition below to understand the reason for what looks like arrant sexism.)

4. "A reception, usually in someone's honor": "The foreign minister's **levee** went unreported in the press because the list of invited guests was withheld from reporters."

5. Formerly, "a reception of visitors held on rising from bed, as by a royal or other personage": "Before introduction of constitutional government, the French monarch customarily received visitors—diplomats, court physicians, nobles, and others—at the time of his **levee** (in French *levé*), that is, while making his morning ablutions upon rising from bed."

Those of us who have read accounts of Lyndon Johnson's years in the White House recall that he was not only the first U.S. president to show reporters the scar left by an abdominal operation but also was known to consult members of his staff while he was using the toilet. Thus, we must not look askance at former royal practices, which may have left their mark on some modern democratic practices.

Especially those of sitting presidents.

lex talionis LEKSS TAL ee OH niss

From Latin, literally, "law of talion," that is, "exaction of compensation in kind."

In English since the end of the sixteenth century, meaning "the principle that a punishment should correspond in degree and kind to the offense of the wrongdoer; retributive justice." Commonly expressed—and mistakenly understood—as "an eye for an eye, a tooth for a tooth": "In his campaign speeches, the former district attorney so misconstrued **lex talionis** that he gave the press the impression that ophthalmic surgeons and dentists would replace judges and prison wardens when he became governor."

Yet there's more than one way to skin a cat.

limousine LIM ə ZEEN

From French, meaning "a type of motorcar." The French limousine *also has the meaning of "long cloak," because such coats were worn by the shepherds of Limousin, a former French province.*

In English since the end of the nineteenth century, **limousine** has two meanings: 1. "any large, luxurious automobile, especially one driven by a chauffeur": "The luxury of the conventional **limousine** of days past has largely been superseded in the public fancy by today's stretch limo, which seems to stretch more and more as the years pass."

2. "A large sedan for transporting passengers to and from an airport, between train stations, etc.": "We customarily engage

a **limousine** and driver to take us to and from Kennedy Airport when we plan to be away from home for more than a few days."

lingua franca LING gwə FRANG kə

From Italian, literally, "Frankish tongue."

And who were the Frankish people? A group of ancient Germanic peoples who, from 768 to 814, ruled over an extensive European kingdom, including most of France, the Low Countries, part of Germany, Austria, Switzerland, and much of Italy. Charlemagne was the greatest Frankish ruler.

In English since the mid-seventeenth century, plural **lingua francas** or **linguae francae** (LING gwee FRAN see), meaning 1. "any language widely used among speakers of different languages": "Pidgin English was the **lingua franca** in New Guinea, where I spent some months during World War II."

2. As **Lingua Franca**, the Italian-Provençal jargon, with elements of other languages, once widely used in eastern Mediterranean ports: "Trade along the Mediterranean coast was facilitated by the **Lingua Franca**, which enabled all sorts of commercial activity to flourish among diverse peoples."

Not to be confused with Esperanto.

litchi LEE chee

From New Latin litchi; *from Chinese* lizhi, *from* li *"scallion"* + zhi *"branch."*

In English since the late sixteenth century, plural **litchis**, also given as **leechee** and **lichee**, meaning 1. "the fruit of a Chinese tree in which a thin, brittle shell encloses a sweet pulp and a single seed": "**Litchis** may be eaten fresh, but they are also canned for export or preserved in syrup."

2. The tree itself: "Arborists are known to admire the evergreen **litchi**, which can be seen in greenhouses of some American botanical gardens."

literati LIT ə RAH tee

From Latin literati, *a plural noun meaning "scholarly people." The Latin singular form* literatus, *used long ago in English, is now rarely seen.*

In English since the early seventeenth century, **literati** means "persons of scholarly or literary attainments"; "intellectuals": "One reviewer suggested the new novel would find few readers among those he called 'the shrinking **literati**,' never making clear whether he was counting heads or commenting on the personalities of intellectual readers."

It is difficult to leave this discussion without calling attention to **glitterati** (GLIT ə RAH tee), a mid-twentieth-century coinage combining "glitter" and "literati." The word "glitterati" may be defined as "wealthy or famous people who conspicuously attend fashionable events that receive notice in the press": "I never fail to enjoy my favorite glossy magazines, which chronicle the almost unreal world of the **glitterati**, a world from which I am otherwise excluded."

But notice that the literati are not included among the glitterati, except for certain authors—the literglitterati?—who make it big and sooner or later become favored dinner and cocktail party guests of the rich and famous.

Stay tuned.

loden LOHD ən

From German Loden, *meaning "a coarse woolen cloth"; tracing back all the way to Old Norse* lothi, *meaning "fur cloak," and* lothinn, *meaning "shaggy."*

In English since the early twentieth century, sometimes called

loden cloth, meaning 1. "a thick, waterproof cloth, used in coats and jackets for cold climates": "The uniform of the 1968 student insurrection was the **loden** coat, fastened in front by leather toggles and rarely if ever cleaned."

2. Also called **loden green**, "the deep olive-green color of this fabric": "No other color would he wear but **loden**, just like all his school friends."

And the French call loden *loden*, of course. But what about the Italians and Spanish? Too warm for loden coats.

lorgnette lorn YET

From the French verb lorgner, *meaning "to squint or to eye furtively"; in French* lorgnette *means "spyglass," and the French word for lorgnette is* lorgnon. *Go figure that one.*

Lorgnette, in English since the end of the eighteenth century, means 1. "a pair of eyeglasses mounted on a handle": "With the advent of contact lenses, fashionable ladies at banquet tables were able to discard their half-glasses and **lorgnettes** without missing any detail of the elaborate gowns worn by other women present."

2. "A pair of opera glasses mounted on a handle": "No proper lady could be seen at the opera without her mother-of-pearl **lorgnette**, behind which—undetected—she could catch forty winks."

Especially welcome after an early dinner.

louche loosh

From French louche, *meaning "cross-eyed, squinting"; from Latin* luscus, *meaning "blind in one eye."*

In French, and in English since the beginning of the nineteenth century, meaning "dubious"; "shady"; "disreputable": "None of us knew exactly when it became the accepted belief that there was something **louche** about Pierre, but certainly from then on we abruptly stopped gossiping whenever he came near."

But how did Latin *luscus* become French *louche*?

We commonly hear people express distrust of anyone who habitually fails to look them in the eye. (Could it be because that person is cross-eyed?) The next step in the intuitive process is to believe that the person in question is shady or disreputable—**louche**.

loupe loop

From French, meaning "a magnifying glass."

In English since the beginning of the twentieth century, meaning "a magnifying glass used by jewelers and watchmakers and by photographers who must examine negatives and slides": "After years of concentration on his work, with his **loupe** most of the time kept in place by a wire running across the top of his bald head, the watchmaker had developed a permanent groove in the skin of his head."

An occupational hazard.

luau loo OW

From Hawaiian lu'au, *meaning "party, feast."*

In Hawaiian, and in English since the mid-nineteenth century, meaning 1. "a feast of Hawaiian food": "Once ashore, we were treated to a magnificent **luau**, with dishes I had never before seen, ample alcoholic drink, and tireless Hawaiian dancers."

2. "A cooked dish of taro leaves, usually prepared with coconut cream and octopus or chicken": "All through the **luau**, the delicious main course, I tried to keep from thinking that what I believed to be chicken was really octopus."

Takes all kinds.

M

maestro MĪ stroh

From Italian maestro, *from Latin* magister, *both meaning "master."*

In Italian, and in English since the end of the eighteenth century, plural **maestros**, meaning 1. "an eminent composer, teacher, or conductor of music": "Few of today's symphonic conductors enjoy the fierce loyalty shown the late Arturo Toscanini, greatest of all **maestros**."

2. As **Maestro**, "a title of respect used in addressing or referring to such a person": "Please keep in mind, **Maestro**, that the car that will take you to the airport will arrive at seven A.M."

3. "A master of any art": "Despite the acclaim for Roberta's early paintings, no one ever thought of her as a **maestro**."

As you can see from the previous sentence, **maestro** is used for both females and males, even though Italian has the feminine form **maestra**. In Italian, **maestra** is used to mean "teacher" or "schoolmistress," but not "master." The history of unequal treatment of women and men being what it is, few of us will be surprised by this usage.

And with the attitudes of many enlightened persons being what they are toward English nouns such as "actress," "aviatrix," "poetess," "sculptress," and the like, we surely cannot anticipate a groundswell of support for "maestra" in English.

You win some, lose some.

Mafia MAH fee ə

From Italian Mafia, *originally meaning "elegance"; "bragging."*

In Italian as *mafia* and *maffia*, and in English since the late nineteenth century, also given as **mafia** and **Maffia**, meaning 1. "a secret organization allegedly engaged in criminal activities in the U.S. and elsewhere": "It is believed that the influence of the **Mafia** in the United States crested in the mid-twentieth century."

2. In Sicily, given as **mafia** or **maffia**, "a spirit of hostility to law, often manifesting itself in criminal acts by a secret organization acting in this spirit": "More than once—especially during wartime—foreign governments have collaborated with the **Mafia** to exploit its members' ability to harass troops occupying Italian soil."

3. Often meaning "any small powerful or influential group in an organization or field"; "clique": "Political writers have used the term Irish **Mafia** in writing about the Democratic Party in Massachusetts."

4. A noun associated with Mafia is **mafioso** (MAH fee OH soh), plural **mafiosi** (MAH fee OH see) and **mafiosos**, in English since the late nineteenth century, meaning "a member of a Mafia": "Once we were told that Danny was a **mafioso**, we

understood why neighborhood storekeepers always treated him with kid gloves."

And tried not to look him in the eye.

mahatma **mə HAHT mə**

From Sanskrit mahatman, *meaning "magnanimous"; from* maha- *"great"* + atman *"soul."*

In English since the mid-nineteenth century, sometimes given as **Mahatma**, meaning 1. "a Brahman sage": "A **mahatma** was one of a class of persons with miraculous powers."

2. Especially in India, "a person held in the highest esteem for wisdom and saintliness": "**Mahatma** Gandhi will always be remembered for his insistence on nonviolence in his country's struggle for independence."

How about those nonviolent nuclear explosions?

mah-jongg **mah jawng**

From Cantonese Chinese ma jiang, *literally, "sparrow," from* má *"hemp"* + qué *"bird."*

In Chinese, and in English since the 1920s, also given as **mah jong**, meaning "a game of Chinese origin played with dominolike pieces, or tiles": "When **mah-jongg** was introduced in England, some people believed it would soon rival the game of bridge in popularity."

It has not.

mahlstick MAHL STIK

From Dutch maalstok, *literally, "painting stick"; from* malen *"to paint"* + stok *"stick."*

In English since the mid-seventeenth century, also given as **maulstick**, meaning "a stick with a padded tip used to support an artist's working hand": "Thackeray wrote that while

Charles V, King of France, was watching his court painter Titian at work, the artist dropped his **mahlstick**, and Charles picked it up for him."

Even a king may bow before first-class talent.

maître d'hôtel MAY **tər doh TEL**

From French maître d'hôtel, *literally, "master of house."*

In French, and in English since the early sixteenth century, plural **maîtres d'hôtel** (MAY tərz doh TEL), meaning 1. "a headwaiter": "My father once told me a **maître d'hôtel** was a headwaiter who could not see a customer until folding money was deposited in his outstretched hand—I'm sure the gibe was not his own."

2. "A butler or steward": "Since few households employ **maîtres d'hôtel** today, temporary employees are brought in for elaborate dinners to fulfill the function these men used to perform."

3. "The manager of a hotel or its dining room": "The **maître d'hôtel** made it clear he was in complete charge of the dining room and would brook no challenge to his authority."

Maître d'hôtel has largely been replaced in American English by the shortened form **maître d'** (MAY tər DEE), plural **maître d's** (MAY tər DEEZ), which may lack the dignity of the full phrase but gets to the point a bit faster.

Yet doesn't get the maître d's attention any sooner.

malaise ma LAYZ

From French malaise, *from Old French* mal *"bad, ill"* + aise *"ease"; with the same meanings as in English.*

In English since the mid-eighteenth century, meaning 1. "bodily discomfort, especially without development of a specific disease": "Our school nurse finds her office crowded on

Mondays with boys and girls complaining of nothing more than **malaise**."

2. "A generalized uncomfortable feeling": "President Carter unintentionally did much to popularize the word **malaise** when he used it in speaking of the need to improve the mood of the nation."

And in doing so fell further in popularity.

The lesson being, never tell a balding man his hair is falling out—unless, that is, you want him to dislike you.

mal de mer MAL də MAIR

From French mal de mer, *meaning "seasickness."*

In English since late in the eighteenth century, with the same meaning: "As soon as food was brought to our table on the first night out, a sudden attack of nausea signaled that **mal de mer** would be my fate for the entire cruise."

A fate worse than death, some sufferers say.

mamzer MOM zər

From Yiddish mamzer, *from Hebrew* mamzer, *meaning "bastard."*

In English since the mid-sixteenth century, also given as **momser** and **momzer**, plural **mamzers** and **mamzerim** (mom ZAY rim), in the Jewish tradition meaning 1. "a bastard"; "an illegitimate child"; "A child born to an unmarried couple is considered a **mamzer**."

2. In slang, "a rascal"; "a despicable person": "After all, it was not as though we were born yesterday; we should have known better than to trust that conniving **mamzer**."

mañana mə NYAH nə

From Spanish, meaning "tomorrow"; also, "in the indefinite future."

As a noun meaning "the indefinite future," **mañana** is considered symbolic of easygoing procrastination: "After retirement from their fast-paced careers in New York City and Hollywood, the couple were grateful for the slow pace of their retirement lives on a tiny Caribbean island, where **mañana** prevails."

Their motto being "Never do today what you can put off until tomorrow."

See **dolce far niente**.

manqué mahng KAY

From French manqué, *past participle of* manquer, *meaning "to lack."*

In French, and in English since the late eighteenth century, meaning "having failed or fallen short"; "unfulfilled or frustrated"; "that which might have been but is not": "James Joyce's Little Chandler saw himself as a poet **manqué** whose literary bent was thwarted by his having to work at a job he hated in order to support his wife and child."

Nothing like hanging on to a rationalization for something that might have been but is not.

masseur mə SUR

From French masseur, *from French* masser, *meaning "to massage"; from Arabic* massa, *meaning "to handle."*

In English since the last quarter of the nineteenth century, meaning 1. "a man who provides massage as his occupation"; the feminine form, **masseuse** (mə SOOSS), appeared in English at about the same time: "**Masseurs** and **masseuses** often find employment in athletic clubs, where members appreciate the benefits of a massage after a vigorous workout."

2. The verb **massage** (mə SAH*ZH*), in English since the late

nineteenth century, is primarily taken to mean to "manipulate the muscles and joints of the body in order to stimulate circulation and relieve stress": "During Michael's training in physical therapy, he became adept at **massaging** patients."

3. But the verb **massage** has a secondary, informal meaning, "to manipulate the presentation of (data, statistics, etc.) so as to give a specific, more favorable result": "The chief financial officer of the company was dismissed when she refused to **massage** her summary of the year's operating figures to protect the price of the company's stock."

It is worth pointing out that the term **massage parlor**, which appeared in English early in the twentieth century, meant "a commercial establishment providing massage for men and women." A massage parlor today is commonly taken to mean "an establishment employing women who appear ready to provide massage but actually offer sexual services for men."

There's the rub.

matériel mə TEER ee EL

From French matériel, *meaning "equipment."*

In English since the second quarter of the nineteenth century, also given as **materiel** (mə TEER ee EL), meaning "arms, ammunition, and all manner of other military equipment": "By war's end, Axis armies had no shortage of **matériel** except for supplies of vital gasoline and oil."

maulstick See **mahlstick.**

mazel tov MAH zəl TAWF

From Yiddish mazltov, *literally, "good luck"; from Hebrew* mazzal tobh, *literally "good star," bringing to mind the English phrase "born under a lucky star."*

In English since the mid-nineteenth century, "an expression of congratulations and good wishes," said especially to Jews on an occasion of good fortune: "When the guests at a wedding hear the groom's heel shatter the wineglass, all present call out, '**Mazel tov**!' "

Surely, the couple will need all they can get.

mea culpa MAY ə KUL pə

From Latin mea culpa, *literally, "(through) my own fault."*

In English since the fourteenth century—Chaucer's time—an exclamation acknowledging responsibility or guilt. The phrase is from the prayer of confession in the Latin liturgy of the Catholic Church, but is widely used outside the confessional: "He seemed not to take criticism seriously, apparently thinking a few taps on his chest and a muttered '**mea culpa, mea culpa**' would get him off the hook."

It's worth trying.

megillah mə GIL ə

From Yiddish megile, *literally, "a scroll"; from Hebrew* məgillah, *literally, "a roll or scroll, especially the portion of a Torah scroll containing the Book of Esther."*

In Yiddish, and in English slang since the mid-twentieth century, also given as **megilla**, meaning 1. "a lengthy, detailed explanation or account": "Don't give me a **megillah**; just tell me whether you really want to go to Grandmother's house for Thanksgiving."

2. "A lengthy and tediously complicated situation": "What started out as a discussion of what to serve at our next cookout became a **megillah** that took all afternoon to settle and ended in canceling the party."

The Book of Esther is read aloud in synagogues during the Jewish festival of Purim and frequently interrupted by children's noisemakers, called gragers, which extend the time needed to complete the reading. Hence the two slang meanings of "megillah."

mélange may LAHN*ZH*

From French mélange, *meaning "a mixture, a medley"; from* mêler, *"to mix."*

In English since the mid-seventeenth century, with the same meaning as in French: "After having lived in Tennessee for five years, María still speaks a **mélange** of Spanish and Portuguese, plus a few words of English."

memento mori mə MEN toh MOR ī

From Latin memento mori, *literally, "remember that you have to die."*

In English since the end of the sixteenth century, meaning "a warning or reminder of death, especially a skull or other symbolic object": "On his desk was his **memento mori**, a photograph of his parents and his uncles, taken a year before all of them died in the Holocaust."

As though he needed to be reminded of his own mortality.

ménage à trois may NAH*ZH* a TRWAH

From French ménage à trois, *literally, "household of three."*

In French, and in English since the last decade of the nineteenth century, meaning "a domestic arrangement in which three people having sexual relations occupy the same household": "Apparently, they had lived in complete harmony as a **ménage à trois** for many years, an arrangement that troubled only their close neighbors."

Take note of how the definition given for **ménage à trois** does not specify the sexes of the people involved, making the definition about as up-to-date—for which read "ambiguous"—as can be. In the past, lexicographers specified a "ménage à trois" as two men and one woman, with one of the men married to the woman.

As you and I know, with affordable housing being in short supply in most places, things have changed. Thus, ignoring the question of whether one of the three participants is married to anyone in the ménage, I count four possible combinations of men and women and trust that some mathematician expert in combinations and permutations will write to tell me whether I am correct.

But the question still remains, Is there anyone among them who knows how to cook?

mensch mench

From Yiddish mentsh, *meaning "a man"; "a human being"; from German* Mensch, *meaning "a person."*

In Yiddish and in informal English since the mid-twentieth century, plural **menschen** (MENCH ən) and **mensches**, meaning "an upright, mature, and responsible person": "It is clear that Michelle is someone you can rely on, a real **mensch** as far as I am concerned."

Notice that **mensch** may be applied to a woman as well as to a man. We need as many **menschen** as possible.

mésalliance MAY zə LĪ ənss

From French mésalliance, *literally, "misalliance."*

In French, and in English since the mid-eighteenth century, also given in English as **misalliance** (MISS ə LĪ ənss), meaning "a marriage with someone who is considered one's social inferior": "In a democratic society, unsuitable marriages— or marriages one's acquaintances consider unsuitable—may sometimes be labeled **mésalliances** on the basis of marked educational and economic differences between bride and groom, not because of contrasting social standings."

At least not openly.

meshuga mə SHUUG ə

From Yiddish meshuge, *from Hebrew* məshugga, *meaning "crazy." Also related to German* meschugge, *with the same meaning.*

In English slang since late in the nineteenth century, also given as **meshugga**, meaning 1. "mad, crazy"; "stupid": "I knew that people in my neighborhood considered me off the wall if not downright **meshuga** because I spent most of my time reading books."

The adjective **meshuga** is closely related to some equally pungent slang nouns. 2. A **meshuganah** (mə SHUUG ə nə), also given as **meshuggane** and as **meshuggener**, for example, came into English from Yiddish late in the twentieth century and means "a crazy person": "Wouldn't you agree that only a **meshuganah** would take three foreign languages, American history, calculus, and physics in the same term?"

3. Another close relative of meshuga is the noun **meshugaas** (MISH ə GAHSS), also given as **mishegaas**, which came into English slang at the beginning of the twentieth century. Meshugaas means "madness, craziness"; "foolishness, nonsense": "His **meshugaas** is leaving crusts of bread outside his front door so the rats that live in the street won't go hungry."

To which one is forced to respond: To each his own meshugaas.

métier MAY tyay

From French métier, *meaning "occupation"; "skill."*

In English since late in the eighteenth century, meaning 1. "one's occupation, trade, or profession": "Fortunately, there is such great demand for his **métier** that he does not have to be concerned about downsizing."

2. "One's forte": "She developed her **métier** as a writer of children's literature from her work as a kindergarten teacher, when she spent many hours telling stories to children."

Talented teacher, fortunate children.

mikvah MIK və

From Yiddish mikve, *from Hebrew* miqweh, *literally, "a collection or mass"; meaning "a ritual bath."*

In Yiddish, and in English since the early nineteenth century, also given as **mikveh** and **mikva**—plural **mikvahs**—a bath in which Orthodox Jews are required to immerse themselves for ritual purification, for example, before the Sabbath and after each menstrual period: "Members of the new synagogue banded together to construct and operate a communal **mikvah**."

minyan MIN yən

From Hebrew minyan, *literally, "a number"; "a reckoning."*

In Hebrew, and in English since the mid-eighteenth century, meaning "the quorum of ten Jewish adult males required to be present for formal worship, with males aged thirteen or older counted as adults": "On many days our little synagogue would not have had a **minyan** without the presence of two or three mourners who daily recited the Kaddish."

In the traditional Orthodox interpretation of **minyan**, women are not counted.

See **Kaddish**.

mirabile dictu mi RAB ə LAY DIK too

From Latin mirabile dictu, *from* mirabile *"wonderful"* + dicere *"to say."*

In English since early in the nineteenth century, usually given as "strange to say" or "marvelous to relate" and generally used sarcastically: "After serving only one term in Congress, he was selected, **mirabile dictu**, by his party as its nominee for Speaker of the House of Representatives."

Whereupon, to no one's surprise, he set out at once to win his party's presidential nomination.

misalliance See **mésalliance.**

mitzvah MITSS və

From Hebrew miswah, *meaning "a commandment."*

In Hebrew, and in English since the mid-seventeenth century, plural **mitzvahs**, meaning 1. "any of the 613 commandments or precepts relating to Jewish religious and moral conduct": "When Fred found out how many **mitzvahs** he would be letting himself in for if he converted to Judaism, his enthusiasm for conversion rapidly drained away."

2. "Any righteous or praiseworthy deed": "She regards visitation of the sick as a **mitzvah** to be undertaken willingly."
3. Mitzvah is best known in the phrase **bar mitzvah** (bahr MITSS və), literally, "son of commandment"; in Hebrew, and in English since the mid-nineteenth century, meaning "a Jewish boy aged thirteen who takes on the responsibilities of an adult under Jewish law." A **bat mitzvah** (baht MITSS və), literally, "daughter of commandment," is a Jewish girl aged twelve who takes on comparable responsibilities. "Our children became **bar mitzvah** and **bat mitzvah** on the same day."
4. The synagogue ceremonies that bestow such status are also known as "bar mitzvahs" and "bat mitzvahs": "The entire family looks forward to Mickey's **bar mitzvah** and Margie's **bat mitzvah**."

Happy times for the principals and for doting parents and grandparents.

modus operandi MOH dəss OP ə RAN dee

From Latin modus operandi, *literally, "mode of operating."*

In English since the mid-seventeenth century, plural **modi operandi** (MOH dee OP ə RAN dee), meaning "the way a person goes about a task, especially the way a felon habitually commits his or her crimes": "My supervisor's **modus operandi** in conducting his annual performance reviews begins with pointing out all the strengths of an employee's conduct before going on to recommend improvements." "Experienced detectives study the **modus operandi** of known criminals and frequently use that knowledge to identify the perpetrator of a crime under investigation."

Fans of TV crime programs are familiar with the abbreviation M.O. for this concept.

modus vivendi MOH dəss vi VEN dee

From Latin modus vivendi, *literally, "mode of living."*

In English since late in the nineteenth century, plural **modi vivendi** (MOH dee vi VEN dee), meaning 1. "way of life"; "manner of living": "Their remarkable **modus vivendi**—indiscriminate use of credit cards—led inevitably to misery."

2. "An arrangement whereby people in a dispute can carry on pending a settlement": "Until company lawyers could work out a reasonable dissolution of the partnership, Smith and Bates agreed to a **modus vivendi** based on a modicum of civility toward one another."

Sometimes easier said than done.

momzer See **mamzer**.

monde See **beau monde.**

mores MOR ayz

From Latin mores, *a plural noun meaning "manners, customs"; singular* mos.

In English since the beginning of the twentieth century, a term in sociology never used in the singular form, meaning "the customs or conventions regarded as characteristic of a community"; "folkways": "The violent **mores** reflected in Hollywood movies and television programs vitiate the beneficial effects on students of years spent in formal schooling and religious training."

O tempora, O mores indeed!

mot juste moh *ZH*UUST

From French mot juste, *literally, "exact word."*

In French, and in English since the beginning of the twentieth century, plural **mots justes** (moh *ZH*UUST), meaning "the word that conveys a desired shade of meaning more nearly precisely than any other": "The novelist's notebooks, with word after word changed, demonstrate her obsessive search for the **mots justes** in every sentence she wrote."

Advice to writers: Heed the wisdom of Voltaire, "The best is the enemy of the good."

A word must be said about the English word **mot**, from the French *mot*, literally "word." A "mot" is a witty saying: "Edwin became known for his sometimes brilliant, usually brittle, **mots**."

We also encounter "mot" in the French *bon mot*, which was taken into English in the mid-eighteenth century, meaning "witty remark or comment"; "clever saying": "When Dorothy Parker, ever ready with a **bon mot**, learned that Calvin

Coolidge, known as 'Silent Cal,' had died, she is said to have remarked, 'How could they tell?' "

moue moo

From French moue, *meaning "a pout."*

In English since the mid-nineteenth century, plural **moues** (moo), meaning "a pouting expression"; "a pout": "Film critics have made much of the ability of the young actress to convey changes in mood, going smoothly from the slightest of **moues** to full-fledged glee, childlike wonder, deep despair—you name it—without uttering a word."

Sometimes, less is more.

mousse mooss

From French mousse, *meaning "moss" and "froth."*

In French, and in English since the end of the nineteenth century, meaning 1. "a sweet dessert of whipped cream as a base, stabilized with gelatin or egg and chilled in a mold": "My affinity for things chocolate has extended to the delicious dish known as chocolate **mousse**, driving yet another nail in my coffin."

2. "An aspic containing puréed meat, vegetables, or fish": "Lately, salmon **mousse** has made its appearance on the menu of my favorite diner."

3. A novel use of **mousse** must also be recognized, meaning "a foamy preparation worked into hair to hold it in place." What will they think of next?

But don't eat the third mousse. Don't even taste it.

muumuu MOO MOO

From Hawaiian mu'u mu'u, *the name of a dress, literally, a "cut-off," so-called because it has no yoke, the usual top section from which the rest of the dress hangs.*

In English since the 1920s, meaning “a long, loose-hanging dress, worn especially by Hawaiian women”: “Travelers to Hawaii have remarked on the beauty of the **muumuu**, the colorful dress urged on Hawaiian women by early Christian missionaries who were offended by the women’s near-nakedness.”

And now sometimes worn by women in other parts of the world.

N

naïf nah EEF

From Middle French naïf, *masculine form of* naïve, *meaning "naive"; from Latin* nativus, *meaning "native."*

In English since the beginning of the sixteenth century, also given as **naif**, as a noun meaning 1. "a naive or inexperienced person": "We all wondered how Jim, by all accounts a hopeless **naïf**, had made his mark in the world of hardball national politics."

2. As an adjective, meaning "naive": "Her **naïf** manner masked a tough inner core that had seen her through the stresses of a childhood of poverty."

See also **faux-naïf**.

nautch nawch

From Hindi nach, *from Prakrit* nachcha, *both meaning "dancing"—Prakrit being any of the dialects of North and Central India, once spoken there in addition to Sanskrit.*

In English since the beginning of the nineteenth century, meaning 1. "in India an exhibition of dancing by professional dancing girls, called **nautch girls**": "Westerners are usually disappointed by **nautch**, finding the entertainment dull and uninventive."

2. Also called **nautch dance**, "a woman's sinuous dance of the Orient, marked by suggestive gyrating of the body": "Fans of hootchy-kootchy take naturally to **nautch**, even though the women who perform the dance are said by Western observers to be less than beautiful."

Take note that the Prakrit word *nachcha* has nothing to do with the English word "cha-cha," which is the American Spanish dance also known as the "cha-cha-cha."

negligee NEG li *ZHAY*

From French négligée, *literally, "neglected," past participle of* négliger, *meaning "to neglect"; from Latin* negligere, *also meaning "to neglect."*

The English **negligee**, also given as **negligée** and as **negligé**, dating from the mid-eighteenth century, means 1. "a woman's light, usually sheer, dressing gown or robe": "When I left for work each morning, my wife was still wearing a **negligee**; what I did not know was that she habitually wore it until lunchtime."

And why not? She spent three hours at her writing before dressing for the day.

2. "Informal attire": "In the evening, Nana usually entertained her male admirers in **negligee**, not dressing formally until it was time to go out to dine."

nexus NEK səss

From Latin nexus, *meaning "a bond, a grip"; from* nectere, *meaning "to bind."*

In English since the mid-seventeenth century, plural **nexus**, meaning 1. "a means of connecting; a tie or link": "Strongest of all ties that bind is cash **nexus**, and it will always be strongest."

2. "A connected series or group": "The investigating committee is part of the **nexus** that has collective oversight of all municipal elections."

nicht wahr ni*kh*t VAHR

From German, literally, "not true."

In German, and in English since the 1920s, meaning, "Isn't it true?" or "Isn't that so?": "Johnson has been pursuing his research without success for more than ten years, **nicht wahr**?"

French, in *n'est-ce pas*, has its own way of expressing **nicht wahr**, as does Spanish in *no es verdad* and Italian in *non è vero*.

No self-respecting language should be without a phrase meaning "nicht wahr."

nihil obstat See **imprimatur.**

ninja NIN jə

From Japanese ninja, *from* nin- *"endure"* + -ja *"person"; meaning "a spy."*

In Japanese, and in English, date of adoption unknown, plural **ninja** or **ninjas**, meaning "a member of a feudal Japanese society of agents trained for espionage, sabotage, and assassination": "I find it disquieting that my country still employs its own **ninjas** whose function is to protect us against criminality, at the same time that we practice legally countenanced criminality."

And now, of course, Hollywood has given us mutant ninja turtles.

What next?

niño NEEN yoh

From Spanish niño, *meaning "a boy or child." Then there is the Spanish* niña, *meaning "a girl or child."*

In English with the same meanings, dates of adoption—no pun intended—unknown.

But why supply this readily available information here? The answer lies in the prominence given by news media to **El Niño**, literally "the child," specifically the Christ child, and meaning "a warm ocean current of variable intensity that develops, usually in late December, along the coasts of Ecuador and Peru. And sometimes causes catastrophic weather conditions": "In recent times, every instance of extraordinary winds, extremes of temperature, flooding, etc., has been blamed on **El Niño**."

But why is the ocean current El Niño named for the Christ child? Because the meteorological phenomenon usually appears close to Christmastime.

nirvana nir VAH nə

From Sanskrit nirvana, *past participle of* nirva, *meaning "to be extinguished," a word that requires some explanation: Here, the goal is enlightenment, which can be achieved only when greed, hatred, and delusion are extinguished.*

In English since the early nineteenth century, meaning 1. "the final goal of Buddhism, freedom from the suffering attendant on the endless cycle of personal reincarnations, as a result of the extinction of individual passion, hatred, and delusion":

"**Nirvana**, we were told, must be the objective of every truly wise man."

2. "A state characterized by freedom from or oblivion to pain, worry, and the external world": "They spend much of their time listening to recordings of sitar music and discussing how they one day will attain **nirvana**."

Nisei **nee say**

From Japanese nisei, *from* ni- *"second"* + sei *"generation."*

In Japanese, and in English since World War II, also given as **nisei**, plural **Nisei** and **nisei**, meaning "an American or Canadian whose parents were immigrants from Japan": "The most highly decorated fighting unit in the U.S. Army of World War II was the 442nd Regimental Combat Team, made up almost entirely of brave **Nisei**."

See also **Issei** and **Sansei**.

noblesse oblige **noh BLESS oh BLEE*ZH***

From French noblesse oblige, *literally, "nobility obliges."*

In French, and in English since the early nineteenth century, meaning "the principle that noble ancestry and privilege entail responsibility": "**Noblesse oblige** holds that people to whom much is given have to give much in return."

Instead of striving steadily to increase the amount available to be given. Without, alas, ever giving.

nolo contendere **NOH loh kən TEN də ree**

From Latin, literally, "I do not wish to contend."

In English since late in the nineteenth century, meaning, "in criminal law a plea in a criminal case by which a defendant accepts conviction but does not admit guilt," also given in jargon as **nolo**: "Jane's attorney encouraged her to avoid a long and expensive trial, which she probably would lose, by pleading **nolo contendere** and accepting a less severe sentence that has been promised."

And that's one way to cop a plea.

nom de plume NOM də PLOOM

An English phrase, plural **noms de plumes** *(NOMZ də PLOOM), coined from French words:* nom *"name +* de *"of"* + plume *"pen"; meaning "pen name"; "a name assumed by a writer."*

Thus, among many literary **noms de plumes**, we have Elia, nom de plume of Charles Lamb (1775–1834); Lewis Carroll, nom de plume of Charles Dodgson (1832–98); George Sand, nom de plume of Lucile Dudevant (1804–76); George Eliot, nom de plume of Mary Ann Evans (1819–80); and Mark Twain, nom de plume of Samuel Clemens (1835–1910).

So if **nom de plume** is an English coinage, what is the French word for "pen name"? *Pseudonyme*, of course. And how do the French define *pseudonyme*? As "nom de plume," of course.

Got it?

non sequitur non SEK wi tər

From Latin, literally, "it does not follow."

In English since the mid-sixteenth century, meaning 1. "in logic an inference or a conclusion that does not follow from its premise": "To say that because a felon has been convicted of committing one heinous crime he will inevitably commit other such crimes is to fall into a **non sequitur**."

2. "A statement containing such an inference or conclusion": "His address to the almost-empty Senate was peppered with **non sequiturs** too numerous to recount."

Not that anyone would ever notice.

nosh nosh

From Yiddish nashn, *from German* naschen, *both meaning "to nibble"; "to eat on the sly." Danish has its* naske *and Swedish has* snaska, *suggesting that nibbling and eating on the sly may well be widespread wherever ample food is available.*

In informal English since the mid-twentieth century, a verb meaning 1. "snack or eat between meals": "Try as I may to resist, I invariably **nosh** midway through the morning and again during the afternoon."

2. "Snack on": "I usually **nosh** a bagel in the morning, a couple of doughnuts in the afternoon, and some nuts and fruit in the evening."

3. **Nosh** also functions as an informal noun meaning "food," especially "a snack": "My favorite **nosh** is a handful or two or three of pistachio nuts."

4. In British slang, a **nosh up** is a large meal: "When my wife and I visit, Dick and Emma always provide a **nosh up** of my favorite foods."

5. Another informal noun is **nosher**, meaning "a habitual and frequent snacker": "I suppose it was my mother's example that qualified me for the dissolute life of a full-fledged **nosher**."

6. The final member of the nosh family—for now, at least—is **nosherei** (NOSH ə RĪ), a slang noun meaning "food for noshing": "I would much rather gorge on tasty **nosherei** while reading a good book than sit through a formal dinner of tasteless food and insipid after-dinner speeches."

Have I made myself clear?

nouveau riche NOO voh REESH

From French, literally, "newly rich."

In French, and in English since the beginning of the nineteenth century, plural **nouveaux riches** (NOO voh REESH), meaning "a person who is newly rich, especially one who displays his wealth ostentatiously": "About the nastiest thing she could think of to say about her in-laws was that they were **nouveaux riches**."

Nouveau riche has so firm a toehold in English that an excellent French-English dictionary gives it as a synonym for the French *nouveau riche*.

If one finds something distasteful about nouveaux riches, it is worth pointing out that French also has an expression for "newly poor." It is, of course, *nouveau pauvre*, which hasn't yet made its way into English. But which of these would you choose to be if you had to be "nouveau" something?

nudnik NUUD nik

From Yiddish nudnik, *a noun made from Russian* nudnyi *"boring, tedious" + the Russian noun suffix* -nik, *suggesting a person connected with the stem preceding it. With this suffix, the word becomes a noun that refers, usually derogatorily or humorously, to a person exhibiting a specified behavior or association. But we must be reminded that the Russian* -nik *is neither intrinsically derogatory nor humorous—see* **sputnik**.

But back to **nudnik** in Yiddish, and in English since the mid-twentieth century, a slang noun meaning "a persistently dull, nagging, and boring pest": "As customer service manager, I spend much of my time dealing with **nudniks** who seem to have nothing to do but pester hardworking people with baseless complaints."

Now that beatniks and peaceniks are no longer with us, the world can concentrate on its no-goodniks and its nudniks.

O

objet d'art awb *zh*ay DAHR

From French, literally, "an art object."

In French, and in English since the mid-nineteenth century, plural **objets d'art** (awb *zh*ay DAHR), meaning "an object of artistic worth or curiosity, especially a small such object": "Bill had forgotten all he ever had known about fine wines and **objets d'art**, but he still considered himself a connoisseur of good writing."

Everybody's a literary critic.

odalisque OHD ə lisk

From French odalisque, *earlier* odalique; *from Turkish* odalik, *from* oda *"chamber"* + -lik *a suffix suggesting "function"; meaning "concubine."*

In French, and in English since the mid-seventeenth century, also given as **odalisk**, meaning 1. "a female slave or concubine in a harem, especially in the seraglio of the sultan of

Turkey": "As an adolescent he dreamt not of sweater girls, but of naked **odalisques** patiently waiting in anticipation of his ardent attentions."

2. As **Odalisque**, "the title of any of a number of representations of such a woman or similar subject, as by Ingres or Matisse": "I was struck by the incongruity of having a nun who is expert in art history stand before the **Odalisque** of Ingres and deliver a television lecture on its artistic quality."

Incidentally, both Italian and Spanish, knowing a good thing when they see one, have *odalisca* in their vocabularies.

oeuvre UH vrə

From French, meaning "a work."

In French, and in English since the last quarter of the nineteenth century, plural **oeuvres** (UH vrə), meaning 1. "the work of a writer, painter, or the like, taken as a whole": "According to Somerset Maugham, an entire shelf of books—representing a writer's substantial **oeuvre**—requires only half a day's effort, every day for a lifetime."

2. "Any of the works produced by a writer, painter, or the like": "He quit work for the day knowing he had accomplished the best writing he had ever done and had found the right publisher for his final **oeuvre**."

Whose firm would soon be swallowed up by a wealthy person entirely ignorant of publishing.

See also **chef-d'oeuvre**.

ombudsman OM bədz mən

From Swedish, meaning "legal representative"; from ombud *"agent"* + -man *suffix, meaning "man."*

In English since the beginning of the twentieth century, plural **ombudsmen** (OM bədz mən), meaning "an official appointed to investigate complaints by individuals against maladministration by persons in authority": "While **ombudsmen** originally were government officials who heard complaints against other government officials, the term now is applied to officials in private industry who perform a comparable function."

Sign of the times: Bowing to pressure from feminist writers, the term of choice now is said to be **ombudsperson**, an authentic Americanism.

omertà **oh MAIR tə**

From dialectical Italian umiltà, *meaning "humility, modesty, self-abasement."*

In Italian, and in English since the beginning of the twentieth century, meaning "secrecy sworn to by oath"; "code of silence": "What once were occasional lapses in **omertà**, the strictly enforced Mafia code, have in recent years become so frequent that the organization may soon face severe diminution of effectiveness."

But don't count on it.

on the qui vive. See qui vive.

origami **OR i GAH mee**

From Japanese origami, oru *"fold"* + kami *"paper."*

In Japanese, and in English since the 1920s, meaning 1. "the traditional Japanese art or technique of folding paper into decorative or representational forms": "She had studied **origami** for many years in Japan before beginning to teach the subject to American adult students."

2. Plural **origamis**, objects made by **origami**: "Each semester her students mount an exhibition of their intricate **origamis** and offer them for sale to eager buyers."

Origami has also been folded into French.
Pun.

outré oo TRAY

From French outré, *past participle of* outrer, *meaning "to exaggerate."*

In French, and in English since the early eighteenth century, an adjective meaning "violating decorum"; also, "beyond the bounds of what is considered proper or usual": "Knowing George would offend my other guests with his **outré** behavior, I decided not to invite him to the dinner party."

If **outré** brings to mind the words "outrage" and "outrageous," be advised they are indeed linguistic cousins of outré.

P

palomino PAL ə MEE **noh**

From American Spanish palomino, *from Spanish* palomino, *meaning "young pigeon"; from Latin* palumbinus, *meaning "resembling a dove," suggesting the use of an admiring term for a beautiful horse. Read on.*

In American Spanish, and in English since the beginning of the twentieth century, plural **palominos**, meaning "a cream-colored or golden horse with a white mane and tail": "At movie theaters showing Westerns on Saturday afternoons, my friends and I knew our cowboy heroes would always wear white hats and ride **palominos**."

While you're contemplating the relationship between a young pigeon and a cream-colored horse, be careful to spell palomino correctly: two "o" 's, not two "a" 's.

Why? If you go from the Spanish *palomino* to the Spanish *palomina*, you are moving from "young pigeon" to "pigeon dung."

No kidding. You could look it up.

pandit. See **pundit.**

paparazzi PAH pə RAHT see

From Italian paparazzo, *the singular form of* paparazzi, *which came into Italian in the mid-twentieth century, meaning "freelance photographer."* Paparazzo *came from the name of a character in Federico Fellini's great film* La dolce vita *(1960). But read on.*

It is said that during production of Fellini's masterwork, he happened to be reading *By the Ionian Sea* (1900), a travel book written by the English novelist George Gissing, in which a hotel keeper had the name Paparazzo. Fellini was taken with the name and gave it to a photographer in *La dolce vita*, who made his living by taking candid photographs of celebrities and selling the pictures to magazines and newspapers. The rest, as they say, is history.

Paparazzo (PAH pə RAHT soh) came into Italian and into English, in about 1965, meaning a freelance photographer, especially one who bedevils celebrities in order to take candid pictures for publication: "As virtually the whole world knows, **paparazzi** will go to almost any lengths to take the pictures they want—especially when a celebrity they are pursuing is a beautiful princess."

So completely absorbed into English is the plural form **paparazzi** that—like the plural form **graffiti** (which see)—it seems to have completely captured the popular mind, so the singular paparazzo is completely unknown. For example, when an English-language newspaper wishes to report the activities of a paparazzo, it refers to him or her as "one of the paparazzi" rather than risk confusing most readers with what they may regard as a typographic error.

Maybe paparazzo, in the closing years of the twentieth century, lost its linguistic function in English since intrepid—and pesky—paparazzi appear always to travel in packs.

papier-mâché PAY **pər mə** SHAY

From French, literally, "chewed paper"; from papier *paper* + mâché *past participle of* mâcher, *meaning "chew"; from Latin* masticare, *with the same meaning.*

In French, and in English since the mid-eighteenth century, also given as **paper-mâché**, meaning 1. "molded paper pulp used for making a variety of articles": "Kindergarten teachers find that most of the children they teach enjoy making masks of **papier-mâché**."

2. As an adjective, meaning "made of papier-mâché": "**Papier-mâché** objects may be painted once they are dry, making them especially attractive to children."

3. Again as an adjective, with the meaning of "false, pretentious, or illusory": "I suppose a politician who has a **papier-mâché** social conscience is not as bad as one who has no conscience at all."

Maybe.

parka PAHR kə

From Aleutian parka, *from Russian* párka, *meaning "jacket made of skin."*

In English since the late eighteenth century, meaning 1. "a hooded fur coat worn in regions of extreme cold": "**Parkas** are essential for anyone traveling to Arctic regions."

2. "A hooded jacket made of wool or windproof material, worn by skiers and others": "Downhill skiers all wore **parkas** once the temperature dropped well below freezing."

3. "Any hooded coat or jacket worn as a raincoat or windbreaker": "Many Maine children wear **parkas** when they go to school in winter."

parvenu PAHR və NOO

From French parvenu, *as a noun meaning "an upstart"; from the past participle of* parvenir, *meaning "to arrive"; from Latin* per *"through"* + venire *"come."*

In English as a noun and an adjective since the end of the eighteenth century, and almost always derogatory.

1. As a noun meaning "a person who has recently acquired wealth, position, or importance, and is thought to lack appropriate manners, dress, etc.": "Who but a snob would consider himself qualified to label someone a **parvenu** because of his manners or dress?"
2. As an adjective, "being or resembling a parvenu": "Donald is seen as a make-believe capitalist, a mortgaged-to-the-hilt **parvenu** real estate wheeler-dealer." "No one ever seems to have as much fun as **parvenu** good-time-Charlies, who don't give a hoot about what people think of their spending habits and unguarded speech."

Parvenu shmarvenu, enjoy yourself.

See also **arriviste**.

passe-partout PASS pahr TOO

From French, from passer *"pass"* + partout *"everywhere."*

In French, and in English since the mid-seventeenth century, plural **passe-partouts** (PASS pahr TOOZ), meaning 1. "something that passes everywhere or provides a universal means of passage": "Knowledge of French used to be the **passe-partout** for travelers in every European country."

2. "A master key"; "a skeleton key": "What they do not have is a **passe-partout** that will open every apartment door in the building."
3. "A picture frame made of two pieces of glass fastened together by adhesive tape": "I fear my old **passe-partouts** may begin shattering because their adhesive tape is drying out."

4. "A kind of adhesive tape used for framing photographs": "**Passe-partout** today is considered old-fashioned and unreliable by most photographers who frame their own prints."

pasticcio. See **pastiche**.

pastiche pa STEESH

From French pastiche, *from Italian* pasticcio, *from Late Latin* pasta, *meaning "pasta."*

In French, and in English since the beginning of the eighteenth century, meaning 1. "an unoriginal picture or musical composition consisting chiefly of motifs or techniques derived from one or more sources": "The orchestra, under the direction of its new conductor, commissioned a new orchestral work, which unfortunately turned out to be little more than a too-familiar **pastiche**."

2. "An incongruous combination of materials, forms, motifs, etc., taken from different sources"; "a hodgepodge": "Some painters have achieved extraordinary effects with their collages, which at first glance may appear to be nothing more than **pastiches** but require artistic skill in assembly."

It must be noted that English also took in the Italian *pasticcio* at the beginning of the twentieth century, with the same meaning as **pastiche**. While "pastiche" has been received in English with such enthusiasm that some French-English dictionaries define the French *pastiche* as the English "pastiche," Italian dictionaries have stayed with their definition of *pasticcio* as nothing more than "meat pie" or "fish pie," in England called a "pasty." But if that is what Italian insists on, don't knock it. After all, we owe the Italians eternal gratitude for inventing the pizza.

Besides, *pasticcio* itself derives from the Italian *pasta*, from the

Late Latin *pasta*, meaning "pasta," and everyone knows what pasta is.

Looks as though all roads still lead to Rome.

pâté de foie gras pah TAY də FWAH GRAH

From French.

In French, and in English since early in the nineteenth century, plural **pâtés de foie gras** (pah TAYZ də FWAH GRAH), meaning "goose-liver pâté": "Few of us studying at the Sorbonne could afford to buy **pâté de foie gras** except on special occasions, when we would pool our resources and buy enough to give each of us one small taste."

A word must be said about the French adjective *gras*, meaning "fat." To encourage the abnormal development of *foie gras*—"fatty liver"—in a goose raised to give its all for a delicious pâté, the poor critter is force-fed. The process of force-feeding, in French called *gavage*, surely makes an animal-lover—as well as the bird itself—gag. But no gourmet dwells on this cruel practice when dipping into pâté de foie gras.

Further, lest it be thought all pâtés are made of goose liver, let it be known that the French and the chefs they have sent abroad for generations have also produced **pâté de campagne**, a coarse pork and liver pâté; **pâté en croûte**, a pâté baked in a pastry; and **pâté maison**, a pâté cooked according to the recipe of the restaurant offering it.

While these various pâtés—and there surely are others—appear frequently on the menus of restaurants in the United States and Great Britain, their names still have a way to go before being considered English words.

patzer PAHT sər

From German Patzer, *literally "a bungler."*

In German, and in English since the mid-twentieth century,

meaning "a casual, amateurish chess player": "The predominant belief is that Florio lacks real talent and will never be anything but a **patzer** despite all the hours he spends at his chess club observing expert players in action."

Once a **patzer**, always a patzer.

peignoir payn WAHR

From French peignoir, *from* peigner, *meaning "to comb"; literally, "a comber," that is, "a garment worn by a woman while her hair is being combed."*

In French, and in English since early in the nineteenth century, meaning 1. "a woman's loose dressing gown": "The newspaper delivery boy was taken aback when his customer, a beautiful woman, came to the door wearing nothing but a sheer **peignoir**."

2. "A gown of terry cloth worn after swimming or after the bath": "At my swim club, women members appear to be trying to outdo one another in the grandness of the **peignoirs** they wear."

Instead of improving their backstrokes.

penchant pah*n* SHAH*N*

From French penchant, *present participle of* pencher, *meaning "to incline" or "learn."*

In French, and in English since the mid-seventeenth century, a noun meaning "a strong inclination, taste, or liking (for something)": "She had a **penchant** for vigorous competitive sports that led young men to admire her but never fall in love with her."

Penchant is a word that clings tenuously to its French pronunciation, pah*n* SHAH*N*, while making strides toward full Americanization and Anglicization, but there is more to the pronunciation story than that.

In England, "penchant" is pronounced PAH*N* shah*n*, a shift in accent from the French pah*n* SHAH*N*. In American speech, two pronunciations are heard: PEN chənt and pah*n* SHAH*N*.

It looks like dealer's choice: Do you want to sound more French or more American?

In this case I vote for the French, because I learned the word as pah*n* SHAH*N* long before dictionaries recognized the more American pronunciation of PEN chənt.

persona non grata pər SOH nə non GRAH tə

From Latin, meaning "an unacceptable person."

In English since the late nineteenth century, plural **personae non gratae** (pər SOH nee non GRAH tee), meaning 1. "a person who is not welcome": "We voted to deny club membership to John because three of our members have voted to declare him **persona non grata**."

2. "A diplomatic representative unacceptable to an accrediting government": "After the Peruvian foreign minister was accused of selling his country's trade secrets, he was declared **persona non grata** by most South American governments."

And when we remove the negative **non** from the phrase, we are left with **persona grata**, plural **personae gratae**, in English meaning "an acceptable person, especially a diplomatic representative acceptable to a foreign country."

"Persona grata" is not heard often, because we do not ordinarily go around announcing that a certain person is welcome. Unless, that is, someone asks us or because his status as persona non grata has been changed.

petit four PET ee FOR

From French, literally, "small oven."

In French, and in English since the late nineteenth century, plural **petits fours** (PET ee FORZ), meaning "a small fancy cake, decorated and frosted": "With our coffee we were served the inevitable dish of conventionally decorated **petits fours**, surely not homemade and certainly anything but tasty."

And how does our excellent French-English dictionary define the French *petit-four*?

Correct. As the English "petit four."

petit mal PET ee MAHL

From French, literally, "small sickness."

In French, and in English since the late eighteenth century, meaning "a mild form of epilepsy with sleepiness or episodic loss of attention": "The manifestations of **petit mal** may be so slight that persons having this condition may believe they suffer from nothing more than occasional headaches."

Yet who would choose to have even the mildest form of **petit mal**?

See also **grand mal**.

petit point PET ee POINT

From French petit point *(pə tee PWAHN), literally, "small stitch."*

In French, and in English since the late nineteenth century, meaning 1. "a small stitch used in embroidery": "I marvel at Frank's devotion to his new hobby, spending hour after hour meticulously stitching his **petit point**."

2. "Embroidery done on a canvas backing and resembling woven tapestry": "Rather than use commercially available printed embroidery canvases, she bought blank canvas, which she then cut and sketched upon for her **petit point**."

And the definition for the French *petit point* supplied by our trusty French-English dictionary? That's right: "petit point."

pickelhaube PIK əl HOW bə

A word few English-speakers know, even though most of them have often seen pictures of the type of helmet it identifies. It is supplied here so you will know what to call the helmet when you next see it.

From German Pickelhaube, *from* Pickel *"pimple" or "pickax"* + Haube *"helmet"; meaning "spiked helmet."*

In English since the late nineteenth century, plural **pickelhauben** (PIK əl HOW bən) and **pickelhaubes**, meaning "a German army spiked helmet of a type worn before and during World War I": "Anyone who has seen pictures of high German officers proudly wearing their **pickelhauben** and sporting rows of medals on their splendid tunics surely understands that the officers were not wearing battle dress."

It is interesting to note that British soldiers once used **pickelhaube** scornfully as a nickname for a German soldier. This is hardly different from the practice of American soldiers who used to refer to their high officers as "brass hats," an allusion to the gold braid they wore on their hats.

This last linguistic observation is old hat. Today's American soldiers and corporation underlings refer to their officers or managers as "the brass" or "the top brass." It also is instructive to know that corporate employees now refer to accountants, lawyers, and other company functionaries as "suits," thus establishing a world-class metaphor.

But surely one must wonder whether the German *Pickel*, which has been translated above as both "pimple" and "pickax," has anything to do with the converted cucumber that English calls a "pickle." Alas, they are strangers to one another. "Pickle" has been in English since the beginning of the fifteenth century, and its association with German lies in the Middle Low German *Pekel*, related to the German *Pökel*, both meaning "brine" and "pickle."

Sorry.

pièce de résistance pee ESS də ri zee STAHNSS

From French, literally, "piece of resistance," that is, "a substantial piece."

In French, and in English since the end of the eighteenth century, plural **pièces de résistance** (pee ESS də ri zee STAHNSS), meaning 1. "the main dish of a meal": "When Norma's **pièce de résistance**, a turkey roasted to juicy perfection, was brought to the table, all present at the feast gazed with delight at the succulent bird."

2. "The most remarkable item in a series or group"; "a special item or attraction": "Tension mounted in the auction room as the hour drew near for bidding on the diamond tiara owned by the late princess, surely the **pièce de résistance** of the sale."

Glittering munificence really grabs people, especially those inclined to show up at auctions.

pied-à-terre pee AY da TAIR

From French, literally, "foot to earth."

In French, and in English since the early nineteenth century, plural **pieds-à-terre** (pee AY da TAIR), meaning "an apartment or small house, for part-time or temporary use": "The generous Egertons have said we may use their attractive flat on Wimpole Street as our **pied-à-terre** whenever we visit London."

Beats a bed-and-breakfast.

Pietà PEE ay TAH

From Italian pietà, *from Latin* pietas, *meaning "piety."*

Also given as **pietà** in Italian, and in English since the mid-seventeenth century, meaning "a painting or sculpture representing the Virgin Mary with the body of the dead Christ on her lap": "When Michelangelo's great ***Pietà*** was exhibited in New York City, a deranged man attacked it and managed to break a piece off the sculpture."

It is enlightening to note that the Latin word *pietas* means "filial" or "parental love" as well as "piety."

pilaf pee LAHF

From Turkish pilav, *meaning "cooked rice"; from Persian* pilaw, *meaning "boiled rice and meat."*

In these languages, and in English in various spellings since early in the seventeenth century, often given as **pilaff** and **pilau**, meaning 1. "an oriental dish of sautéed rice steamed in bouillon, often with poultry, shellfish, or meat": "In New York City, there are as many types of **pilaf**—most of them worth trying—as there are Middle Eastern restaurants, many of them worth avoiding."

2. "A dish of rice cooked in meat or chicken broth": "What passes for **pilaf** in some restaurants is nothing more than overcooked rice that has stood for hours and then is doused with canned chicken broth prior to serving."

piquant PEE kənt

From French piquant, *present participle of* piquer, *meaning "to prick or sting."*

In French, and in English since the early sixteenth century, an adjective meaning 1. "agreeably pungent or sharp in taste": "The chef's **piquant** sauces are attracting knowledgeable diners to our restaurant."

2. "Agreeably stimulating, interesting, or attractive": "She is

known for her sense of humor and **piquant** smile, characteristics that can be counted on to open the purses of potential donors to our charity."

3. "Of an interestingly provocative or lively character": "We agreed the new dean's **piquant** wit would set the desired tone for what we hoped would be an interesting meeting."

It would be the first ever.

pissoir pee SWAHR

From French pissoir, *from* pisser, *meaning "urinate."*

In French, and in English since the early twentieth century, meaning "a street urinal for public use," usually blocked from view by a low wall, screen, or the like: "As far as I am concerned, the institution of the **pissoir**, which offers democratic relief to all male pedestrians, is just one more bit of evidence that French culture leads the world."

While the French have other terms for this convenience, including *urinoir* and *vespasienne*, only *pissoir* has moved from French into English. But while we can readily comprehend the French *urinoir*, we may have trouble with *vespasienne*. Be aware that French has *colonne vespasienne*, literally, "Vespasian column," from the name of the Roman Emperor Vespasian, more properly Titus Flavius Sabinus Vespasianus. But why does this mean "public urinal"?

Because Vespasian, in his wisdom, saw fit to introduce a tax on public lavatories. And one can easily imagine generations of coarse men and mischievous boys taking revenge on Vespasian's tax policies by relieving themselves publicly at the base of a Roman column.

Not unlike dogs taking delight in spraying a modern municipal fire hydrant.

pita PEE tah

From Modern Greek petta *or* pitta, *meaning "bread, cake, pie"; in Turkish given as* pide, *and in Aramaic as* pitta, *with the same meanings.*

In American English since the mid-twentieth century, also given as **pita bread**, meaning a round, flat Middle Eastern bread, often cut open and filled with meat, peppers, etc., to make a sandwich: "After we had a few olives with our drinks of ouzo, we tucked into a delicious lunch of **pita** overstuffed with slices of lamb, onion, and tomato."

pizza PEET sə

From Italian pizza, *meaning "pie"; from Greek* pétea *meaning "brain," and Greek* petítes, *meaning "bran bread."*

In English since early in the twentieth century, also given as the tautological **pizza pie**, meaning "a flat, baked pie of Italian origin, consisting of a thin layer of bread dough topped sometimes with cheese and spiced tomato sauce, and often garnished with pepperoni slices, anchovies, mushrooms, etc.": "**Pizza** is the ultimate gift of Neapolitan cuisine to the world, uniting Italians and all others in homage to the joys of the tomato, mozzarella cheese, and olive oil."

Baked in a **pizzeria** (PEET sə REE ə), a place where pizzas are baked or sold, and eaten straight from the oven.

Not warmed up in a microwave oven from the frozen state. Ugh!

placebo plə SEE boh

From Latin placebo, *literally, "I shall please" or "I shall be acceptable," from* placere, *meaning "to please."*

In English since the late eighteenth century, plural **placebos** and **placeboes**, meaning 1. "a medicine intended to cure by reassuring the patient rather than by offering pharmacological effect": "Patients unaware that their physicians are prescribing **placebos** often show marked alleviation of their symptoms."

2. "Such a medicine given in a controlled trial"; "a dummy pill": "Pharmacologists regularly test promising new drugs by administering them to half the patients in a test program and administering **placebos** to the rest."

With both groups led to think they are receiving a promising new drug.

plat du jour PLAH də *ZH*UUR

From French, literally, "dish of the day."

In French, and in English since the beginning of the twentieth century, plural **plats du jour** (PLAHZ də *ZH*UUR), meaning "the featured dish of the day on a restaurant menu": "On our trip through France we saved money and were able to sample a great variety of food by always ordering the **plat du jour** at every restaurant we stopped at."

A good technique, especially if you have trouble reading French menus or making up your mind.

See also **du jour**, which indicates the broad possibilities of this ordinary French phrase, literally, "of the day," when wrapped in a mantle of contemporary English.

poi poi

From Hawaiian poi.

In Hawaiian, and in English since the early years of the nineteenth century, meaning "a Hawaiian dish made of the root of the taro": "After fermenting, **poi** is moistened, pounded, baked, and then eaten with the fingers."

If you have the opportunity to taste this dish, it is worth knowing the accepted procedure for eating this finger food. Dip your fingers into the bowl of poi, move your fingers around, pull them out, and then suck them clean.

A dish reviled by some, but said by others to be finger-lickin' good.

porte-cochere PORT koh SHAIR

From French porte-cochère, *from* porte *"gateway"* + cochère *(from* coche, *meaning "coach"); literally, "a gate for coaches."*

In French, and in English since the end of the seventeenth century, also given as **porte-cochère**, meaning 1. "a covered carriage entrance leading into a courtyard": "New York City still has a number of former mansions, now desirable apartment houses, that have **porte-cocheres** extending from the street into handsome courtyards."

2. "A covered area at the door of a building for sheltering persons entering and leaving automobiles": "The cover provided by our **porte-cochere** is especially welcome when we entertain friends of advanced age."

poseur poh ZUR

From French poseur, *from* poser, *meaning "to pose"; literally, "a poser."*

In French, and in English since the late nineteenth century, plural **poseurs**, meaning "a person who puts on airs": "The jockeying for class leadership began in his first week at Harvard, when **poseurs** tried to outdo one another in displaying cool composure and sophistication."

While many others were wondering whether they would ever feel comfortable being at the school.

powwow POW wow

From Narragansett powwaw, *meaning "Indian priest, magician"; from Algonquian* pawewa, *literally, "he dreams," suggesting that the powers of the Indian priest derive from his visions.*

In English since the early seventeenth century, a noun meaning 1. "a conference with Indians or between Indians": "When the **powwow** concluded, it was obvious that the truce that had been declared would not last for very long."

2. Informally, "any conference or political meeting": "Our leaders agreed to hold one more **powwow** with management before having the membership take a strike vote."

3. As a verb, meaning "to hold a powwow": "The radical minority group declared its opposition to the proposal that we continue to **powwow** until we have selected a full slate of candidates for leadership positions."

4. Informally, "to confer": "When I was a child, my father insisted that the entire family **powwow** at the dinner table to prevent minor differences from becoming big ones."

Another American Indian word that has survived and flourished in English.

précis pray SEE

From French précis, *originally a noun use of the adjective* précis, *meaning "cut short."*

In French, and in English since the mid-eighteenth century, meaning 1. as a noun, plural **précis** (pray SEEZ), "a concise summary": "The instructor asked all of us to write **précis** of an essay by E. B. White."

2. As a verb, "make a précis of": "I was told the essay I selected for the assignment was too compressed to **précis**."

protégé PROH tə ZHAY

From French protégé, *literally, "protected," past participle of* protéger; *from Latin* protegere, *both meaning "to protect."*

In French, and in English since the late eighteenth century, a noun meaning "a person under the patronage of someone interested in his or her career": "James has reached the stage of his life in which he feels uncomfortable thinking of himself as a younger man's **protégé**, but in fact that is precisely what he is."

While **protégé** is used in English to accommodate both sexes, French—as it so often does—has a feminine form, *protégée*, which has also come into English. The attitudes of feminists being what they are, chances are **protégée** (PROH tə ZHAY) soon enough will depart from English.

Until then, "protégée" may be used to characterize a girl or woman under someone's patronage.

provenance PROV ə nənss

From French provenance; *from French* provenir, *from Latin* provenire, *both meaning "to come forth."*

In French, and in English since the mid-nineteenth century, also occasionally given as **provenience** (proh VEE nee ənss), said of an artwork, meaning "origin, place of origin"; "pedigree": "Before the dealer would consider purchasing the painting, she insisted on seeing its **provenance**, the complete and verifiable record of its passage from the artist through the painting's successive owners."

The frequency of art thefts being what it is.

pumpernickel PUM pər NIK əl

From German Pumpernickel, *properly Westphalian dark rye bread.*

The German word *Pumpernickel* had an earlier sense of lout or stinker, from *pumpern* meaning "to fart," and *Nickel*, a pet form of the name Nikolaus, in English called Nicholas. One can guess that it was applied to heavy dark bread because of the passing effect of the bread on the digestive system.

In English since the mid-eighteenth century, meaning a coarse, dark, slightly sour bread made of unsifted rye: "When I'm in the mood for a sandwich lunch, I reach for two thick slices of **pumpernickel**, with almost any sliced meat for the filler, plus a slathering of English mustard, a thick slice of onion, and a bottle of dark beer."

Or two.

And after the aforementioned sandwich lunch—alert to the etymology of pumpernickel—a walk alone in the forgiving seclusion of a woods. Or didn't you notice the "passing effect of the bread" above?

pundit PUN dit

From Hindi pandit, *from Sanskrit* pandita, *meaning "learned man."*

In English since the mid-eighteenth century, meaning 1. "a learned person, expert, or authority": "The late A. L. Rowse was looked upon as the **pundit** of Elizabethan literature and the last word on Shakespeare's life and works."

2. "A person who makes comments and judgments, especially in an authoritative manner"; "a critic or commentator": "Much fun is made of TV **pundits**, who can be rousted out of bed and within minutes deliver themselves of sententious, indecipherable, and unreliable wisdom on any subject whatsoever, including subjects they've never heard of before."

3. As **Pandit** (PUN dit), capitalized when used as a title of respect, meaning in India "a man esteemed for his wisdom"; "a pundit": "People of my generation remember with respect **Pandit** Jawaharlal Nehru, the first Indian prime minister."

putz putss

From Yiddish puts, *literally, "finery," possibly from* putsn, *a verb meaning "cleanse, shine"; from German* Puts, *meaning "ornaments, adornment."*

In Yiddish, and in English slang since the beginning of the twentieth century, a vulgar term for 1. "penis": "Group showers in infantry barracks I have known inevitably gave rise to comparisons of the sizes of soldiers' **putzes**."

2. "A fool, a jerk"; also, "an objectionable person": "If he is as much of a **putz** as you say he is, how did he ever manage to become a law school dean?"

It is interesting to note that in the 1998 campaign for a U.S. Senate seat, the Republican candidate referred to his Jewish rival, a Democrat, as a **putz head**. The incident, which became an overnight scandal, is said to have cost Republican support among Jewish voters, who well knew the word "putz" in both its meanings.

So, before you use colorful language in your next campaign for public office, be sure you know all the meanings of the words you intend to use.

Q

quahog KWAW hawg

From Narragansett poquaûhock.

In American English since the mid-eighteenth century, also given as **quahaug**, meaning "an edible clam inhabiting waters along the Atlantic coast": "Some gourmets esteem the succulence of the **quahog**, eaten raw of course."

Narragansett is the language of the Narragansett Indians, a tribe of the Algonquian family formerly located in Rhode Island and now almost extinct. Yet, lovers of edible bivalves still are grateful to the Narragansetts for naming the **quahog**, and horse-racing devotees are indebted—as one might expect—to Narragansett for the name of Narragansett Park, a racetrack in Pawtucket, Rhode Island, sponsored by the Narragansett Racing Association.

For another word from Narragansett, see **sachem**.

quattrocento KWAH troh CHEN toh

From Italian quattrocento, *literally, "four hundred"; here short for* mil quattro cento, *meaning "1,400."*

In English since the late nineteenth century, and also given as **Quattrocento**, meaning the fifteenth century, used in reference to the Italian art and literature of that time: "Since the retirement of Professor Eggers, our art history journal has paid little attention to the rich **quattrocento**."

See also **trecento**.

quiche **keesh**

From French quiche, *from Alsatian* Küche, *diminutive form of German* Küchen, *meaning "cake."*

In English since the mid-twentieth century, meaning "a dish made of a pastry shell filled with eggs and usually cheese and other ingredients": "**Quiches** have found a place on many restaurant menus in recent years, mystifying many of us who for a long time have regarded it as a woman's dish."

But now, apparently, even real men eat quiche.

quidnunc **KWID nungk**

From Latin quid nunc, *meaning, "What now?"*

In English since the beginning of the eighteenth century, meaning "a busybody, a person eager to know the latest news and gossip": "Until his final days, Herbert remained the quintessential **quidnunc**, never overlooking idle gossip, no matter how trivial or far-fetched."

quinella **kwi NEL ə**

From American Spanish quiniella, *meaning "a soccer pool."*

In English since the mid-twentieth century, also given as **quinela** and **quiniela** (keen YEL ə), meaning 1. "a type of bet on a horse or dog race in which the bettor must select the first two finishers without specifying their order": "The old-timer watched with fascination as bettors lined up to risk—and surely lose—their money on **quinellas**, sucker bets."

2. A race in which such bets are made: "The seventh race at our local track is usually a **quinella**, selected for this bet so no one will leave for home with as much as two dollars in his pocket."

The odds are a lot better than the odds on winning a state-run lottery, which isn't saying much.

qui vive kee VEEV

From French, literally, "(long) live who?," a sentry's challenge, meaning "whose side are you on?"

It must be noted that "long live . . . "—you fill in the rest—was customarily used as a password, so the sentry's challenge *qui vive?* was intended to elicit the correct response: for example, the Revolution, the king, or the like. If the response was incorrect . . .

In English since the early eighteenth century, in the phrase **on the qui vive**, meaning "on the alert"; "watchful": "When news of the prison break spread through town, everyone suddenly was **on the qui vive**, and guns of every sort appeared in the hands of ordinarily mild-mannered men and women."

The most dangerous of gunslingers.

quondam KWON dəm

From Latin quondam, *an adjective meaning "former, onetime."*

In English since the end of the nineteenth century, with the same meaning: "It is in the nature of things that if you live long enough, most of your friends will become your **quondam** friends, the phenomenon being explained not by inconstancy but by the passage of time and the inevitability of death."

R

raconteur RAK ən TUR

From French raconteur, *meaning "storyteller"; derived from* raconter, *meaning "relate."*

In French, and in English since the early nineteenth century, meaning "a person good at recounting interesting stories and anecdotes": "In Ron's prime, everyone agreed he was unsurpassed as a **raconteur**, but time and the early onset of senility took their toll, leaving him without an audience and without stories to tell."

The feminine form **raconteuse** (RAK ən TUUZ), in English since the mid-nineteenth century, plural **raconteuses** (RAK ən TUU ziz), is hardly ever heard and is presumed to be on its way out.

ragout ra GOO

From French ragoût, *meaning "a stew"; from* ragoûter, *meaning "to restore the appetite of."*

In French, and in English since the mid-seventeenth century, meaning "a highly seasoned stew of meat or fish, with or without vegetables": "What could be better on a winter evening than to sit down to a dinner of bread, wine, and a marvelous **ragout**?"

Yet, as we think of the reality of a savory ragout set on a table before us, awaiting frontal attack with knife and fork, there appears to be no connection between *ragoûter*, "restore the appetite of," and ragout, "a highly seasoned stew." Surely such a stew would take the edge off an ordinary mortal's appetite.

The only obvious explanation is that men and women of centuries past had enormous capacities and could do justice to a ragout merely as a warm-up for a main course.

Maybe they were the so-called real men who didn't eat quiche.

raison d'être **RAY zohn DE trə**

From French, literally, "reason for being."

In French, and in English since the mid-nineteenth century, plural **raisons d'être** (RAY zohnz DE trə), meaning "a rational justification for one's existence": "Writing poetry for its sake alone, not for love of money, is surely his **raison d'être**."

ramada **rə MAH də**

From American Spanish ramada, *meaning "an open shelter"; from Spanish* enramada, *meaning "arbor, bower"; from* enramar, *meaning "intertwine branches."*

In English since the mid-nineteenth century, meaning "an open shelter, often with a dome-shaped thatched roof": "Once we had built our **ramada** on the beach in front of our modest summerhouse, we looked forward to a simple and idyllic existence."

It is interesting to learn this humble origin of the name of the

Ramada Inns, the highly successful chain of air-conditioned motels that offer shelter but otherwise bear no resemblance to the ramadas common in the early American Southwest.

rara avis RAIR ə AY viss

From Latin, literally, "a rare bird."

In English since the beginning of the seventeenth century, plural **rarae aves** (RAIR ee AY veez), meaning "a rarely encountered person or thing"; "a rarity": "In her long career in the school system, Sylvia was that rarest of **rarae aves**, someone who never lost her love of literature and could pass on that love even to indifferent students."

If only such teachers were less rare.

ratatouille RAT ə TOO ee

From French ratatouille, *from* touiller, *meaning "to stir up."*

In French, and in English since late in the nineteenth century, meaning "a vegetable stew of Provence, typically made of eggplant, peppers, tomatoes, onions, etc.": "When I see the kitchen worktable covered with fresh vegetables, I know the star of the evening meal will be a delicious **ratatouille**."

It is interesting to note that modern French also uses *ratatouille* as a slang pejorative, meaning "a bad stew" and "lousy food." But this may be an example of regional French scorn—envy?—for things Provençal.

And English does not use **ratatouille** pejoratively.

realpolitik ray AHL poh li TEEK

From German Realpolitik, *from* real *"real"* + Politik *"politics."*

In German, and in English since the early twentieth century, also as **Realpolitik**, meaning "practical politics," especially policies based on power rather than on ideals: "We look back with special distaste to the era when **realpolitik**—as practiced by self-serving academics on temporary duty in Washington, D.C., who were projected into national prominence—was the order of the day in formulating United States foreign policy."

And a **realpolitiker** (ray AHL poh LEE ti kər) is "a practical politician," a person who advocates or practices realpolitik.

réchauffé **ray shoh FAY**

From French réchauffé, *past particle of* réchauffer, *meaning "reheat," from* re- *"again"* + échauffer *"to warm up"; from Latin* calefacere, *meaning "to make warm."*

In English since the end of the eighteenth century, as a noun, meaning 1. "a warmed-up dish of food": "Because Joyce had prepared so much food for the family Thanksgiving, all the meals served for the rest of that week would certainly be **réchauffés**."

2. "Anything old or stale brought into service again": "Halfway through the first chapter of his recent novel, I realized that the book was nothing more than a **réchauffé** of his earlier work, and there was no point in reading further."

3. As an adjective, said of food, meaning "reheated"; of opinions, writing, ideas, etc., meaning "rehashed": "The dinner was a tour de force—without exception everything was **réchauffé**, from the opening salvo of réchauffé noodle pudding and continuing with réchauffé every other dish served—extending even to the réchauffé gossip."

The wine was room temperature.

recherché **rə SHAIR shay**

From French recherché, *past participiple of* rechercher, *meaning "search for carefully."*

In French, and in English since the early eighteenth century, an adjective with several interesting meanings: 1. "sought out with care": "Finally, the **recherché** guest of honor arrived, asked to rest for a moment, and snoozed contentedly for the rest of the evening."

2. "Very rare, exotic, or choice"; "arcane"; "obscure": "Trevor made an audible show of sniffing the air and said, 'Surely you have some **recherché** dry rot somewhere in your darling little house.' "

3. "Of studied refinement or elegance"; "precious"; "affected"; "pretentious": "At her mother's insistence, Emily prepared a **recherché** luncheon, which required hours of shopping to find just the right tablecloths and serviettes, the purchase of two dozen crystal goblets, and the hiring of a cook and two uniformed waitresses."

Only the food was ordinary.

réclame ray KLAHM

From French réclame, *from* réclamer, *meaning "ask for"; from Latin* reclamare, *meaning "cry out against."*

In French, and in English since the mid-nineteenth century, meaning 1. "publicity"; "notoriety, self-advertisement": "She's always willing to offer substantial discounts to jet-setters for the **réclame** their patronage induces among social climbers."

2. "Hunger for publicity"; "talent for getting attention": "His **réclame** had changed him almost overnight from a principled young artist to a despicable self-promoter."

And wealthy artist.

redivivus RED ə VEE vəss

From Latin, meaning "renewed, renovated"; from re- *"again"* + vivus *"living, alive."*

In English since the mid-seventeenth century, an adjective meaning "returned to life"; "reborn, renewed": "As we listened to the marvelous music the young pianist was playing, my companion whispered, 'Surely a Horowitz **redivivus**.' "

Note that **redivivus** always follows the noun it modifies: Picasso redivivus, Mantle redivivus, and the like.

reductio ad absurdum ri DUK tee OH AD ab SUR dəm

From Latin, literally, "reduction to the absurd."

In English since the early eighteenth century, in logic meaning "a method of refuting a proposition by showing that its logical consequence would be absurd": "My teacher illustrated **reductio ad absurdum** by reciting a familiar absurdity, 'The more you sleep, the longer you live; sleep all the time, and you'll live longer than anybody.' "

Absurd enough for you?

restaurant RESS tər ənt

From French restaurant, *present participle of* restaurer, *meaning "to restore"; from Latin* restaurare, *"to restore."*

The meaning of this word, used in English since at least 1820, is well understood. It is included here as an interesting example of differences between American and English pronunciation of words taken from French.

First consider the French pronunciation of **restaurant**: RESS tə RAH*N*. The use of italics in *N* indicates that its sound is almost unvoiced.

In American English, "restaurant" is usually pronounced RESS tər ənt or RESS tə RAHNT. In British English, the preferred pronunciation is RESS tə RAH*N*. As in French, the final *t* is unvoiced, and *n* is almost unvoiced.

We are accustomed to the unvoiced final *t* in many words of French origin. Consider, for example, the word *chalet*. In French it is pronounced shah LAY. And while Americans pronounce it sha LAY, the British typically pronounce it SHA lay.

Cousins often disagree. But they agree here on not really pronouncing the final *t*.

restaurateur RESS **tə rə** TUR

From French restaurateur, *meaning "an owner or manager of a restaurant." In English with the same meaning since the late eighteenth century.*

It is clear that this English word is not applied to an owner or manager of your favorite diner or fast-food establishment but is reserved for a person associated with something at the very least a little more grand.

What better source than French for giving us words dealing with the preparation of food and its enjoyment? Consider **sauté** (which see), court-bouillon (and bouillon alone), as well as **gourmet** (which see), among hundreds of other terms. It's almost as if we can't be considered serious cooks or diners without using adoptions from French.

But on to a brief but important discussion of the pronunciation of "restaurateur." Whether we use this word in England or in the United States, its correct pronunciation is RESS tə rə TUR; in France, ress taw ra TUR.

Notice that there is no *n* in the spelling or pronunciation of "restaurateur," yet too many people are misled by the spelling and pronunciation of "restaurant" and manage to squeeze an *n* into restaurateur. Small wonder the most permissive of dictionaries now accepts the spelling "restauranteur."

But for you and me, a real no-no.

rickshaw RIK shaw

Shortened from Japenese jinrikisha, *literally, "man power," from* jin *"man"* + riki *"strength"* + sha *"vehicle."*

In Japanese, and in English since the late nineteenth century, also given as **ricksha**, **rikisha**, and **rikshaw**, meaning "a two-wheeled, cartlike passenger vehicle, pulled by one person": "A misguided person at the meeting of environmentalists shocked us by proposing to reduce air pollution in our cities by replacing automobiles with **rickshaws**, like those he had formerly seen on the streets of China and Japan."

And allowing Toyota and Nissan automobiles to rust away, while at the same time increasing human misery under the guise of saving the environment.

Imagine!

ricochet RIK ə SHAY

From French, meaning "a rebound, a bounce."

In English since the mid-eighteenth century, with the same meaning, especially 1. "a rebound of an object from the surface against which it hits a glancing blow": "Everyone who has experienced the perils of gunfire in a city street knows that the chance of injury to innocent bystanders is greater from the **ricochet** of bullets than from a direct hit."

2. Also used as a verb in English—the French verb is *ricocher*, meaning "rebound, ricochet." The English verb, more formally, means "to rebound from a surface as a missile does when it strikes with a glancing blow": "We lay flat behind the boulders while the enemy soldier kept on firing, and we could hear his bullets **ricochet** all around us."

And, believe it or not, all that came to my mind was to wonder whether I was lying prone or supine.

risqué ri SKAY

From French risqué, *past participle of* risquer, *meaning "to risk."*

In French, and in English since the mid-nineteenth century. Said of a story, song, film, etc., meaning "daringly close to impropriety"; "off-color"; "slightly indecent": "Most of the audience reacted to the comedian's **risqué** stories initially with uncomfortable laughter and cold stares, and then by leaving the auditorium long before the program was slated to end."

roman à clef roh MAH nah KLAY

From French, literally, "novel with a key."

In French, and in English since late in the nineteenth century, plural **romans à clef** (roh MAH*N* zah KLAY), meaning "a novel in which actual persons are introduced under fictitious names": "Aldous Huxley's novel *Point Counter Point* is classified as a **roman à clef** since many of its characters are recognizable as prominent literary and political figures of Huxley's time."

roué roo AY

From French roué, *past participle of* rouer, *literally, "to break on the wheel"; used as a noun.* Roué *was the term applied individually to the profligate companions of the French Duc d'Orléans (c. 1720), suggesting that they deserved to be broken on the wheel.*

In French, and in English since the end of the eighteenth century, meaning "a dissolute and licentious man"; "a debauchee, a rake": "People still considered Douglas a **roué** long after old age had reduced him to the status of harmless spectator of the game of life."

For those whose reading has not included tales of punishment in years gone by, it must be noted that "breaking on a wheel," mentioned in the first paragraph above, is a form of torture in which the victim is stretched until he or she is disjointed, and an iron bar is employed to break the long bones of the body.

In justice to medieval torturers, however, it must be said that an executioner usually administered the coup de grâce—you fill in the details—to put the poor wretch out of his misery.

See **coup de grâce**.

S

sabotage SAB ə TAHZH

From French sabotage, *from* saboter, *meaning "to make a mess of"; "to botch."*

In French, and in English since the mid-nineteenth century, meaning 1. "any underhanded interference with production, work, etc., especially by enemy agents during wartime or by employees during a labor dispute": "Acts of **sabotage** by union members stiffened the resolve of management to fight the union."

2. "Any undermining of a cause": "The social worker characterized her client's behavior as **sabotage** of her husband's earnest efforts to keep the couple together."

3. As a verb, meaning "injure" or "attack by sabotage": "No one really believed the press was guilty of **sabotaging** the president's reelection campaign."

A word related to sabotage is **saboteur** (SAB ə TUR), meaning "a person who commits or practices sabotage": "The executive's assistant, considered to be the person most influential in promoting the company's enlightened personnel policies, in reality functioned as a **saboteur** of employees' interests."

Most people know **saboteur** but do not find it easy to pronounce. Understand that "saboteur" does not rhyme with "sewer."

sachem SAY chəm

From Narragansett sâchim *or* saunchum, *meaning "a chief."*

In American English since the early seventeenth century, meaning 1. "the supreme chief of some North American Indian tribes": "He came to the fort as his tribe's **sachem**, fully empowered to initiate trade between his people and the settlers."

2. In slang, "a political party leader, particularly one of twelve former high officials governing the Tammany Society, in New York City": "Few contemporary party **sachems** of major American cities are willing to accept an openly gay candidate for mayor."

safari sə FAHR ee

From Swahili safari, *from Arabic* safar, *meaning "a journey."*

In Swahili, and in English since the late nineteenth century, meaning 1. "an expedition, for hunting, exploration, or tourism, especially in eastern Africa": "Men who once served hunters and explorers now work as tour guides for wealthy tourists on motorized photo **safaris**, who think they are roughing it while spending their time photographing African wildlife."

2. "The hunters, guides, vehicles, and other equipment forming such an expedition": "Businesses that supply **safaris** stand ready to organize everything needed for the comfort of

tourists, from guides and porters to almost every imaginable personal convenience."

3. As a verb, meaning "to go on a safari": "At the insistence of the bridegroom, the couple arranged to **safari** on their honeymoon and, to the surprise of their friends, enjoyed every minute of the experience."

A new safari term arose in the 1970s—**safari park**—meaning "a parklike zoo in which wild animals are kept in the open for tourists to observe from their buses or cars."

Shades of Stanley and Livingstone.

salmagundi SAL mə GUN dee

From Middle French salmingondin, *now given as* salmigondis, *meaning "hodgepodge"; a compound of* salemine *"salted food"* + condir *"to season."*

In French as *salmigondis*, and in English as **salmagundi** since the mid-seventeenth century, meaning 1. "a dish of cubed poultry or fish, chopped meat, anchovies, onions, oil, etc., often served as a salad": "Everyone looked forward to Sunday night and Grandmother's **salmagundi**, which she called her 'chop suey,' even though she had never tasted that dish."

2. "Any mixture or miscellaneous collection": "While at Skidmore College, he edited the interesting journal called ***Salmagundi***, which lived up to its name and surprised me with its broad-ranging subject matter every time I came upon a copy."

It is interesting to note that "salmagundi" is pronounced almost identically with French *salmigondis*. In case you wondered.

samizdat SAH miz DAHT

From Russian samizdat, *the abbreviation of* samoizdátel'stvo, *from* samo- *"self"* + izdate'stvo *"publishing house."*

In Russian, and in English since 1965, in the former U.S.S.R. meaning 1. "the clandestine or illegal copying and distribution of literature"; "underground press": "Novels of certain authors were made available only by **samizdat**, but nevertheless were widely read."

2. "A text or texts that are self-published": "Many literary people believe that as the American publishing industry declines, we may one day see important literature in English appear only as **samizdat**."

No sooner coined in Russian than adopted in English—how quickly words can move from language to language in this exciting time of accelerating communication!

samovar SAM ə VAHR

From Russian samovár, *from* samo- *"self"* + varit *"to boil"; literally, "self-boiler."*

In Russian, and in English since the early nineteenth century, meaning "a metal urn, used especially by Russians for heating water to make tea": "When my grandfather fled Russia to avoid military service, the only thing of value he took with him was his **samovar**, which he had received as a gift from his grandmother."

What's life without a glass of hot tea?

sang-froid sah*n* FRWAH

From French, literally, "cold blood."

In French, and in English since the mid-eighteenth century, meaning "coolness of mind"; "composure in the face of danger": "The epitome of **sang-froid** is the Hollywood actor Clint Eastwood, who looks always as though he doesn't know you but wouldn't mind shooting you in cold blood."

One would expect that any foreign term adopted in English and retained for well over two centuries might acquire something approaching an English pronunciation. But this is not the case with **sang-froid**, which is pronounced sahn FRWAH in French and in American English; as SAHN frwah in British English. And the two English pronunciations will never approach English in their sounds.

Sansei sahn say

From Japanese sansei, *from* san *"three" or "third"* + sei *"generation"; literally, "third generation."*

In Japanese, and in English since the beginning of World War II, also given as **sansei**, with plurals **Sansei** and **sansei**, meaning "a grandchild of Japanese immigrants to the United States or Canada": "Sociologists have pointed out that **sansei** typically are well-educated high-achievers, who have succeeded in gaining entry to all the professions."

Despite the fact that first-generation Japanese-Americans—Issei—had spent World War II in U.S. internment camps, while their sons—Nisei—were fighting heroically as soldiers in the United States Army.

See **Issei** and **Nisei**.

sarong sə RONG

From Malay sarung *or* sarong, *literally, "a sheath."*

In English since the early nineteenth century, meaning "a loose-fitting garment, consisting of cloth tucked around the waist or under the armpits, worn especially by men and women of the Malay Archipelago": "Once the **sarongs** of the Malays and the Javanese were seen in Hollywood movies starring Dorothy Lamour, they were widely albeit unsuccessfully imitated by Western designers of ladies' dresses."

But not by designers of men's clothing. No one thought for a moment that Western men would ever wear sarongs.

sashimi sah SHEE mee

From Japanese sashimi, *from* sashi *"pierce"* + mi *"flesh."*

In Japanese, and in English since the late nineteenth century, meaning "a dish of thinly sliced raw fish, artfully arranged and served with grated radish or ginger and soy sauce": "Half the fun of eating **sashimi** is watching the highly trained Japanese chef slice and garnish the raw fish."

For the name of a related dish, which includes rice as well as raw fish, see **sushi**.

sati su TEE

From Hindi and Urdu, from Sanskrit sati, *literally, "faithful wife."*

In English since the late nineteenth century, also given as **suttee** (su TEE), meaning 1. "a former Hindu practice in which a widow immolated herself on the funeral pyre of her husband": "To the Western mind, it is inconceivable that a woman would willingly perform **sati**, that is, allow herself to be burned to death alongside the corpse of her husband."

2. "A woman who thus immolates herself": "In the Western press it was widely reported that the widow, in accordance with custom, died a **sati**."

But how did this custom arise? In Hindu mythology, Sati, the wife of Rudra, a Vedic god, immolated herself after a quarrel between her father and her husband. Another account holds that Sati, the wife of the god Shiva, who was reborn as Parvati but was still the wife of Shiva, died by throwing herself into the sacred fire.

So maybe **sati** or **suttee** isn't as terminal as one might think—that is, for anyone married to a god.

sauna SAW nə

From Finnish, meaning "a steam bath."

In Finnish, and in English since the late nineteenth century, a noun meaning 1. "a bath that uses dry heat to induce sweating": "Back when men were men, bunches of leafy birch twigs were made available to whisk up the circulation and increase the effectiveness of the **sauna**."

2. "A bathhouse or room, usually of wood, equipped for such a bath": "Our **sauna** was a crude one-room shack built by an unskilled carpenter."

3. As a verb, "to take a sauna": "In our little Vermont community, populated by descendants of Finnish immigrants, any evening invitation in winter included an opportunity for men and women to **sauna**, then roll naked in the snow, sauna again, and then—after dressing, to be sure—to gulp down potent whiskey before eating an enormous supper."

What could be better?

sauté soh TAY

From French sauté, *past participle of* sauter, *meaning "to leap or cause to toss."*

In French, and in English since the beginning of the nineteenth century, an adjective meaning 1. "quickly and lightly fried or browned in a little fat": "Anyone owning a frying pan can perform minor miracles with veal or fish **sauté** plus the wine of one's choice."

2. As a verb, cook in this manner: "I would rather **sauté** a single slice of beef than order in a Chinese takeout of many courses rapidly congealing in their cardboard containers."

3. As a noun, "a dish of sautéed food": "The newly married young man smiled smugly as he said, 'It's just a little **sauté** I learned in my bachelor days' and proceeded to serve sliced shoe leather burned to a crisp."

Ugh!

savant sa VAHNT

From French savant, *meaning "learned," from* savoir, *"to know"; from Latin* sapere, *"to be wise."*

In French, and in English since the beginning of the eighteenth century, meaning "a person of profound or extensive learning; a learned scholar": "In my years on the university campus, I attended many lectures given by colleagues recognized as **savants**, whose erudition and insights never failed to impress me."

The masculine French adjective *savant* has its feminine form, *savante*, which is almost never heard in English.

See also **idiot savant**.

savate sə VAT

From French, literally, "an old shoe."

In French, and in English since the mid-nineteenth century, meaning "a type of boxing in which blows may be delivered with the feet as well as with the fists": "I enjoy watching a prizefight, but **savate** with its kicking repels me."

But why call the sport **savate**? Because the contestants wear *savates*, meaning "light shoes that resemble slippers."

savoir-faire SAV wahr FAIR

From French, literally, "to know how to do."

In French, and in English since the beginning of the nineteenth century, meaning "knowledge of how to behave in any situation"; "tact": "Bill did not learn much about European history in his year at Oxford, but he surely acquired more than enough **savoir-faire** to earn him a welcome anywhere."

Which may turn out to be worth more than profound academic learning.

sayonara sī ə NAHR ə

From Japanese sayonara, *for* sa *"that"* + yo *"appearance"* + nara *"if it be."*

In Japanese, and in English since the late nineteenth century, an interjection meaning "good-bye, farewell": "Even as she whispered **sayonara**, something inside me said I would never see her again."

The stuff grand opera thrives on.

schadenfreude SHAHD ən FROI də

From German Schadenfreude, *from* Schaden *"harm"* + Freude *"joy."*

In German, and in English since the mid-nineteenth century, meaning "malicious enjoyment of another's misfortune": "Frank, always assiduous in protecting his pension money by buying United States Treasury bonds, could not deny that he experienced **schadenfreude** when the stock market crashed, wiping out the paper fortunes of millions of people—but not his own modest nest egg."

Giving rise to the inevitable Itoldyouso.

schlag shlahg

From Austrian German Schlag, *short for* Schlagobers; *from* schlagen *"to beat"* + Obers *"cream"; meaning "whipped cream."*

In German, and in English since the mid-twentieth century, in Viennese cuisine meaning "whipped cream, used especially as a topping for cake, coffee, etc.": "When you visit Vienna, forget your diet and treat yourself whenever possible to a delicious torte with a generous dollop of **schlag**."

Yum!

schlemiel shlə MEEL

From Yiddish shlumiel, *from Hebrew Shelumiel, a proper name.*

In the Old Testament, Shelumiel was the head of the tribe of Simeon in Numbers, who assisted Moses with the census. In the Talmud he is said to have met with an unhappy end.

In Yiddish, and in English slang since the late nineteenth century, meaning "an awkward and unlucky person for whom things never turn out right"; "a born loser": "A wag has described a **schlemiel** as someone who falls on his ass and breaks his nose."

Awkward and unlucky.

schlep shlep

From Yiddish, shlepn, *from German* schleppen, *both meaning "to drag."*

In Yiddish, and in English slang since the early twentieth century, a verb meaning 1. "to carry, to lug": "The girls pooled their remaining cash and hired a porter instead of **schlepping** their heavy suitcases from the airline baggage room all the way out to the parking lot."

2. "Move slowly, awkwardly, or tediously": "By the end of the convention's second week, they were too tired to **schlep** from booth to booth."

3. As a noun, "something that is tedious, slow, or awkward"; "a drag": "The couple decided to move to Manhattan because it was too much of a **schlep** to commute from Staten Island to the city every day."

4. A closely related noun, **schlepper** (SHLEP ər), in English since the 1930s, meaning "a pauper, a beggar"; "a hanger-on"; also, "a jerk": "I knew at once she had brought home

yet another **schlepper**, someone who obviously would never amount to much."

She might have been better off befriending alley cats.

schlock **shlok**

From Yiddish shlak, *meaning "an apoplectic stroke"; "an evil"; "a nuisance"; perhaps from Yiddish* shlogn , *meaning "to strike."*

In Yiddish, and in English slang since the beginning of the twentieth century, also given as **schlocky** (SHLOK ee), an adjective meaning 1. "cheap, trashy": "He survived for years by writing **schlock** novels as fast as he could—under a pen name, of course."

2. As a noun, "something of cheap or inferior quality"; "junk": "All the shops in the new mall that sell upscale, quality merchandise are thriving, but those that sell **schlock** are sure to be gone before the year is out."

schmaltz **shmahltss**

From Yiddish shmalts, *perhaps from German* Schmaltz, *both meaning "fat, drippings."*

In Yiddish, and in informal English since the 1930s, also given as **schmalz** (shmahltss), meaning 1. "fat or grease, especially that of a chicken": "As an omnivorous child, I made many an after-school snack of a slice of corn bread spread thickly with **schmaltz** and topped with a slice or two of Bermuda onion."

Followed by a nap.

2. "Exaggerated sentimentality, as of music or soap operas": "All through the two hours of radio soaps, Helen and Maud never stopped ironing shirts while tears ran unimpeded down their faces—the **schmaltz** was doing its job."

When English latches onto a first-class, expressive noun, it usually wastes no time before putting the noun through its paces. Thus, **schmaltz** led to the adjective **schmaltzy** (SHMAHLT see), with its inevitable comparative and superlative forms **schmaltzier** and **schmaltziest**.

3. While it may be a stretch to think of fat or drippings as "schmaltzier" or "schmaltziest," there is no problem in characterizing soap operas in this way: "Afternoon audiences appear to prefer the **schmaltziest** story lines imaginable, as long as there is nothing subtle about the sex scenes."

Always appealing to lonely senior citizens.

schmear shmeer

From Yiddish shmirn, *from German* schmieren, *both meaning "to smear, to grease."*

In Yiddish, and in English slang since the mid-twentieth century, also given as **shmear**, a noun meaning 1. "a dab, as of cream cheese, on a bagel or the like": "At about nine every weekday morning, attractive young editors crowd into the luncheonette on our corner and, without saying a word, put down exact change for a **schmear** and a container of coffee to go—the entire transaction taking about fifteen seconds."

2. Usually given as **the whole schmear**, meaning "everything possible"; "every aspect of the situation": "Do you think they are going to go for **the whole schmear** or just for the trimmed-down version?"

3. "A bribe"; "bribery"; "flattery": "If the young actor goes to the meeting without me, they'll turn on the **schmear**, and he'll sign anything they wave in front of him."

So where we have a wonderfully versatile noun, we're bound to have a verb.

4. "Spread, smear": "When you see a big buffet laden with hors d'oeuvres—and no chairs or dining table—there'll be no dinner, so be sure to **schmear** everything you want on bread or crackers and lay it on thick."

It'll keep you until morning.

schmooze **shmooz**

From a Yiddish verb schmuesn, *meaning "chat, gossip"; from a Yiddish noun* schmues, *from a Hebrew noun* shəmu'os *meaning "rumors, gossip."*

In Yiddish, and in English slang since the end of the nineteenth century, also given as **schmoose** and **schmoos**. 1. A verb meaning "chat idly"; "gossip, sometimes with a hidden motive": "The agent spent the entire evening at the producer's side, **schmoozing** so engagingly that the poor man had no idea he was being rolled."

2. As a noun, "chatter"; "conversation, especially of a satisfying nature": "There is nothing like a long **schmooze** with an old friend to help me forget my problems."

3. As a noun, **schmoozer** (SHMOOZ ər), meaning "a practitioner of the art of schmoozing": "My best friend, a **schmoozer** par excellence, drops in on weekends to regale me with the latest neighborhood news."

And have a couple of beers.

schmuck **shmuk**

From the vulgar Yiddish word shmok, *literally, "a penis."*

In Yiddish, and in vulgar English since the late nineteenth century, also given as **shmuck**, meaning "a contemptible, obnoxious, or objectionable person"; "a fool": "Try as I will, I cannot understand how a **schmuck** like Jules is taken seriously."

schnapps shnahpss

From German Schnaps, *meaning "a shot of whiskey, gin, spirits, etc."; from Dutch* snaps, *meaning "a gulp or mouthful," from* snappen, *meaning "to seize, to snatch."*

In German, and in English since the beginning of the nineteenth century, also given as **schnaps**, meaning 1. "any strong spirit, in Europe especially a drink of Hollands gin, slivovitz, aquavit, or kirsch": "My father was fond of saying water is for washing, milk is for babies, and **schnapps** is for drinking."

2. "A drink of schnapps": "Let's have a **schnapps** before we go out to face the world."

Nothing like the strong stuff to buck up one's spirits.

schnook shnuuk

From Yiddish shnuk, *meaning "snout" or, more likely, from German* Schnucke, *meaning "a sheep."*

In American slang since the mid-twentieth century, meaning "a simpleton"; "a sucker": "When I realized Ed was taking me for a **schnook**, I began to bet recklessly until I knew I had him bamboozled and proceeded to clean him out."

Which thought lends credence to the hypothesis that **schnook** derives from the German for "sheep." After all, sheep and schnooks are regularly shorn, but unlike sheep, schnooks also are frequently taken to the cleaners.

schnorrer SHNOR ər

From Yiddish shnorer, *meaning "beggar, sponger"; from German* Schnurrer, *meaning "scrounger, tramp"; from* schnurren, *meaning "to go begging."*

In English since the end of the nineteenth century, a slang noun, also given as **shnorrer**, meaning "beggar, moocher, especially a person who habitually borrows or lives at the expense of others with no intention of repaying": "Help that **schnorrer** once, and he'll never stop putting the arm on you."

séance SAY ahnss

From French séance, *literally, "a sitting"; from Latin* sedere, *meaning "to sit."*

In French, and in English since the end of the eighteenth century, meaning especially 1. "a meeting in which a spiritualist tries to communicate with the spirits of the dead": "Most of the persons attending the **séance** appeared to believe the charlatan was actually talking with Olga's dead aunt."

2. "A session or sitting, as of an organization": "The first **séance** of the year was abruptly terminated after lunch, when the presiding officer and other members suddenly took ill."

Something wrong with the food, wouldn't you suppose?

seersucker SEER SUK ər

From Hindi sirsakar, *from Persian* shir o shakar, *literally, "milk and sugar."*

In English since the early eighteenth century, meaning 1. "a striped cotton or linen cloth woven with a puckered surface:" "On Wall Street years ago, the end of summer was signaled by the abrupt appearance of subdued dress, displacing straw hats and **seersucker** suits."

2. "A garment made of seersucker": "Sam and his fiancée showed up at the garden party in matching blue and white **seersuckers**."

The last time they were to agree on anything.

seraglio si RAL yoh

From Italian serraglio, *meaning "harem"; from Turkish* saray, *meaning "palace"; from Persian* saray, *with the same meaning.*

In English since the late sixteenth century, plural **seraglios**, meaning 1. "the part of a Muslim house or palace in which wives and concubines are secluded"; "a harem": "Much to my dismay, the four wives and two concubines of the host were all exceedingly fat, well past middle age, and nondescript—nothing like what I expected to find in a **seraglio**."

2. In the past, "a Turkish palace, especially that of the sultan": "The word **seraglio** summons up dreams of palatial structures, infinite wealth, hundreds of servants, and beautiful dancing girls—all serving the needs of one powerful ruler."

Incidentally, **seraglio** made its way into French as *sérail*, into Spanish as *serallo*, and into German as *Serail*.

It should be pointed out that the Italian *serraglio* also is taken to mean "a cage for wild animals"; "a menagerie as well as a seraglio." But why not? Lurking in the shadows behind *serraglio* is the Italian verb *serrare*, meaning "lock up."

shampoo sham POO

From Hindi campna, *meaning "to press."*

In English since the mid-eighteenth century, a verb meaning 1. "to wash the head or hair, especially with a preparation that does not leave a soap film": "Alice had her hairdresser **shampoo** her hair once a week."

2. "Clean (rugs, upholstery, or the like) with a special preparation": "The company bought a machine for **shampooing** its carpeting twice a month."

3. As a noun, "the act of shampooing": "I decided to ask for a **shampoo** and set, in addition to a haircut."

4. "A preparation used for shampooing": "We were well advised to buy three bottles of our favorite **shampoo** for our biking trip through Yugoslavia."

Shampoo may have been in short supply there.

sherbet SHUR bit

From Turkish serbet, *from Persian* serbet, *from Arabic* sarba, *meaning "a drink"; from Arabic* sariba, *a verb meaning "to drink."*

In English since the end of the sixteenth century, meaning "a frozen, fruit-flavored water ice, with milk, egg white, or gelatin added": "Many flavors of **sherbet** and ice cream are available on restaurant dessert menus, yet I am never tempted to order anything but chocolate ice cream."

Of course, when dining at a tony restaurant, you might want to order sorbet, but when it arrives, don't act surprised when it turns out to be sherbet.

And if you order sherbet in Britain, expect to be served a drink made of fruit juice diluted with water and ice. Or if you order sherbet in Australia, expect to see a glass of beer or some other alcoholic drink put down in front of you.

shibboleth SHIB ə lith

From Hebrew shibboleth, *meaning both "ear of corn" and "freshet." And "freshet" is to be understood as meaning "a sudden rise in the level of a stream."*

Put aside for a moment your wonder about what the two meanings of the Hebrew word *shibboleth* have to do with the meanings of the English "shibboleth."

Shibboleth, in English since the late fourteenth century, means

1. "a catchword or slogan of a party, sect, etc.": "Once the terms 'pro-life' and 'pro-choice' were firmly established as **shibboleths**, they ensured that we would never have a completely rational debate on the legality of abortion."
2. "A peculiarity of pronunciation or behavior that distinguishes a particular group of persons": "Their distinctive pronunciation of 'Harvard Yard' was the **shibboleth** that marked them forever as native Bostonians, never to change."

In Judges, in the Old Testament, the story is told of the Gileadites' use of *shibboleth* as a test word to screen fleeing Ephraimites, who could not pronounce the sound *sh*.

So whether the Hebrew word *shibboleth* means "ear of corn" or "freshet," we will long have "shibboleth" as an English word with its distinctive meanings, as is known full well by all students urgently building their vocabularies before sitting for college entrance examinations.

shish kebab SHISH kə BOB

From Turkish sis kebab, *from* sis *"skewer"* + kebap *"roast meat."*

In Turkish, and in English since the early twentieth century, meaning "a dish consisting of cubes of marinated meat and vegetables grilled and served on skewers": "I particularly like the cherry tomatoes and sliced green peppers that contrast so well with the flavor of the meat in **shish kebab**."

See also **kabob**.

sine die SĪ nee DĪ ee

From Latin sine die, *from* sine *"without"* + die *"day."*

In English since the early seventeenth century, meaning "without fixing a day for future action or meeting": "The national chairman adjourned the party convention **sine die**, and the thousands of delegates moved rapidly toward the exits, happy in the knowledge that they had nominated a winning ticket."

Maybe.

sine qua non SĪ nee kwah NOHN

From Latin (causa) sine qua non, *literally, "(cause) without which not," from* sine *"without"* + qua *"which"* + non *"not."*

In English since the late sixteenth century, meaning "an indispensable condition or qualification"; "something essential": "Competency in advanced computer programming is a **sine qua non** today for most high-paying jobs, except in the traditional professions of medicine and law."

And it could prove valuable even there.

sirocco sə ROK oh

From French sirocco *and* siroco, *from Italian* sirocco *and* scirocco, *all meaning "a sultry southeast wind"; ultimately from Arabic* sharuk, *meaning "east wind." Portuguese has* xarouco, *and Spanish has* siroco, *both meaning "sirocco."*

In English since the early seventeenth century, also given as **scirocco** (shə ROK oh), meaning 1. "a hot, dust-laden wind blowing from northern Africa and affecting parts of southern Europe": "I always made sure to leave sunny southern France as soon as the horrid **sirocco** began to blow each year."

2. "A warm, sultry south or southeast wind accompanied by rain, occurring in the same regions": "He was experiencing the depression associated with the onset of the **sirocco** and familiar to all of us living on the Mediterranean."

3. "Any hot, oppressive wind": "It is not uncommon for us to have to put up with a **sirocco** every time El Niño kicks up its heels."

slalom SLAH ləm

From Norwegian slalam, *from* sla *"sloping"* + lam *"track."*

In Norwegian, and in English since the early twentieth century, as a noun meaning 1. "a downhill ski race over a winding and zigzag course marked by gates, gates being a pair of poles separated from one another by a small open space": "Our skiers did exceptionally well last year in the giant **slalom**."

2. "Any winding or zigzag course for automobile drivers, canoeists, or water-skiers": "Spectators flocked to the shores of the lake to enjoy the water-skiing exhibition, particularly the drenching **slalom**."
3. As an adjective, "of a zigzag course with obstacles": "Older children in the school devised a **slalom** course for roller skaters."
4. As a verb, "ski in or as if in a slalom": "Mary enjoyed **slaloming** downhill, following a self-contrived course of demanding twists and turns that existed only in her imagination."

Incidentally, French has also adopted the noun *slalom*, and German has its own *Slalom*.

slivovitz SLIV ə vitss

From German Sliwowitz, *from Bulgarian* slivovitza, *from Serbo-Croatian* sljivovica, *from* sljiva, *meaning "plum."*

In English since the end of the nineteenth century, also given as **slivovic** and **slivowitz**, meaning "a plum brandy, usually colorless and slightly bitter": "Several central and eastern European countries claim to have invented **slivovitz**, proving they all know a good drink when they meet one."

If only they had chosen an easily pronounceable name for it.

slogan SLOH gən

From Scots Gaelic sluagh-ghairm, *from* sluagh *"army"* + gairm *"cry," literally, "a war cry."*

In English since the beginning of the sixteenth century, meaning 1. "a distinctive cry, phrase, or motto of any party, group, or person"; "a catchword or catch phrase": "Some advertising agencies specialize in devising logos and **slogans** for manufacturers of consumer goods."

2. "A war cry or battle cry, as formerly used among the Scottish clans": "'Geronimo,' introduced by U.S. paratroopers in World War II, is the latest addition to the long list of **slogans** used by armies in centuries past."

slurp slurp

From Dutch slurpen, *from German* schlürfen, *both meaning "to swig"; "to eat greedily or noisily."*

In English since the mid-seventeenth century, a verb meaning 1. "to eat or drink noisily": "Everyone at the table but Elsa suddenly became aware that she was **slurping** her soup."

2. As a noun, meaning "the sound made in slurping": "The boy finished his after-dinner chocolate milk with three satisfyingly resonant **slurps** and one profound belch."

To the mortification of his grandmother.

smorgasbord SMOR gəss BORD

From Swedish smörgsbord, *from* smörgs *"sandwich"* + bord *"table."*

In Swedish, and in English since the end of the nineteenth century, also given as **smörgasbord**, meaning 1. "a buffet course or meal of various hot and cold hors d'oeuvres, salads, meats, etc.": "It takes a strong appetite and plenty of akvavit for an American to do justice to an authentic Swedish **smorgasbord** and then be able to eat again at any time during the next day."

2. "An extensive array or variety": "Rebecca's **smorgasbord** of earrings, nose rings, and other bangles set tongues wagging all through the room."

No telling what young people will do next.

soigné swahn YAY

From French soigné, *from the past participle of* soigner, *meaning "take care of."*

In French, and in English since the early nineteenth century, feminine form **soignée**, meaning 1. "well-groomed": "I felt completely out of place among all the **soignée** women at the charity fashion show."

2. "Meticulously or elegantly done": "How surprised we were to discover that a modestly priced restaurant—actually a neighborhood diner—could serve food genuinely **soigné**.

Wait till word gets out.

soiree swah RAY

From French soirée, *from* soir, *meaning "evening"; from Latin* serus, *meaning "late" or "too late."*

In French, and in English since the early nineteenth century, also given as **soirée**, meaning "an evening party or social gathering, especially one held in a private house": "Our **soirees** originally were looked on as musical evenings at home, but later became a kind of discussion group dealing with current political issues."

And most of the pleasure was lost.

solecism SOL ə SIZ əm

From French solécisme, *from Latin* solecismus, *from Greek* soloikismos; *from* soloikos, *meaning "speaking incorrectly."*

But there is more to the story. Sóloi was the name of a Greek city in Cilicia, an ancient country in southeast Asia Minor, where a corrupt form of Athenian Greek was spoken. Thus, when ancient Greeks disparaged the Greek spoken in Sóloi as *soloikismos*, they were laying the groundwork for a word that would eventually become "solecism."

In French, and in English since the late sixteenth century, meaning 1. "an ungrammatical usage": "A locution such as 'the media was'—instead of 'were'—is so common that some lexicographers no longer characterize it as a **solecism**."

2. "Any blunder or impropriety in manners": "Today we ban smoking in schools and offices as an offense against health, but not too long ago, smoking in the street was considered an unpardonable **solecism**."

3. "Any error or inconsistency": "Many people consider the criminalization of marijuana a **solecism** that will inevitably be abandoned."

Worth all the trouble we've gone to? I hope so.

sommelier SUM əl YAY

From French sommelier, *meaning "wine waiter"; from earlier French* sommerier, *from* sommier, *meaning "a person appointed to arrange for transportation"; from* somme, *meaning "a burden"; from Late Latin* sagma, *meaning "horse load"; from Greek* ságma, *meaning "pack saddle."*

A long journey from "pack saddle" to "wine waiter."

In French, and in English since the early twentieth century, in a restaurant or club meaning "a person in charge of wines": "A first-class **sommelier** will help a customer choose his wines, bring to the table the wines selected, and uncork and pour them."

And usually with the best of intentions, see that the advantages of high-priced wines are not overlooked.

soubrette soo BRET

From French soubrette, *from Provençal* soubreto, *feminine form of* soubret, *meaning "coy"; from Latin* superare *meaning "to be above."*

In French, and in English since the mid-eighteenth century, meaning 1. "a lady's maid as a character in a play or opera, especially one who is pert or coquettish": "She soon tired of playing **soubrettes** in summer-stock productions of shallow comedies."

2. "An actress playing a soubrette": "I found the **soubrette** just a few inches too thick in the waist to be credible."

3. "Any pert or lively young woman": "The partners in Rosalie's firm look upon her as an unsophisticated **soubrette** who cannot be taken seriously even though they select her to write challenging briefs."

You can't please everybody.

soufflé soo FLAY

From French soufflé, *past participle of* souffler, *meaning "to blow, to puff"; from Latin* sufflare, *meaning "to breath on, to blow on," from* sub *"under"* + flare *"to blow."*

In French, and in English since the beginning of the nineteenth century, as a noun meaning 1. "a light baked dish made by beating egg yolks and other ingredients with egg whites": "As long as the chef is given sufficient notice, he will be happy to prepare as many of his signature chocolate **soufflés** as you wish."

2. As a verb, "to make light, to make puffed up, as by beating and cooking": "When many boiled potatoes go uneaten, I usually **soufflé** them for the next day's lunch."

3. As an adjective, also given as **souffléed**, meaning "made light and frothy": "She was especially skilled at preparing my favorite cheese omelet **soufflé**."

soupçon soop SAW*N*

From French soupçon, *from Middle French* sospeçon, *from Latin* suspicio, *all meaning "a suspicion."*

In French, and in English since the mid-eighteenth century, said of a flavoring or quality meaning "a trace, a very small amount": "In preparing lamb dishes, the chef is careful not to use more than a **soupçon** of garlic." "Even after the suspect claimed he was the serial killer responsible for the deaths of so many young women, a **soupçon** of anxiety was prevalent that would not be fully dispelled for a long time."

spritzer SPRIT sər

From German Spritzer, *meaning "a splash"; from German* spritzen, *meaning "to spray, to squirt."*

In English since the mid-twentieth century, meaning "a tall drink of chilled white wine and soda": "My wife, eschewing martinis and Bloody Marys, usually has a glass of white wine or a **spritzer** before dinner."

A wise woman.

sputnik SPUUT nik

From Russian spútnik, *literally, "a traveling companion"; from* s- *"with, together"* + put *"way" or "journey"* + -nik *a noun suffix.*

In Russian, and in English since 1957, sometimes given as **Sputnik**, meaning "a Soviet unmanned artificial earth-orbiting satellite": "When the first **sputnik** was launched, the U.S. space program went into overdrive in an effort to catch up with the U.S.S.R."

And succeeded.

stampede stam PEED

From American Spanish estampida, *meaning "crash, uproar"; from Spanish* estampar *"to stamp"* + -ida *a noun suffix.*

In English since the beginning of the nineteenth century, meaning as a noun: 1. "sudden fright and scattering of a herd of animals, especially of horses or cattle": "Any sudden, unexpected movement or loud noise was enough to cause a **stampede** that could have threatened the lives of the cowboys who were leading their livestock to market."

2. "Any uncontrolled general flight or rush": "The **stampede** that erupted in the crowded nightclub ended in disaster when people found that all exits had been locked shut."

3. As a verb, "to scatter or flee in a stampede": "Many people were trampled to death by members of the audience who **stampeded** out of the burning building." "A few of the wild horses **stampeded** the rest, and it took days to round up all the frightened creatures."

4. As a verb, "to act hurriedly or unreasoningly": "As soon as the Ohio delegates switched their votes, state after state **stampeded**, and our candidate swept to victory."

But that was just for the nomination—the election, the hard part, remained to be won.

status quo STAY təss KWOH

From Latin, literally, "the state in which," meaning "the existing state of affairs."

In English since the early nineteenth century, with the same meaning as in Latin: "Conservatives in Congress seem satisfied with the **status quo**, so there is no expectation of making progress on campaign finance reform."

A related phrase from Latin is **status quo ante** (STAY təss kwoh AHN tay), literally, "the state in which before," meaning the previously existing state of affairs.

In English since the late nineteenth century, with the same meaning as in Latin: "When the war ended, every attempt was made to revive the economy of the defeated nation, all the while knowing it would take decades to achieve **status quo ante**."

Alerting all of us to the dangers implicit in fomenting warfare.

stele STEE lee

From Greek stéle, *meaning "a standing block."*

In English since the late eighteenth century, also given as **stela** (STEE lə), plural **stelae** (STEE lī) and **steles** (STEE leez), meaning in archaeology "an upright slab or pillar, used especially as a gravestone and bearing inscriptions and designs": "During most of their vacations they travel to Central America to make rubbings of designs on Incan **stelae**."

stevedore STEE vi DOR

From Spanish estibador, *meaning "stevedore"; from* estibar, *meaning "to stow a cargo"; from Latin* stipare, *meaning "to pack together."*

In English since the late eighteenth century, as a noun meaning 1. "a person employed in loading and unloading cargo ships": "The availability of materials-handling equipment at dockside reduces the requirement that **stevedores** be exceptionally strong, thus making possible an increased number of women employed on the waterfront."

2. As a verb, "load or unload a cargo"; "load or unload a ship": "He **stevedored** in New Orleans until he began to play an important role in organizing the longshoremen's union and soon became president of the union."

stiletto sti LET oh

From Italian stiletto, *diminutive of* stilo, *meaning "dagger"; from Latin* stilus, *meaning "stylus."*

In Italian, and in English since the end of the sixteenth century, plural **stilettos** and **stilettoes**, meaning 1. "a short, thick-bladed dagger": "Sure enough, when the police frisked their prisoner, they found he had a **stiletto** encased in a leather sheath tied to his ankle."

2. "A pointed instrument for making eyelet holes in needlework": "Either a sturdy needle or a **stiletto** is used for making the holes that are required."

By the 1950s, some women took to wearing shoes with **stiletto heels**, a replacement for what earlier had been called "spike heels." The wearer's own heels stood several inches above the floor, and the shoe heels at bottom could just about cover a Lincoln penny: "No ordinary male observer can fathom how a woman thus shod can walk, much less dance or run, without breaking an ankle or two."

Do you suppose an HMO will pay for fixing ankles broken in this way?

strabismus strə BIZ məss

From New Latin strabismus; *from Greek* strabismós; *from* strabós, *meaning "squinting."*

In English since the end of the seventeenth century, in ophthalmology meaning "crossed eyes"; "an inability to direct the gaze of both eyes to the same object simultaneously"; also, "squinting": "**Strabismus** is a disorder that can be corrected today by a relatively simple operation in which the surgeon shortens an eye muscle in the crossed eye."

strudel STROOD əl

From German Strudel, *literally, "whirlpool, eddy."*

In German, and in English since the late nineteenth century, meaning "a baked dessert made of rolled-up layers of flaky pastry with a filling, usually fruit": "No one who has ever spent even a few days in Vienna forgets the miracle of **strudel**, particularly the *Apfelstrudel*." Apple strudel, that is. Nor forgets the inches that indulgence adds to the waist.

suave **swahv**

From French suave, *from Latin* suavis, *meaning "sweet, agreeable."*

In French, and in English since the beginning of the fifteenth century, said of persons or their speech or manner, meaning "polite or superficially polite, smoothly agreeable"; "bland, soothing, mollifying": "The young man's **suave** manner captivated young women and scared their fathers half to death." All of whom could tell a sweet-talker from a mile away.

sub rosa **sub ROH zə**

From Latin, literally, "under the rose"; meaning "secretly, in secret"; "in strict confidence."

In English since the mid-seventeenth century, with the same meaning: "The operation was carried off **sub rosa** from start to finish, which accounts for its complete success as a military action, and for its failure as a political action when word of it leaked out long after the operation was finished."

A word must be said about the literal meaning of **sub rosa**, "under the rose." In mythology Cupid is said to have given a rose to Harpocrates, the god of silence, as a bribe not to spill the beans about the love affairs of Venus. Much later, in historical time, the rose was sculpted in the ceilings of banquet rooms to remind guests that what was said at the table was not to be repeated outside the room.

Maybe a sculptor should have been hired to adorn the ceiling of the Oval Office.

succubus SUK yə bəss

From Medieval Latin succubus, *a masculine form with feminine meaning of Late Latin* succuba, *meaning "a prostitute"; from Latin* succubare, *from* sub- *"under"* + cubare *"to lie (in bed)."*

In English since the mid-fourteenth century, plural **succubi** (SUK yə BĪ), meaning 1. "a demon in female form said to have sexual intercourse with sleeping men": "Some male psychiatrists consider that accounts of **succubi** at work may well be nothing more than examples of wish fulfillment."

2. "Any demon or evil spirit": "When an attractive widow bought a house nearby, the women of the neighborhood shunned her as a **succubus** who would destroy their marriages."

3. "A loose woman or prostitute": "For many years he had sustained a relationship with a **succubus** that did not come to light until the day when she appeared at his hospital bedside just before he died."

But **succuba**, from Late Latin, is a feminine form of succubus that is sometimes seen in English. Its definition? "A succubus, a prostitute." So little is gained from having the word "succuba."

A word must be said here about the related word **incubus** (IN kyə bəss), from Latin *incuba*, meaning "nightmare"; from *incubare*, meaning "to lie on."

In English since the thirteenth century, plural **incubi** (IN kyə bī) and **incubuses**, meaning "a succubus" but also meaning "a nightmare as well as someone or something that weighs heavily on the mind": "Racial prejudice, incurable and vile, to this day is an **incubus** that will not be dispelled."

sui generis SOO Ī JEN ər iss

From Latin, literally, "of its own kind."

In English since the late eighteenth century, an adjective phrase meaning "unlike anything else, unique": "After long deliberation, the chief justice announced that the court would hear the complaint, deeming it worthy of judicial consideration on the grounds that it was **sui generis**." "The department tolerated the erratic behavior of its chairman, because of his reputation for **sui generis** contributions to scholarship."

sukiyaki SUU **kee YAH kee**

From Japanese sukiyaki, *from* suki *"slice"* + yaki *"broil."*

In Japanese, and in English since the early twentieth century, meaning "a Japanese dish of thin slices of beef fried with vegetables and bean curd, especially in sugar, broth, and soy sauce": "In Japanese restaurants in the United States, pork and chicken may be offered in **sukiyaki** in place of beef."

Perhaps because pork and chicken usually are cheaper than beef.

sushi SOO **shee**

From Japanese, literally, "it is sour."

In Japanese, and in English since the end of the nineteenth century, meaning "cold boiled rice flavored with rice vinegar, usually rolled in seaweed and served with raw fish": "In a restaurant my wife favors, **sushi** is formed into long seaweed-wrapped rolls before being sliced into bite-size pieces."

If you don't want rice with your raw fish or seaweed, see **sashimi**.

suttee. See sati.

swami SWAH **mee**

From Hindi swami, *meaning "master"; from Sanskrit* svami, *from* svamin, *meaning "master, prince."*

In Hindi, and in English since the mid-eighteenth century, plural **swamies**, meaning 1. "a male Hindu religious teacher"; also used as an honorific: "Acting out of respect, the teacher's students always addressed him as **Swami**."

2. "A person of great learning and judgment"; "a pundit": "While today we may refer to political commentators as pundits, in years gone by they were often called **swamies**."

And usually were as far off the mark as the current crop of commentators, but not as highly paid.

T

table d'hôte TAH bəl DOHT

From French, literally, "the host's table."

In French, and in English since the early seventeenth century, plural **tables d'hôte** (TAH bəlz DOHT), meaning "a meal of designated dishes served at a fixed time and price in a hotel or restaurant": "At our hotel, the clerk gave us a list of nearby restaurants, including two that advertised **tables d'hôte.**"

In the Middle Ages, before the restaurant era, the **table d'hôte** was "a common table"—the host's table—for guests of an inn and for others who might wish to be accommodated.

You can be sure servings of meat and drink were generous.

taboo tə BOO

From Tongan tapu *or Fijian* tabu, *both meaning "forbidden, prohibited."*

In English since the late eighteenth century, also given as **tabu**, a noun meaning 1. "a prohibition or restriction imposed by social custom": "**Taboo** remains an effective force today in regulating marriages in certain societies."

2. Among Polynesians, "an act or system of setting apart a person or thing as cursed or sacred": "The islanders still observe **taboo** despite the intrusion of Western influences on their lives."

3. As an adjective, "prohibited or consecrated"; "avoided or prohibited by social custom": "The names of certain gods were **taboo** words until recently."

4. As a verb, "prohibit or forbid by authority or social influence"; "put under a taboo": "From that point on, tribal law **tabooed** marriage between first cousins."

But why did some clever person see fit to call his perfume Tabu? And why has Tabu been so popular?

Perhaps because of the excitement implicit in something forbidden?

tabula rasa TAB yə lə RAH ssə

From Latin, literally, "scraped tablet," meaning "a clean slate."

In English since the early sixteenth century, plural **tabulae rasae** (TAB yə LEE RAH see), meaning 1. "a mind, especially at birth, viewed as having no innate ideas": "Parents of a newborn child—surely a **tabula rasa**—face an extraordinary challenge, knowing that everything they do or say or feel may shape the entire life of their child."

2. "Anything existing undisturbed in its original, pure state, or restored to this state": "With the site cleared of all debris, the architects had a **tabula rasa** on which to bring to life their dreams of dignified housing for the disabled."

It doesn't hurt to restore an institution to its original state, if the original was worthy.

talisman TAL iss mən

From French talisman *or Spanish* talismán, *both meaning "amulet"; perhaps from Arabic* tilasm *or from Greek* télesma, *meaning "payment"; from* telein *meaning "to complete."*

In English since the early seventeenth century, meaning 1. "an object worn as an amulet or charm, supposed to avert evil or bring good luck to the wearer": "He never went anywhere without his **talisman**, a gold ring his father had given him to ward off sinister influences."

2. "Any ring, stone, or other object thought to act as a charm": "He thought of his dog-eared copy of Psalms as a **talisman**, to be read in occasionally, but to be near him always."

In case he wants to lie down in green pastures and read a few verses.

tamale tə MAH lee

From Mexican Spanish tamales, *singular* tamal; *from Nahuatl* tamalli, *Nahuatl being a language spoken in central Mexico.*

In Mexican Spanish, and in English since the late sixteenth century, plural **tamales**, meaning "a Mexican food of seasoned meat and cornmeal dough, wrapped in corn husks and baked": "I miss the characteristic smells of the Mexican capital, especially the rich aroma of cooking corn and burning coals tended by women selling **tamales** to passersby."

Note that tamale appeared in English first as "tamal," before becoming **tamale**, both spellings construed as singular forms of the Mexican Spanish *tamales*.

tchotchke CHAHCH kə

From Yiddish tshatshke, *from Polish* czaczko; *from Russian* tsatska, *meaning "trinket, diamond."*

In Yiddish, and in informal American English since the mid-twentieth century, also given as **tsatske** (TSAHTSS kə) and **chotchke**, meaning 1. "trinket, ornament, souvenir": "No matter how firm Sylvia's resolve not to spoil her grandchildren, she returned from every business trip and vacation with a bagful of **tchotchkes** for them."

2. Also given as **tchotchkeleh** (CHAHCH kə lə) or **tsatskeleh** (TSAHTSS kə lə), "a pet name for a pretty girl or woman": "Soon there was no doubt in his mind—his employer's daughter was much more than a mere **tchotchkeleh** and would have to be dealt with seriously."

Which might include asking her to marry him.

terra cotta TER ə KOT ə

From Italian terra cotta, *literally, "baked earth"; from Latin* terra cocta; *from* terra *"earth"* + cocta *"baked or cooked," with* cocta *being the past participle of* coquere, *meaning "to bake" or "cook."*

In English since early in the eighteenth century, meaning 1. "a hard, fired clay, usually brownish-red in color when unglazed, used in modeling and for tiles and bricks": "The Romans have left us numerous examples of their work in bronze and **terra cotta**."

2. "Something made of terra cotta": "She took a liking to **terra cottas** and before long had acquired a sizable number of distinguished pieces by well-known sculptors."

3. "The color of terra cotta": "The carpeting you have selected is so close to **terra cotta** that your mahogany furniture will merge well with it."

4. As an adjective, "made of terra cotta, of the color of terra cotta, etc.": "This year's garden catalogs show new bulbs of interesting colors, including a **terra cotta** tulip that I particularly like."

Incidentally, the French call **terra cotta** *terre cuite*, literally, "cooked earth," also translated as "baked clay." *Cuite* is the past participle of *cuire*, meaning "to cook."

But read on.

terra incognita TER ə in KOG ni tə

From Latin, literally, "an unknown land."

In English since the early seventeenth century, meaning 1. "an unknown or unexplored region": "Imagine the bravery of early explorers of the New World willing to navigate on the basis of charts showing they faced **terra incognita**."

2. "An unexplored subject or area of study": "The philosopher's musings went deeply into **terra incognita**, leaving most listeners mystified and the rest bored."

You can't please everybody.

terrazzo tə RAZ oh

From Italian, meaning "a terrace"; "a balcony."

In English since the late nineteenth century, meaning "a flooring material of marble chips and cement polished after being laid down": "While my wife studied the old paintings high on the walls of the cathedral, I examined the **terrazzo** I walked on, marveling at the craftsmanship of masons whose efforts had withstood centuries of footsteps."

And the polishing of those floors by millions of pairs of shoes.

testis TESS tiss

From Latin, literally, "a witness," meaning "testicle."

In English since the late seventeenth century, plural **testes** (TESS teez), with the same meaning: "His physician gave him the unhappy news that his cancer was untreatable except by removal of one of his **testes**."

But how does a word with the literal meaning of "witness" come to mean "testicle"? No one is certain, but the educated guess is that the testis was witness—evidence, that is—of virility, and manliness was much esteemed.

tête-à-tête TAYT ə TAYT

From French, literally, "head to head."

In French, and in English since the late seventeenth century, plural **tête-à-têtes** (TAYT ə TAYTSS), a noun meaning 1. "a private conversation or interview, usually between two people": "No one at the party was unaware that Hilda and her sister had been deep in a **tête-à-tête** for more than an hour."

2. As an adjective, "private, confidential"; "involving two people": "Their regular Wednesday **tête-à-tête** luncheons at the sidewalk café inevitably became the subject of much gossip."

3. As an adverb, "face to face"; "together in private": "They resolved never to be seen again sitting **tête-à-tête**, lest the nature of their relationship be misunderstood."

thesaurus thi SOR əss

From Latin thesaurus, *from Greek* thesaurós, *meaning "treasure, treasury, storehouse."*

In English since the early eighteenth century, plural **thesauruses** and **thesauri** (thi SOR ī), meaning 1. "a dictionary of synonyms and antonyms": "As the writer grew older, he found he was turning increasingly to his **thesaurus** for help in recalling precise words he needed."

2. "Any comprehensive reference book": "One of the books he kept near at hand on his desk was a marvelous **thesaurus** of boxing terms."

3. "Any computerized thesaurus, especially one for use in indexing and information retrieval": "After a few years'

experience, professional indexers find they rarely have to resort to their **thesauruses**, even when compiling complex indexes."

thug **thug**

From Hindu thag, *literally, "a rogue"; "a swindler."*

In English since early in the nineteenth century, meaning 1. "a vicious or brutal ruffian, robber, or murderer": "After **thugs** beat a storekeeper cruelly, they had no trouble extorting protection money from every business in the area."

2. In history, and usually given as **Thug**, "a member of a religious organization of robbers and assassins in India": "We are told that the **Thugs** were vigorously prosecuted by British rulers from 1831 on—with mass arrests and executions common—so that the Thugs virtually ceased functioning in the decades that followed."

An instance in which the promise of quick and cruel punishment had a beneficial effect.

tinnitus **ti NĪ təss**

From Latin tinnitus, *meaning "a tinkling, a jingling"; from* tinnire *meaning "to ring, to tinkle."*

In English since the late seventeenth century, in medicine meaning "a sensation of buzzing or ringing in the ears": "The principal symptoms the patient complained of were vertigo, persistent headache, and **tinnitus**."

tokus TUU *khə*ss

From Yiddish tokhes, *meaning "buttocks"; from Hebrew* tahath, *meaning "under."*

In Yiddish, and in English slang since the beginning of the twentieth century, also given as **tochis** and **tuchis**; and by children and their well-intentioned but misguided parents as

tush, **tushie**, and **tushy**; all meaning "the buttocks"; "the anus": "The boss told me to get off my **tokus** and do some work." "The pain deep in his **tokus** was no ordinary ache."

The children's versions of tokus given here—"tush," "tushie," and "tushy"—reflect the reluctance of parents and grandparents to deal directly with the names of certain body parts when speaking with their little darlings. Thus, while in standard English adults are apt to say "backside" when they mean "buttocks," "tush" and the other forms represent a comparable linguistic aversion.

See also **tutu**.

tong tong

From Cantonese t'ong, *in Mandarin* táng, *meaning "meeting place"; "hall."*

In Chinese, and in English since the late nineteenth century, meaning "a fraternal or secret society of Chinese in the United States, commonly considered to be associated with criminal activities": "Decades ago in San Francisco's Chinatown, rival **tongs** fought one another for control of illicit gambling enterprises." "**Tongs** in the United States are believed to have had roots in tongs, political organizations, back in China."

touché too SHAY

From French touché, *literally, "touched, hit"; past participle of* toucher, *meaning "to touch."*

In French, and in English since the late nineteenth century, meaning 1. "in fencing, an exclamation used to acknowledge a hit": "In a few more seconds, he once again said '**Touché**'—for the fifth time—and the match was over."

2. "A spoken admission of a valid point or justified accusation

made by another person": " '**Touché**,' I said, to which he responded, 'It's about time,' and there the unpleasant scene ended."

tournedos TUUR ni DOH

From French tournedos; *from* tourner *"to turn"* + dos *"back"; from Latin* dorsum *"back."*

In French, and in English since the late nineteenth century, plural **tournedos** (TUUR ni DOHZ), meaning "small slices of fillet of beef, served with various sauces": "Of all the steak dinners I have eaten, **tournedos** with a green salad and a bottle of Burgundy surely is my favorite."

Medium rare, please.

tourniquet TUR ni kit

From French tourniquet, *possibly from Old French* tournicle, *meaning "a coat of mail"; associated with* tourner, *meaning "to turn."*

In French, and in English since the end of the seventeenth century, meaning "a device or bandage applied tightly around a person's or other animal's limb for slowing the flow of blood through an artery by compression": "Before stitching up the lacerated hand, the surgeon applied a **tourniquet** above the patient's wrist."

It should be pointed out that while French uses *tourniquet* with the same meaning as in English, another meaning of the French *tourniquet* is "turnstile." But the first French meaning of *tourniquet* in our favorite French-English dictionary is given as "tourniquet."

Tower of Babel. **See babel.**

tracasserie **tra KASS ə ree**

From French tracasserie, *meaning "harassment"; from* tracasser, *meaning "to worry"; "bother oneself or others"; "harass."*

In French, and in English since the early eighteenth century, meaning "a state of annoyance or disturbance"; "a petty quarrel"; "a fuss": "Once the honeymoon was over, their marriage settled into a continuing series of **tracasseries**, and neither spouse could see a way to improve their situation."

Dear Abby:

trachoma trə KOH mə

In Greek trákhoma, *meaning "roughness"; from* trakhys *"rough"* + -oma *a suffix used in naming a tumor.*

In English since the late seventeenth century, meaning "a chronic, contagious disease of the eye with granulation and scarring": "In a thorough examination, the ophthalmologist always looks for signs of **trachoma** and other pathological conditions."

trattoria TRAH tə REE ə

From Italian trattoria, *meaning "restaurant"; from* trattor, *meaning "restaurateur"; from* trattare, *meaning "to treat."*

In Italian, and in English since the early nineteenth century, meaning "an Italian restaurant, usually informal or inexpensive": "I have always felt more comfortable having a meal in my neighborhood **trattoria** than in a fine restaurant offering elaborate dishes."

Served by slow and bored waiters, all unimpressed by my presence or my choice of food.

trauma TROW mə

From Greek traûma, *meaning "a wound."*

In English since the late seventeenth century, plural **traumas** and **traumata** (TROW mə tə), meaning 1. "any injury to the body; a condition resulting from this": "While at first glance the effects of the crash did not appear serious, he did suffer the **trauma** of shock, unnoticed at first, but which required emergency treatment."

2. "In psychiatry, an experience that produces psychological injury"; "the injury caused": "Much is now being made of childhood **traumas** that, untreated, are said to result in lifelong emotional disability."

And in the hands of a slick lawyer . . .

trecento **tray CHEN toh**

From Italian trecento, *literally, three hundred; short for* mille trecento, *literally, 1,300, meaning the years between 1300 and 1399.*

In English since the early nineteenth century, also given as **Trecento**, meaning "the fourteenth century, especially as a period of Italian art, architecture, etc.": "Giotto is one of the painters whose works are often cited as exemplars of the flourishing of the great **trecento**."

trek **trek**

From Afrikaans trek, *from Dutch* trek, *meaning "journey, expedition"; from* trekken, *a verb meaning "pull; migrate."*

In English since the early nineteenth century, as a noun meaning 1. "a journey, especially an arduous or dangerous journey": "Never again will our commune undertake a **trek** as arduous as the one we made entirely on foot to the interior of Costa Rica."

2. As a verb, "to travel or migrate, especially slowly or with difficulty": "No matter what you think of the apartheid-minded South Africans of recent times, you must admire the

courage of their ancestors, who **trekked** into the Transvaal and established productive agriculture there."

triage tree AH*ZH*

From French triage, *meaning "a sorting"; from* trier, *meaning "to sift."*

In French, and in English since the early twentieth century, meaning as a noun 1. "in medical practice, the sorting of wounded soldiers or accident victims to decide treatment priority in order to increase the number of survivors": "Devotees of American television's *M*A*S*H* series will forever recall the actions of the harried medics whose first job was to perform **triage** when battle casualties were brought in."

2. "Determination of priorities in responding to a crisis of any sort": "Our decision on whether to market on the Internet will not be made until a **triage** is conducted to determine how scarce company resources should be allocated to achieve best company-wide long-term results."

3. As an adjective, "pertaining to the task of triage": "Under ideal circumstances, senior medical officers head up our **triage** teams."

4. As a verb, "perform the task of triage": "Anyone who must **triage** a large-scale medical emergency has to be kept continuously informed of the number of nurses and physicians on duty, the number of hospital beds and operating rooms available, essential medical supplies, and the like."

An awesome responsibility.

tribade TRIB əd

From sixteenth-century French tribade, *meaning "a lesbian"; from Latin* tribas, *from Greek* tribás, *meaning "a rubbing"; from* tribein, *meaning "to rub."*

In English since the end of the sixteenth century, meaning, in the words of the venerable *Oxford English Dictionary*, "a woman who is said to practice unnatural vice with other women"; in modern lexicography, "a lesbian": "In the history of jurisprudence we see many examples of accusations and convictions of pedophiles and **tribades**."

But the more interesting linguist aspect of tribade is its etymology. As given above, it derives ultimately from a Greek verb meaning "to rub." And this stems from a sexual act involving rubbing and, to a degree, resembling sexual intercourse.

Again, as you might expect, there is the word **tribadism**, which can be defined as "lesbianism."

But, before leaving the subject, one must wonder just what the Oxford lexicographers meant by "practice unnatural vice." And whether we can look more kindly on natural vice.

troglodyte TROG lə DĪT

From Latin troglodyta, *from Greek* troglodytés, *literally, "one who creeps into holes"; a "cave dweller."*

In English since the mid-sixteenth century, meaning 1. "a cave dweller"; "especially in prehistoric times, a caveman": "Archaeologists working in western Africa have uncovered fresh evidence of burial places of early **troglodytes**."

2. "A person living in seclusion"; "a hermit": "From middle age on, he lived as a **troglodyte**, plotting his revenge against society and avoiding contact with people except for sending the occasional letter bomb."

3. "A person ignorant of affairs of the world": "I don't know how you can consider marrying a **troglodyte** who hasn't read a book or a newspaper since he left high school."

He's probably not even on the Internet.

trompe l'oeil **trawmp LOI**

From French, literally, "(it) deceives the eye."

In French, and in English since the late nineteenth century, meaning 1. "visual deception of the eye; an optical illusion": "To decorate her living room, she hired a painter who could paint imaginary book shelves holding sets of imaginary leather-bound classics, altogether achieving a well-nigh perfect **trompe l'oeil**."

2. As an adjective, said of a painting, "designed to make a viewer think the objects represented are real": "The artist should use false perspectives to heighten the realism of **trompe l'oeil** paintings."

trousseau **TROO soh**

From French trousseau; *from Old French* troussel, *diminutive of* trousse, *meaning "a parcel"; from* trousser, *meaning "to fasten."*

In French, and in English since the early nineteenth century in the present sense, plural **trousseaux** (TROO sohz) and **trousseaus**, meaning "a bride's collection of clothing, linens, etc., gathered in preparation for her marriage": "Susan has finally decided she will never marry and is giving away, piece by piece, the marvelous **trousseau** she collected over the years."

How sad!

tsatske. See tchotchke.

tsunami **tsuu NAH mee**

From Japanese tsunami, *from* tsu *"harbor"* + nami *"waves."*

In Japanese, and in English since the end of the nineteenth century, plural **tsunamis**, meaning "an unusually large sea wave produced by a seaquake, earthquake, or undersea volcanic eruption": "One of the all-time greatest **tsunamis**, created off Chile by a 1960 earthquake, was reported to have been traveling at a speed of four hundred miles an hour when it hit Japan."

And did lots of damage.

tundra TUN drə

From Russian túndra, *from Lappish* tundra, *meaning "a flat, elevated area."*

In English since the mid-nineteenth century, meaning "a vast, nearly level, treeless region of Alaska and northern Russia, usually marshy with underlying permafrost": "As a result of ignorance, we tend to overlook the persistent environmental damage to the brittle **tundra** that is caused by our Arctic oil exploration."

tutu TOO too

From French tutu, *a child's alteration of* cucu, *diminutive of* cul, *meaning "buttocks."*

In French, and in English since the beginning of the twentieth century, meaning "a short, full skirt of layers of tulle, worn by ballerinas": "The pretty young snowdrops in their **tutus** danced their way across the stage and into the hearts of the audience."

The French word *cul*, you will recall, is associated with **tutu**. How did this come about? One guess is that a dancer wearing the stiff tutu shows a bit of underwear, and a child seeing this might well be amused by the sight.

Perhaps calling out—in French, of course—"Mother, see the lady's *cucu*." And from there a short step to tutu.

And maybe not.

U

ukase yoo KAYSS

From French ukase, *from Russian* ukáz, *meaning "edict, ordinance"; from Russian* ukazati, *meaning "to show, to indicate, to order."*

In English since the early eighteenth century, meaning 1. "any proclamation or order by an absolute or arbitrary authority": "Cotton Mather is said to have issued a **ukase** barring women from kissing their babies on Sundays."

2. "In czarist Russia, a pronouncement of the czar having the force of law": "The czar was encouraged to issue a **ukase** barring publication of foreign literature."

ukulele YOO kə LAY lee

From Hawaiian 'ukulele, *literally, "a leaping flea." Why this was the name given to the ukulele will be explained shortly.*

In Hawaiian, and in English since the end of the nineteenth century, also given as **ukelele**, meaning "a small, four-string guitar associated with Hawaiian music, but also heard in jazz bands": "The **ukulele** is said to be a development of a Portuguese musical instrument brought to Hawaii late in the nineteenth century."

But why was this innocuous instrument called *'ukulele*, a leaping flea? Because a British army officer named Edward Purvis is said to have popularized the ukulele at the court of King Kalakaua, and his lively playing style gave him the nickname *'ukulele*. And from there it was an easy move to calling his instrument a ukulele. That's why.

And when you hear a ukulele played expertly, you'll see how appropriate leaping flea is.

urbane ur BAYN

From Middle French urbain, *from Latin* urbanus, *both meaning "urban"; from Latin* urbs, *meaning "a city."*

In English since the early sixteenth century, an adjective meaning 1. "having the polish regarded as characteristic of sophisticated social life in major cities": "His **urbane** father fools me not for a moment—the man is a thoroughgoing boor."

2. "Reflecting sophistication and elegance, especially in language": "Throughout the essay we are impressed by an **urbane** tone surprising in one so young."

The related noun **urbanity** (ur BAN i tee) came into English hard on the heels of **urbane** and, unsurprisingly, means the quality of being urbane: "Roger exuded **urbanity** in everything he wore, in every mannerism he affected, and in every word he uttered; small wonder the men of the town detested him."

urinoir. See **pissoir.**

utopia yoo TOH pee ə

From New Latin utopia, *literally, "not a place"; from Greek* ou *"not"* + topos *"a place." The word* **utopia** *was coined by Sir Thomas More (1478–1535).*

In English since 1551, the year of publication of an English translation of More's political fable *Utopia*, which More published in Latin in 1516. Utopia was the name chosen by More for his imaginary island, described as a place enjoying perfection in law, politics, etc.

In English, meaning 1. "an imagined perfect place or state of things": "People dreamed of a socialist **utopia**, where coconuts, liberty, and human rights drop from trees, and no one need worry about getting into a first-class nursery school or paying for an education at a college of his or her choice."

2. "Any visionary system of political or social perfection": "During the Great Depression in the United States, earnest university students spent much of their time designing—of course without much success—**utopias** in which unemployment, hunger, and privation would not exist."

Get real!

uxorious uk SOR ee əss

From Latin uxorius, *meaning "fond of a wife"; from* uxor *"a wife"* + -ius *"characterized by."*

In English since the end of the sixteenth century, meaning 1. "doting upon, or obsessively fond of, one's wife": "An **uxorious** young husband surely does not know it, but he is laying a firm foundation for a future as full-time henpecked husband."

2. "Showing such fondness": "From Gerald's **uxorious** treatment of his wife, catering to her every wish, you would think she were a fragile porcelain doll."

How did it happen that uxorious, which formerly meant "fond of a wife," came to mean "doting upon one's wife"? A reasonable inference is that fondness, even doting, is thought to be acceptable in a wife, but not in a husband. So when men began to openly show tenderness toward their wives, they were considered something less than masculine—they were acting like wives!

And real men can't countenance such behavior.

V

vade mecum VAY dee MEE kəm

From French vade mecum, *meaning "pocketbook"; from Latin* vade mecum, *literally, "go with me."*

In English since the early seventeenth century, plural **vade mecums**, meaning 1. "a book for ready reference"; "handbook"; "manual": "He bought a pocket-size German-English dictionary, intending it to serve as his **vade mecum** during his two months in Germany."

2. Anything useful a person carries about for frequent or personal use: "Until recently, John's **vade mecum** had been his slide rule, which he finally replaced with a pocket-size electronic calculator."

Things, even words, have a way of going out of date. But Spanish still has its *vademécum*, Italian its *vademecum*, and German its *Vademekum*, all translated into English as "vade mecum."

valet va LAY

From French valet, *from Middle French* vaslet, *meaning "a squire"; from Medieval Latin* vassus, *meaning "a manservant, a retainer."*

In French given as *valet de chambre*, in English since the mid-sixteenth century, meaning 1. "a man's personal attendant who takes care of clothes, etc.": "Frederick invariably addressed his **valet** as 'my man,' much to the annoyance of his wife, who had married a penniless and modest young man and watched him degenerate into an insufferable prig with a personal fortune in the millions."

2. "A man employed by a hotel to perform similar duties for hotel guests": "Bill hated the too-wealthy Wall Streeters who left $1,000 suits in a heap on a hotel bedroom floor for their **valets** to pick up and take away for cleaning."

3. "A parking attendant at a restaurant, hotel, or other establishment": "Davis had learned not to tip a **valet** who parked his car until it had been returned, so he could see whether it arrived unscathed."

Things you learn.

vamoose va MOOSS

From Spanish vamos, *meaning "let's go."*

In American slang since the early nineteenth century, meaning "to depart hurriedly"; "decamp": "Once we heard the police car's siren, we knew it was time to **vamoose**."

A vital element of street smarts.

vaporetto VAP ə RET oh

From Italian vaporetto, *meaning "a small steamboat"; from Italian* vapore, *from Latin* vapor, *both meaning "steam."*

In Italian, and in English since the early twentieth century, plural **vaporettos** and **vaporetti** (VAP ə RET tee), meaning in Venice "a motorboat used to carry passengers along a canal": "The only efficient way to get about in Venice is by motorboat, especially by **vaporetto**, a relatively inexpensive and commodious means for carrying dozens of passengers at a time."

Of course, if you stay at one of the wonderful and expensive Venetian hotels, you will be provided, usually without charge, with a driver and fast motorboat holding no more than six passengers.

But why call the motorboats carrying people on the canals of Venice **vaporetti**, which translates literally as "small steamboats"? Because the original vaporetti were powered by steam.

Yet, the Venetian gondoliers are still paddling their gondolas. And singing Verdi and Puccini.

All's right with the world.

vatic VAT ik

From Latin vates, *meaning "prophet; poet."*

In English since the end of the sixteenth century, meaning "pertaining to or characteristic of a prophet"; "prophetic"; "inspired": "Sybil's uncanny **vatic** powers, displayed in her weekly newspaper column, were the talk of the village."

Surely, the similarity in spelling of **vatic** and Vatican must not go unnoticed. The Vatican, the papal residence, was established on *Vaticanus Mons*, Vatican Hill, of ancient Rome. In Roman times, the hill was the headquarters of the *vaticinatores*, the soothsayers or prophets. And today, among other words from *vates*, we have the elegant verb **vaticinate** (və TISS ə NAYT), meaning "to prophesy," and the equally elegant noun **vaticination** (və TISS ə NAY shən), meaning "prophecy and the act of prophesying."

vendetta ven DET ə

From Italian vendetta, *meaning "revenge, vengeance"; from Latin* vindicta, *meaning "vengeance."*

In English since the mid-nineteenth century, meaning 1. "a blood feud in which the family of a murdered person seeks vengeance on the slayer or the slayer's family, especially as once practiced in Corsica and Sicily": "The implacable family of the murdered young girl sought out and killed her slayer, sparking a **vendetta** between two families that did not end until virtually the entire village had been wiped out."

2. "Any prolonged and bitter rivalry or feud, as in politics": "Once reckless taunts and accusations were aired in the Democratic Party primary, a **vendetta** erupted that ruined the party's electoral chances for years to come."

verboten vər BOHT ən

From German verboten, *past participle of* verbieten, *meaning "to forbid."*

In English since World War I, meaning "forbidden, as by law"; "not allowed, prohibited": "Hans, in speaking of his childhood, said that during the war everything pleasurable in his country was **verboten** except for a few things that were specifically permitted."

Hyperbole?

vertigo VUR ti GOH

From Latin vertigo, *meaning "whirling, dizziness"; from* vertere, *meaning "to turn."*

In English since the early sixteenth century, plural **vertigoes** and **vertigines** (vər TIJ ə NEEZ), meaning "a dizzying sensation of tilting within stable surroundings or of being in tilting or whirling surroundings"; "dizziness": "A great number of the patients referred to the neurologist complained of persistent migraine and occasional **vertigo**."

Other languages have their words for **vertigo**. French has *vertige*. Spanish has *vértigo*, which it defines as "vertigo" but also as "a fit of madness." And Italian has *vertigine*.

Vertigo has a related word, **vertiginous** (vər TIJ ə nəss), an adjective meaning "affected with vertigo," but also used figuratively to mean "apt to change quickly"; "unstable": "As the prices of stocks rose to **vertiginous** heights, my wife became increasingly cautious about her investments."

As well she might.

verve vurv

From French verve, *meaning "vigor, enthusiasm"; from Latin* verba, *meaning "words."*

In English since the late seventeenth century. In modern senses since the mid-nineteenth century, meaning 1. "in literary or artistic work, enthusiasm, intellectual vigor, spirit": "The only writer at the party whose work could reasonably be said to possess **verve** was a woman in her early nineties who said she had been writing for many decades and had never been published."

2. "Vivaciousness"; "liveliness"; "animation": "Everyone enjoyed the evening thoroughly, well aware it did not stem from the sorry excuse for food Michael served, but from Mary's **verve**, which infused the table talk and inspired welcome lightheartedness."

veto VEE toh

From Latin, literally, "I forbid."

In English since the early seventeenth century, plural **vetoes**, meaning 1. "the constitutional power of one branch of government to reject a decision of another branch": "The president is expected to issue a **veto** if the Senate and House do not eliminate the harshness of their proposed medical insurance legislation."

2. "An emphatic prohibition of any sort": "As expected, his mother had the power of **veto** on the guest list for Ruth's slumber party."

3. As a verb, "reject a bill by exercising a veto"; also, "prohibit emphatically": "The president's husband urged her to **veto** the defense appropriations bill." "At our family council meetings, everyone has a vote on family matters, but Father may **veto** any decision he does not agree with."

via dolorosa VEE ə DOHL ə ROH sə

From Latin, literally, "sorrowing road."

In English since the beginning of the twentieth century, as **Via Dolorosa**, meaning 1. "the route believed to have been taken by Christ through Jerusalem to Calvary": "In the **Via Dolorosa**, a procession of believers was moving slowly, pausing periodically to commemorate Christ's passage along the road."

2. As **via dolorosa**, "any prolonged ordeal that has to be borne with fortitude": "From that day on, Clarence knew each step in the rest of his lifelong **via dolorosa** was going to be more difficult than the last."

Life just ain't a bowl of cherries.

viaticum vī AT i kəm

From Latin viaticum, *neuter of* viaticus, *meaning "pertaining to a road or journey"; from* viare, *meaning "to travel"; from* via, *meaning "road."*

In English since the mid-sixteenth century, plural **viaticums** and **viatica** (vī AT i kə), meaning 1. "money or other necessities for a journey"; also, "travel expenses, especially those paid to a public servant for a trip that is part of the official's duties": "It is dispiriting to read of trips to luxurious vacation resorts by public servants, supposedly to transact government business and often involving generous **viaticums**." 2. "The Eucharist or Communion administered to a person who is dying or in danger of death": "All of us felt comforted by the presence of a priest who would stay with us at the side of our wounded leader and administer the **viaticum** when needed."

For a journey from which there is no verifiable return.

vichyssoise VISH ee SSWAHZ

From French vichyssoise, *shortened from* crême vichyssoise, *literally, "cream soup of Vichy," Vichy being the name of a city in central France.*

In French, and in English since the early twentieth century, meaning "a soup, usually served cold, made with potatoes, leeks, and cream and characteristically garnished with chopped chives": "Despite competition from too heavily seasoned gazpacho as an introduction to a hot-weather meal, expertly prepared **vichyssoise** will always be number one on the gourmet's summer soup parade."

The city of Vichy is blessed by many for giving birth to this soup, as it formerly was blessed for the quality of its mineral water. Properly called **Vichy water**, it was widely sold and soon came to be called **Vichy**.

But then came World War II, when much of France was occupied by Nazi forces. Under the leadership of Marshal Henri Pétain, a government was established in the unoccupied part of the country in 1940, with its capital in—you guessed it—Vichy. As a result, "Vichy" became a synonym for any government that collaborates with an enemy country.

So it is easy to see why the mineral water identified with Vichy rapidly lost its cachet. You win some and you lose some.

vignette vin YET

From French vignette, *literally, "a little vine," so called from the vinelike decorations supplied in early books.*

In French, and in English since the mid-eighteenth century, meaning 1. "a brief descriptive account, anecdote, or essay"; "a character sketch": "Many of her most successful books have been collections of **vignettes** of her family's life on the prairie."

2. "In photography, a portrait showing only the head and shoulders of the subject, with the edges gradually shading into the background": "Our town had a photographer who specialized in creating **vignettes**, and when they were no longer in vogue, he found himself without clients."

3. "An engraving or drawing that is shaded off gradually so as to leave no definite line at the border": "These days one rarely sees a book illustrated with **vignettes**, because such engravings or drawings appear old-fashioned to modern readers."

4. As a verb, "soften the edges of (a photograph or picture), in the manner of a vignette": "He set up interchangeable, neutral backgrounds in his studio for photographs he intended to **vignette**."

virago vi RAH goh

From Latin virago, *meaning "a female warrior," from* vir *"a man"* + -ago *a suffix suggesting "resemblance."*

In English since the end of the tenth century, meaning "a dominating or abusive woman"; "a scold, a shrew": "Warned by his father that the woman he wanted to marry was surely a

virago, Mark decided to put off any idea of marriage until he had further opportunity to judge her temperament."

Formerly, a **virago** was also defined as "a woman of masculine strength or spirit, an amazon," but this meaning has disappeared.

Just in time, considering modern attitudes toward the sexes.

virtuoso VUR choo OH ssoh

From Italian virtuoso, *meaning "skilled, versed"; from Late Latin* virtuosus, *meaning "virtuous."*

In Italian, and in English since the early seventeenth century, plural **virtuosos** and **virtuosi** (VUR choo OH see), meaning as a noun 1. "a person who excels in performance of music": "Everyone who heard the young woman's piano debut recognized her immediately as a **virtuoso**."

2. "A person who has special knowledge of or taste for the fine arts"; "a connoisseur": "The outstanding quality of early Greek statuary is immediately apparent to **virtuosi**."

3. As an adjective, meaning "characteristic of a virtuoso": "The senator was known as a **virtuoso** fund-raiser." "Her **virtuoso** solo piano performance brought invitations from orchestras all over the world." An additional adjective, with the same meaning, is **virtuosic** (VUR choo OSS ik).

4. More useful than "virtuosic" is the noun **virtuosity** (VUR choo OSS i tee), meaning "the character, skill, or ability of a virtuoso": "The first violinist's **virtuosity** sets him apart from the rest of the string players in the great orchestra."

vis-à-vis VEE zə VEE

From French, literally, "face to face"; from Old French vis *"visage"* + à *"to"* + vis *"visage"; from Latin* visum, *meaning "a vision, a sight."*

In French, and in English since the early eighteenth century, as an adverb meaning 1. "facing one another": "Although the man and woman sat **vis-à-vis** for their evening meal, they seemed never to look at one another and surely never spoke."

2. As an adjective, meaning "face-to-face": "Everyone thought that a single meeting **vis-à-vis** with the Chinese foreign minister was all the United States diplomat needed to launch an effective rapprochement between the two nations."

3. As a preposition, meaning "compared with, in relation to": "In deciding whether to make a donation to a charity, Craig always considers the organization's amount of business expenses **vis-à-vis** the amount it spends to help people in need."

4. As a noun, plural **vis-à-vis**, meaning "a counterpart"; "an opposition number": "Whoever was in charge of seating arrangements for the conference saw to it that my **vis-à-vis** was a person I would surely admire." "She and her **vis-à-vis** in London had never met, but they got along famously in their telephone conversations."

Maybe it was just as well they had never met. They could have disliked one another.

vista VISS tə

From Italian vista, *meaning "a view"; feminine form of* visto, *the past participle of* vedere, *meaning "to see"; from Latin* videre, *meaning "to see."*

In Italian, and in English since the mid-seventeenth century, meaning 1. "a view or prospect, especially one that affords pleasure to a viewer": "On the first full day of my visit, Jack took me on a long hike to the top of his property, from where we could enjoy the **vista**."

2. "A far-reaching mental view": "Her rosy **vista** of our country's economic future did not jibe with the pessimistic views of most economists."

Suggesting that "one man's meat is another man's poison."

vodka VOD kə

From Russian vódka, *diminutive form of* vodá, *meaning "water."*

In Russian, and in English since the late eighteenth century, meaning 1. "an unaged, colorless distilled spirit, made originally in Russia by distillation of potatoes, grain, etc.": "Resumption of the sale of **vodka** at a reasonable price was the key demand of striking workers."

2. "A shot of vodka": "Again he called to the bartender, this time saying he wanted **vodka** straight."

Using the word for "water" in naming the favorite drink of Russians is a marvelous example of the use of euphemism.

See **eau de vie** and **whiskey** for additional examples of the use of euphemisms.

vol-au-vent voh loh VAH*N*

From French, literally, "flight in the wind."

In French, and in English since the early nineteenth century, meaning "a shell of puff pastry filled with chopped meat, vegetables, etc., in sauce": "A first-class **vol-au-vent**, in contrast with an Italian lasagna, manages to be light as well as delicious and satisfying."

Not that there's anything wrong with being devoted to a first-class **lasagna**.

volte-face vohlt FAHSS

From French volte-face, *meaning "a turnabout"; from Italian* voltafaccia, *from* voltare *"to turn"* + faccia *"face."*

In French, and in English since the beginning of the nineteenth century, plural **volte-face**, meaning "a reversal of attitude, opinion, or position in an argument": "We have become inured to the sudden **volte-face** of the tobacco companies in defending themselves against charges of ignoring informed medical research into the hazards of smoking."

Well, you can't blame them for trying.

voyeur **vwah YUR**

From French voyeur, *literally, "one who sees," meaning "a Peeping Tom"; from* voir *"see"* + -eur *a suffix taken as "one who."*

In French, and in English since the end of the nineteenth century, meaning "a person who obtains sexual gratification by observing sexual acts or organs, especially secretively": "The patient, a **voyeur** of long standing, and his unconventional therapist spent hours together examining photographs of couples engaged in sexual intercourse, an activity they both appeared to enjoy."

Two words associated with "voyeur" are the noun **voyeurism** and the adjective **voyeuristic**, the former meaning "the practice of obtaining sexual gratification by observing sexual acts or organs"; the latter meaning "characteristic of voyeurs."

To each his own.

waffle WOF əl

From Dutch wafel, *from Middle Low German* wafel, *both meaning "a waffle."*

In English since the mid-eighteenth century, meaning 1. "a batter cake with a pattern of deep indentations on each side, formed by the gridlike design on the two parts of the metal utensil in which it is made": "An essential part of the **waffle** is the accompanying generous serving of Vermont maple syrup, which imparts a distinctive flavor to the dish."

2. Waffle also has other meanings, the most current one as a verb being "speak or write equivocally": "Instead of responding directly to a question, politicians and other masters of obfuscation will avoid giving a direct answer, preferring instead to **waffle**."

To the exasperation of the questioner.

wampum WOM pəm

From Algonquian wampum, *short form of* wampumpeag;

from wap *"white"* + umpe *"string"* + -ag *a plural noun suffix.*

In English since the early seventeenth century, meaning 1. "strings of cylindrical beads made from shells, formerly used by North American Indians for ornamentation or as money": "The settlers became aware that they were being offered **wampum** in exchange for any kind of manufactured goods, and that the settlers could make a considerable profit by sending strings of beads back to England for sale to dealers in curios."

2. Informally, "money": "It became clear to Charley's family that he needed **wampum** badly and would stop at nothing to get it—nothing except looking for a job, that is."

Weltanschauung VELT AHN SHOW **uung**

From German Weltanschauung, *literally, "world-view"; from* Welt *"world"* + Anschauung *"perception."*

In German, and in English since the mid-nineteenth century, plural **Weltanschauungen** (VELT AHN SHOW uung ən) and **Weltanschauungs**, meaning "the view of life of a person or group"; "a philosophy of life, particularly a conception of the universe and humanity's place in it": "Peoples of different languages, experiences, and social systems may have dissimilar **Weltanschauungen** and find it difficult to get along as neighbors."

Unless they make a special effort to achieve comity.

Weltschmerz VELT SHMAIRTSS

From German Weltschmerz, *literally, "world-pain"; from* Welt *"world"* + Schmerz *"pain."*

In German, and in English since the late nineteenth century, also given as **weltschmerz**, meaning "a pessimistic view of life"; "an apathetic or vaguely yearning attitude": "When I was a college student in the depths of the Great Depression, all the undergraduates I knew were afflicted with what we called 'terminal **Weltschmerz**'; to feel optimistic was unthinkable."

But all that changed on the day Pearl Harbor was bombed.

whiskey HWISS kee

From Irish uisce beatha *or Scots Gaelic* uisge beatha; *in Scotland and Ireland also given as* usquebaugh, *later given as* whiskybae, *which was shortened to "whiskey" or "whisky." All these terms may be translated as "water of life," and all are translations of the Latin* aqua vitae, *literally, "water of life."*

In English since the beginning of the eighteenth century, given as **whisky** for Scotch and Canadian whiskey, as **whiskey** for Irish and American whiskey, meaning 1. "an alcoholic liquor distilled from a mash of grain, especially barley, rye, or corn": "In recent years a particular type of Scotch **whisky**, called single malt, has justifiably become quite popular."

2. "A drink of whiskey": "At my club, I ordered my usual **whiskey** and a splash of water and sat with it for almost an hour."

I wanted to keep a clear head.

wiener WEE nər

From German Wiener, *short for* Wiener Wurst, *literally, "Viennese sausage."*

In English since the mid-nineteenth century, meaning "frankfurter, hot dog": "The quintessential American picnic includes an ample supply of **wieners** and buns, cole slaw, potato salad, and watermelon, plus at least one keg of beer."

Since both the "wiener" and the "frankfurter" are named for their European cities of origin, one might assume that

Vienna and Frankfurt compete for hot dog preeminence. As far as is known, however, such rivalry does not exist. Could it be that the world knows the best hog dogs are always made in the United States? And that Coney Island, in New York City, is the best place to go for experiencing this culinary delight?

And that eating the English excuse for a hot dog at a soccer—football, that is—match is apt to be a terminal experience?

See also **frankfurter** and **wiener schnitzel**.

wiener schnitzel VEE nər SHNIT səl

From German Wiener Schnitzel, *literally, "Viennese veal cutlet";* Schnitzel *meaning "a shaving," from* schnitzeln, *meaning "to whittle."*

In English since the mid-nineteenth century, also given as **wiener schnitzel à la Holstein** (ah lah HOHL stīn), meaning "a fried breaded veal cutlet, variously garnished and usually coated with egg or served with a fried egg on top": "Who can resist the succulence of a **wiener schnitzel** accompanied by a pitcher of lager beer?"

won ton WON TON

From Cantonese Chinese wahn t'an, *meaning "a dumpling."*

In English since the early twentieth century, in Chinese cooking meaning 1. "a dumpling filled with minced pork and spices, usually eaten boiled in soup, but sometimes fried": "**Won tons** are not unlike ravioli in appearance and consistency but, not surprisingly in Chinese cuisine, are never served with a tomato sauce."

2. "A soup containing won tons": "The menu of a Chinese restaurant of small reputation often will offer **won ton soup**, terming it 'won ton (kreplach) soup,' unwittingly suggesting

that kreplach, a popular item of Jewish cuisine, itself contains minced pork." Oy vay!

For the uninitiated, it is worth pointing out that kreplach, plural as well as singular, from Yiddish *kreplech*, from German *Krappel*, meaning "a fritter," are pockets of noodle dough filled with chopped chicken liver, kasha, and the like and usually served in soup.

But in traditional Jewish cookery, never, repeat never, filled with pork—raw, minced, fried, or any other style.

XYZ

Xanthippe zan TIP ee

From Greek, the name of the ill-tempered wife of the philosopher Socrates.

In English since the late sixteenth century, also given as **Xantippe**, meaning "an ill-tempered woman, particularly an ill-tempered wife"; "a shrew": "The judge showed Tom great sympathy in his divorce suit when Tom testified he had married in haste, expecting a sweet-tempered mate and got instead a veritable **Xanthippe**."

So well established is this meaning that no one will ever name a daughter Xanthippe. Tiffany, Chelsea, and all the rest are acceptable.

xylophagous zi LOF ə gəss

From Greek xylophágos, *from* xylo *"wood"* + -phagos *"eating."*

In English since the early eighteenth century, an adjective meaning 1. "of certain insects or larvae, feeding on wood":

"Entomologists call attention to the role of **xylophagous** insects in returning the wood of downed trees to the forest soil."

2. "Destructive of timber": "Once **xylophagous** larvae are detected in a stand of valuable trees, the trees must be treated quickly in order to prevent serious damage."

yacht yot

From Dutch jaghte, *short for* jaghtschip, *meaning "a hunting ship"; from* jaght *"chase"* + schip *"a ship"; from* jagen, *meaning "to hunt."*

In English since the mid-sixteenth century, meaning 1. "a water vessel designed and used for pleasure cruising, racing, and the like": "**Yachts** for a long time have been the luxuriously appointed vessels of choice for royalty and business titans."

2. As a verb, "sail or cruise aboard a yacht": "Today, while many people speak of sailing somewhere, seldom do we hear that somebody intends to **yacht** anywhere."

And **yachtsmen** (YOTS mən), originally meaning "persons who yacht," refer to themselves as "sailors," even when they are members of a **yacht club**. If you ask them why they belong to their yacht clubs, they will tell you they enjoy sailing.

Even when the drinks and food served at the club are especially attractive.

yahoo YAH hoo

A word of British English origin that readily made its way into American English from the time of its coinage as ***Yahoo*** *by the English satirist Jonathan Swift (1667–1745) in his* Gulliver's Travels *(1726).*

Yahoo means 1. "any member of a race of brutes human in form but exhibiting all the vices of human beings": "Gulliver found that the **Yahoos** were dominated by the Houyhnnyms, a race of horses endowed with all the finer qualities of mankind and the ability to reason."

2. As **yahoo**, meaning "a yokel, a lout"; "a boorish person": "At the town meeting last year, my neighbors and I—all newcomers—were treated as **yahoos** whenever one of us tried to speak, so we were unable to make our position clear on the proposed changes in zoning."
3. "A coarse or ill-mannered person": "We found the nominees for school superintendent generally acceptable, the exception being a **yahoo** who somehow had managed to acquire academic credentials but surely would antagonize the professional staff."

The Internet now boasts its own **Yahoo!** (complete with exclamation point). This is the proprietary name of an Internet feature that may be thought of as a kind of directory—an electronic index called "a search engine"—that helps users by finding information being sought. It is reasonable to conjecture that the name was selected by its inventors as a celebratory exclamation akin to the American **yahoo**, the unrestrained cry of a cowboy on gaining control over a fractious wild horse, or of a boisterous cowboy galloping into town and firing his pistol into the air to signal to the world that he's ready for some likker and wimmin.

This derivation reflects a childhood centered about Saturday afternoons at the Arch or the Superior. For a dime, a child could see at least two cowboy movies as well as the latest episode of a thriller serial, a short comedy, and a newsreel.

yakuza **YAH kuu** ZAH

From Japanese yakuza, *from* ya *"eight"* + ku *"nine"* + -za *"three"; from the worst hand in the card game known as* yakuza—*an 8, a 9, and a 3.*

In Japanese, and in English since the mid-twentieth century,

plural **yakuza**, meaning 1. "a Japanese criminal organization, which may be thought of as the Japanese Mafia": "Many businesses in modern Japan are preyed upon by a **yakuza**, which uses threats and strong-arm tactics to extort illicit payments from them."
2. "A member of this organization"; "a gangster or racketeer": "Matsumoto's heart sank when he saw three burly **yakuza** enter his shop—he knew at once what they were about, because they wore expensive shoes, dark, well-tailored suits, and menacing expressions."
Could they have learned this from Hollywood gangster movies?

yam yam

From Portuguese inhame *or Spanish* iñame, *considered to be African in origin.*

In English since the late sixteenth century, meaning "the sweet potato, an edible starchy tuber of a tropical plant, genus *Dioscorea*": "Although most of my friends think they have to serve their baked **yams** with marshmallow coatings, I am always gratified to see the properly golden tuber standing on the table before me."
Saying, "Try me, I am delicious."

yarmulke YAHR məl kə

From Yiddish, yarmolke, *from Polish* jarmulka, *both meaning "a cap."*

In Yiddish, and in English since the end of the nineteenth century, meaning "a skullcap worn by Orthodox Jewish males and, during worship, by other Jewish males as well": "Ezra wore a **yarmulke** under his hat so that whenever he removed his hat indoors his head would not be uncovered, not even for a moment."
God forbid!

yashmak yahsh MAHK

From Arabic yasmak, *from Turkish* yasmak, *meaning "a veil."*

In English since the mid-nineteenth century, meaning "the double veil worn by a Muslim woman in public to conceal all of her face except for her eyes": "It is interesting to observe that even young Muslim women studying at the best Middle Eastern universities are more apt than not to wear **yashmaks**."

yen yen

From Chinese yan, *meaning "a craving"; "an addiction."*

In English since late in the nineteenth century, primarily as a noun meaning "a desire or craving and associated at first with opium addiction"; less frequently, as a verb meaning "to have a craving"; "yearn"; "desire strongly": "Once Adam sniffed the air and detected the unmistakable aroma of a charcoal fire doing its thing, his **yen** for barbecue quickly overpowered his resolve to eat sensibly, and he set to work demolishing a large plate of fatty ribs and what looked to me like an entire pound of baked beans."

yenta YEN tə

From Yiddish yente, *originally a female personal name.*

In Yiddish, and in English slang since the early twentieth century, meaning "a busybody, a gossip"; "a noisy, vulgar woman": "Together with the other neighborhood **yentas**, she quickly established her apartment as an informal headquarters for public discussion of all manner of juicy rumor, innuendo, and scandal."

The discussion group met every weekday afternoon.

yeti YET ee

From Tibetan yeh-teh, *literally, "a little manlike animal."*

In Tibetan, and in English since the early twentieth century, also given as **Yeti**, meaning "a large unidentified animal variously described as bearlike, manlike, and half man half beast that is said to exist in the Himalayas": "While **yeti** is the name used by the Sherpas to describe a creature never seen by a reliable witness, the rest of us usually call it the Abominable Snowman."

yodel YOHD əl

From German jodeln, *from Bavarian dialect* jodln, *literally, "to utter the syllable* jo,*" in English written as* **yo***.*

In German, and in English since the early nineteenth century, as a verb meaning 1. "sing or warble a musical call, with the voice continually alternating between falsetto and normal pitch in the manner of Tyrolean mountaineers": "It takes more than lederhosen and a few buckets of beer to enable a marcher in a Wilhelm Tell Day parade to **yodel** passably well."

2. As a noun meaning "a song or refrain sung in this manner": "While there is a certain charm in listening to someone's authentic **yodels** for a few minutes, any such performance lasting an hour or more drives me up the wall."

yogurt YOH gərt

From Turkish yoghurt, *also given as* ***yoghurt*** *and* ***yoghourt***.

In Turkish, and in English since the early seventeenth century, meaning "a semisolid food prepared from milk fermented by added bacteria and sometimes flavored or sweetened": "So now, when **yogurt** is available in many flavors and processed to resemble second-rate ice cream, you can be sure that whatever benefits the food originally provided are lost in the overguzzling of out-of-control health-food fanatics."

zabaglione ZAH bəl YOH nee

From Italian zabaglione, *a variant form of* zabaione, *an Illyrian drink, Illyria being an ancient country along the east coast of the Adriatic Sea.*

In Italian, and in English since the end of the nineteenth century, meaning "an Italian dessert served either hot or cold, made of whipped and heated egg yolks, sugar, and wine, usually Marsala": "Remember that a meal at some of the finest restaurants in Florence or Rome is not complete without a generous serving of the heavenly froth that is **zabaglione**."

zaftig ZAHF tik

From Yiddish saftik, *literally, "juicy, succulent"; from German* saftig, *meaning "juicy."*

In Yiddish, and in English slang since early in the twentieth century, also given as **zoftig**; said of a sexy woman, meaning "plump, curvaceous"; "stacked": "One of our mischievous games was to watch young women go by and rate their figures audibly on a scale from one to ten, from hopelessly skinny to big-time **zaftig**."

Boys.

Zeitgeist TSĪT GĪST

From German, from Zeit *"time"* + Geist *"spirit."*

In German, and in English since the late nineteenth century, meaning "spirit of the times"; "the trend of thought or feeling that marks a particular period of time": "The dramatic alteration in the nation's **Zeitgeist** that accompanied military defeat on the Continent persisted for a decade."

ziggurat ZIG uu RAT

From Assyrian ziggurat*u*, *literally, "a pinnacle."*

In English since late in the nineteenth century, "a pyramidal tower in ancient Mesopotamia, perhaps surmounted by a temple and consisting of a great number of stories, with an ascent winding around the outside of the structure that gave the appearance of a series of terraces": "The first **ziggurat** is thought to have dated from the third millennium B.C. and may have been the legendary Tower of Babel."

zombie ZOM bee

From Kongo nzambi, *meaning "god"*; zumbi, *meaning "fetish." Kongo is a Bantu language of west central Africa.*

In English since the beginning of the nineteenth century, meaning 1. "in voodoo, a corpse said to be revived by witchcraft, usually for some evil purpose": "**Zombies** are generally considered by Haitians and West Africans to be mute and to lack will."

2. In early-twentieth-century informal English, meaning "an automaton"; "a slow-witted, dull, or apathetic person": "Members of the opposition party were **zombies**, never consulted by their leadership and without a voice in making policy."

3. In World War II, a tall mixed drink—"death in a glass"—consisting of various types of rum, liqueur, and fruit juices: "Anyone who ordered a **zombie**, known for its lethality, was looked upon either as a neophyte in the world of barhopping or as a potential suicide."

The alcoholic drink called "zombie" may have disappeared, as far as is known. Perhaps no one has survived to order the drink more than once.

zuchetto zoo KET oh

From Italian zuchetta, *a diminutive of* zucca, *meaning "a gourd or head."*

In Italian, and in English since the mid-nineteenth century, plural **zuchettos** and **zuchetti** (zoo KET ee), meaning "a small skullcap worn by Roman Catholic ecclesiastics": "In accordance with tradition, priests wear black **zuchettos**, bishops wear violet, cardinals red, and popes white."

Good to know.

zugzwang TSOOK TSVAHNG

From German Zug *"move"* + Zwang *"compulsion, obligation."*

In German, and in English since the end of the nineteenth century, "the obligation in chess to make a move even when the move will be disadvantageous": "I stared at the board for several minutes before concluding that there was no way I could get out of the dratted **zugzwang**."

And all I could do was look as though I knew something my opponent did not.

zwieback ZWĪ BAK

From German Zwieback, *literally, "twice-baked," from* zwie *or* zwei *"twice"* + backen *"bake."*

In German, and in English since the end of the nineteenth century, meaning "a special egg bread that is sliced after baking and toasted until the slices are dry and crisp": "Babies in their first year used to be given **zwieback** routinely to help them get through the rigors of teething."

Today, at least in U.S. cities, they are more likely to gnaw on bagels.